12/23

First Vision

First Vision

Memory and Mormon Origins

STEVEN C. HARPER

OXFORD
UNIVERSITY PRESS

OXFORD
UNIVERSITY PRESS

Oxford University Press is a department of the University of Oxford. It furthers
the University's objective of excellence in research, scholarship, and education
by publishing worldwide. Oxford is a registered trade mark of Oxford University
Press in the UK and certain other countries.

Published in the United States of America by Oxford University Press
198 Madison Avenue, New York, NY 10016, United States of America.

© Oxford University Press 2019

CIP data is on file at the Library of Congress
ISBN 978-0-19-932947-2

To mjh and HKH

Contents

PART III: CONTESTED MEMORY

Acknowledgments

This book began to take shape in my mind during a 2008 seminar led by Richard Bushman. For many reasons, it would not have come to pass without him. It depends, too, on other mentors including the late Milton Backman, the late Richard Anderson, James Allen, and Dean Jessee.

When I began working on this book I was on the Church History and Doctrine faculty at Brigham Young University. Then I spent six years at the Church History Department of The Church of Jesus Christ of Latter-day Saints before returning. Both departments provided time and funds and support without which this book would not exist. I thank Brent Top, Richard Bennett, Dana Pike, and Alex Baugh in Provo. I thank Reid Nielson, Matthew Grow, Matthew Godfrey, Jay Burrup, and Chad Orton in Salt Lake City.

The *Joseph Smith Papers* underpins all of part I. Thanks to everyone who has contributed in any way to that monumental project. Thanks also to the many colleagues who generously shared their research, including Scott Esplin, Sherilyn Farnes, Chad Foulger, Matthew Godfrey, Scott Hales, Emily Jensen, Robin Jensen, Hannah Jung, Katherine Kitterman, Mark Ashurst-McGee, Dallin Morrow, Cameron Nielsen, Jacob Olmstead, Ardis Parshall, Brian Reeves, Richard Saunders, and Jed Woodworth. Jed also sharpened my analysis. So did Ann Taves, David Grua, and Kathleen Flake. Kathleen navigated New Orleans in the process.

Many people facilitated my research. I thank Glenn Rowe and Brandon Metcalf at the Church History Library, Wayne Sparkman at the Presbyterian Church of America Historical Center, Emily Reynolds at the Wheatley Institution, and the staff members of Special Collections at the J. Willard Marriott Library and of the L. Tom Perry Special Collections at the Harold B. Lee Library.

I thank Anna Godfrey for sharing her story with me. I thank Dustin Harding and Stewart Peterson for granting interviews. Both have portrayed Joseph Smith experiencing his first vision. I thank my colleagues at the Church History Library for listening to, encouraging, and critiquing my ideas. I thank Ann and John Lewis for supplemental research funds.

Thanks to Cynthia Read at Oxford University Press for supporting this book and many others. Thanks, too, to Salma Ismaiel and to Prabhu Chinnasamy, for the painstaking work of shepherding the manuscript toward publication. Thanks to Chris Williams for the index.

I thank Spencer Fluhman generally for encouragement and specifically for recommending Elise Petersen as a research assistant. Elise did much of the work on which this book depends. I am particularly grateful to her for all she did and how she did it. Kendra Williamson is an exceptionally good editor who has rescued my work many times. When I changed my mind about how to write this book halfway through, Kendra came to the rescue again. I thank her for that.

Jennifer Sebring is my reason to write, to even continue breathing. It's not so much for her but because of her.

I hope the book brings everyone who contributed to it a sense of satisfaction without any sense of responsibility for its defects or shortcomings. Those are mine.

Introduction

A Boy Who Asked God a Question

Joseph Smith (1805–44), founder of The Church of Jesus Christ of Latter-day Saints,[1] remembered that his first audible prayer, uttered in the woods near his parents' home in western New York State, resulted in a vision of heavenly beings who forgave him and told him Christianity had gone astray. "The Mormon narrative," according to a 2012 blog post, "seems to always start with a young boy who asked God a question one spring morning in 1820."[2] That may have been true in 2012, but it hasn't always been so.

When and why and how did Joseph Smith's "first vision," as Latter-day Saints now know the event, become their seminal story? What challenges did it face along the way? What changes did it undergo as a result? Can it possibly hold its privileged position against the tides of doubt and disbelief, memory studies, and source criticism—all in the information age?

The historical record includes four primary accounts—1832, 1835, 1838/ 39, and 1842—of the theophany dictated or written by Joseph Smith, revised copies of most of these, and five secondary accounts written by contemporaries who heard him relate the event. Smith described his vision regularly beginning at least by the mid-1830s, which is later than saints typically assume but earlier than scholars have thought.

The accounts of Smith's vision are both little known and, paradoxically, much contested. Many believers assume full awareness of the experience as they have received it through a redacted, canonized 1838/39 account in Smith's manuscript history and subsequent rehearsal in sermons, lessons, art, music, film, and pageantry, yet they are understandably unaware of the complex and mysterious processes of memory formation and re-formation either in Smith's mind or their own.

Scholars of this evidence, meanwhile, enjoy increasing awareness of the thick, complex historical record, but much of the resulting scholarship is partisan. It debates, often naïvely, the reliability of Smith's memory, also unaware of the processes of memory formation and re-formation in Smith's mind and in the minds of saints following after him. The debate is obstructive and almost fruitless.[3] So long as it continues, otherwise thriving Mormon studies will not learn from memory studies, which long ago stopped asking "how accurately a recollection fitted some piece of a past reality" and started investigating "why historical actors constructed their memories in a particular way at a particular time."[4]

Investigating "the composition of multiple narratives of an experience from different points of view," wrote religion scholar Ann Taves, "is an excellent way to examine how interpretations of an experience develop over time."[5] Fortunately, Taves and Robert Rees have recently begun thinking of the complicated historical record as "a resource for revealing the relationship between what people remember and the ideological dilemmas of their past and present."[6] This book follows their lead.

It also charts substantial new historiographical territory. It aims the light of memory studies, amassed over the past century, at Joseph Smith's narratives, as well as the secondary accounts of his vision and the rich historical record surrounding their compositions. In a way, this book is a travel narrative—the travel of memory through time—telling the odyssey of Smith's vision from its obscure origins to its current situation as the genesis of The Church of Jesus Christ of Latter-day Saints.

■ ■ ■

Memory is more mysterious, complex, and meaningful than we may think, if we think about it at all. Memory is more process than entity. It is also "an umbrella term under which congregate myriad phenomena."[7] This book is only about the *formation* of Joseph Smith's memories of his first vision, the memories of it shared by various groups, and the *re-formation* of these memories from Smith's time until ours.

The process of constructing enduring memories is termed *consolidation*. "Consolidation refers to the idea that memory is not fixed at the time of learning but continues to change and be reorganized as time passes."[8] When consolidation does not occur, memory evaporates. When it does, stable but not static memories form.[9]

Memories can consolidate within both individuals and groups. Thomas Anastasio and his colleagues theorized that "individual and collective memory formation are examples of analogous processes that occur on different levels."[10] The British psychologist Frederic Bartlett (1886–1969) was the first to notice the value of using groups to analyze how individuals remember and vice versa, but that insight went little noticed until Anastasio and his colleagues articulated their "three in one" model of memory consolidation that this book applies to the historical record of Joseph Smith's first vision.

The theory holds that an entity—whether an individual like Joseph Smith or a group like modern Mormons or their critics—embody three components or capacities that cooperate to consolidate memories: (1) storage, (2) selection and relation, and (3) generalization and specialization. To put it another way, both individuals and groups *store* stable memories and new information in a buffer, *select* items from this buffer and *relate* those items to each other, and, lastly, make these memories enduring in a process that turns the information into *general* knowledge with *specialized* elements. Anastasio and colleagues further explained: "The consolidation process dynamically structures the knowledge that individuals and collectives extract from their environments and makes it consistent with their ongoing experience."[11]

Whether in individuals or groups, memory consolidation takes time. Then the process continually recurs, as what has been consolidated shapes new memories. There are no better nor more interesting examples of how memories (individual and collective) consolidate and recur than the memories of Joseph Smith's first vision.

■ ■ ■

This is not a book for those interested in determining whether the vision actually happened, and if so whether it was in 1820 or 1824, or which of Smith's vision memories is more authentic or accurate than others. Expecting autobiographical memories—that is, memories recollected about one's own life—to be either accurate or inaccurate is a false dilemma. Memories like Smith's vision accounts (as well as the memories of his followers and critics) are not accurate *or* distorted. They are both.[12] And they are both objective *and* subjective.[13]

The historian's tools are unfit for the task of determining the veracity of Smith's first vision; however, they are well suited to evaluate the culture of his vision memories. They are also fit to examine the environments in which Smith consolidated his memories, as well as the culture those memories created, at least in part.

This book, therefore, does not engage the event itself (which cannot be accessed by historians), but the recorded memories of it (which can). To that end, Smith's vision is a subjective reality in all that follows. The goal is to explain how he remembered his first vision, how others have remembered it, and what difference those memories have made over time. The book tells what Smith's various vision records reveal about the nature of memory both individual and collective, about the culture of Mormonism, and about the cultures in which it emerged and has since lived.

Put most simply, the book shows that the mere survival of Smith's vision memory depended on numerous contingencies, and the fact that it has become the genesis story of the Latter-day Saints was anything but inevitable.

Notes

1. This is the official name of the church. Its style guide calls for the first reference to use the full name. It objects to *Mormon Church* or *Mormonism*. The term *Mormon* and its variants will therefore be used sparingly, generally only in quotes or titles or adjectivally as in the subtitle *Mormon Origins*. Shortened references to the institution will prefer *the church* and describe its members as *Latter-day Saints* or, simply, *saints*. See http://www.mormonnewsroom.org/style-guide.
2. Rachael Givens, "Mormonism and the Dark Night of the Soul," accessed September 12, 2012, http://www.patheos.com/blogs/peculiarpeople/2012/09/mormonisms-dark-night-of-the-soul/.
3. Gregory A. Prince, "Joseph Smith's First Vision in Historical Context: How a Historical Narrative Became Theological," *Journal of Mormon History* 41, no. 4 (October 2015): 74–94; Stan Larson, "Another Look at Joseph Smith's First Vision," *Dialogue: A Journal of Mormon Thought* 47, no. 2 (Summer 2014): 37–62; Dan Vogel, *Joseph Smith: The Making of a Mormon Prophet* (Salt Lake City: Signature, 2004), xv.
4. David Thelen, "Memory and American History," *Journal of American History* 74, no. 4 (March 1989): 1117–29.
5. Ann Taves, *Religious Experience Reconsidered: A Building Block Approach to the Study of Religion and Other Special Things* (Princeton, NJ: Princeton University Press, 2009), 71.
6. David Middleton and Derek Edwards, eds., *Collective Remembering* (London: Sage, 1990), 3. See Robert A. Rees, "Looking Deeper into Joseph Smith's First Vision: Imagery, Cognitive Neuroscience, and the Construction of Memory," *Interpreter: A Journal of Mormon Scripture* 25 (2017): 67–80; Ann Taves and Steven C. Harper, "Joseph Smith's First Vision: New Methods for the Analysis of Experience-Related Texts," *Mormon Studies Review* 3 (2016): 53–84.

7. Thomas J. Anastasio, Kristen Ann Ehrenberger, Patrick Watson, Wenyi Zhang, *Individual and Collective Memory Consolidation: Analogous Processes on Different Levels* (Cambridge, MA, and London: MIT Press, 2012), 4.

8. Larry R. Squire, "Biological Foundations of Accuracy and Inaccuracy in Memory," in *Memory Distortion: How Minds, Brains, and Societies Reconstruct the Past*, ed. Daniel L. Schacter (Cambridge, MA: Harvard University Press, 1995), 198.

9. Consolidation also includes the combination of separate items to compose memories, as well as strengthening and solidifying and adapting memories beyond their earliest composition. See Anastasio et al., *Individual and Collective Memory Consolidation*, 2, 5.

10. Anastasio et al., *Individual and Collective Memory Consolidation*, 2.

11. Anastasio et al., *Individual and Collective Memory Consolidation*, 6.

12. C. R. Barclay, for instance, observed that people he studied "retained the general meaning of their experiences, even though they were wrong about many particulars." "Schematization of Autobiographical Memory," in *Autobiographical Memory*, ed. D. C. Rubin (Cambridge: Cambridge University Press, 1986), 97.

13. Edmund Blair Bolles, *Remembering and Forgetting: An Inquiry into the Nature of Memory* (New York: Walker, 1988), 58, 64–65.

PART I

JOSEPH SMITH'S MEMORY

1

A Few Days After

Some few days after I had this vision I happened to be in company
with one of the Methodist Preachers who was very active in the before mentioned religious excitement and conversing with him on the
subject of religion I took occasion to give him an account of the vision which I had had. I was greatly surprised at his behaviour, he
treated my communication not only lightly but with great contempt,
saying it was all of the Devil, that there was no such thing as visions
or revelations in these days, that all such things had ceased with the
apostles and that there never would be any more of them.

—Joseph Smith, 1838/39[1]

According to the historical record, between 1820 and at least 1830, Joseph
Smith (see Figure 1.1) told only one person about his vision of God and
Christ. He remembered that it did not go well. A few days after the vision, he "happened to be in company" with a Methodist preacher who had
stirred many souls (including his) to seek salvation. "I took occasion to give
him an account of the vision," Smith remembered eighteen years later. "I
was greatly surprised at his behaviour, he treated my communication not
only lightly but with great contempt." The minister said Smith's story was
of the devil, visions had ended with the apostles, and there would never be
another one.[2]

That rejection powerfully influenced the ways Smith's memories consolidated. Assuming that Joseph Smith's autobiographical ability developed as
it does in most children and teens, he began as a young child to organize
his experiences into memorable cultural scripts. These prescriptions, along
with his parents' validation, shaped his childhood sense of himself. Then
Smith sought the approval of a clergyman he respected, but he was off
script.

The resulting rejection fractured Joseph Smith into an *ought self*, pre-
scribed by cultural authorities like the clergyman, and an *actual self*, or what
he knew from his own experience. Smith had approached God in crisis,

Figure 1.1 Joseph Smith Jr. (1805–44) experienced his first vision of deity around 1820 and founded The Church of Jesus Christ of Latter-day Saints in 1830.

Portrait by Danquart Anthon Weggeland. Courtesy The Church of Jesus Christ of Latter-day Saints.

desperate for salvation. Instead of assuring Smith that the resolution to his crisis was real, the minister's rejection caused dissonance within Smith—a divided self he innately had to reconcile.[3] But the gap between his culture's expectations and his actual experience was too wide to reconcile.

Susan Engel, a scholar of autobiographical memory in children, observed that "narrative descriptions of specific past experiences are first constructed with others."[4] Joseph Smith's memory of his experience formed and re-formed as he told it. He remembered that telling his story "excited a great deal of prejudice against me among professors of religion and was the cause of great persecution which continued to increase."[5] Seeking validation, he got rejection instead. According to the Methodist preacher—a religious expert—Smith had not seen God after all. It was a jarring experience to have his spiritual crisis resolved one day and the resolution rejected days later.

The preacher's rejection upset Smith's memory, with long-term effects. He learned through experience that making his memory public made it con-testable. Engel explained that "once we recall with or for others, the process of remembering depends as much on motivation and social context as it does on any neural network."[6] Such circumstances often cause people to re-cast their past so that it conforms with their culture. The minister's rejection hindered Smith's willingness, and perhaps even his ability, to tell his story.[7] Finding that telling hurt and disrupted the story, he could have conformed, altering his memory as needed to make his experience acceptable.

Instead, he kept it to himself for years—even a decade, according to the historical record. Then after years of "serious reflection," struggling for some alternative, Smith embraced the identity of the persecuted visionary. He was like Paul before King Agrippa, relating

> the account of the vision he had when he saw a light and heard a voice, but still there were but few who believed him, some said he was dishonest, others said he was mad, and he was ridiculed and reviled, but all this did not destroy the reality of his vision. He had seen a vision and he knew he had, and all the persecution under Heaven could not make it otherwise, and though they should persecute him unto death yet he knew and would know to his latest breath that he had both seen a light and heard a voice speaking unto him and all the world could not make him think or believe otherwise. So it was with me.[8]

Assuming the persecuted visionary identity, Smith likewise embraced his vision:

> I had actualy seen a light and in the midst of that light I saw two personages, and they did in reality speak unto me, or one of them did, And though I was hated and persecuted for saying that I had seen a vision, yet it was true and while they were persecuting me reviling me and speaking all manner of evil against me falsely for so saying, I was led to say in my heart, why persecute me for telling the truth? I have actually seen a vision, and who am I that I can withstand God or why does the world think to make me deny what I have actually seen, for I had seen a vision, I knew it, and I knew that God knew it, and I could not deny it.[9]

There is no evidence in the historical record that Joseph Smith told anyone but the minister of his vision for at least a decade. In that period the minister's rejection turned Smith inward, where he wrestled with how to remember and represent the experience. The enduring influence of rejection, together with what happened to Smith as time passed, shaped each version of the story he decided to tell.[10]

Notes

1. "History, 1838–1856, volume A-1 [23 December 1805–30 August 1834]," 3–4, in The Joseph Smith Papers, accessed May 6, 2019, https://www.josephsmithpapers.org/paper-summary/history-1838-1856-volume-a-1-23-december-1805-30-august-1834/3

2. Karen Lynn Davidson, David J. Whittaker, Mark Ashurst-McGee, and Richard L. Jensen, eds., *Joseph Smith Histories, 1832–1844*, vol. 1 of the Histories series of *The Joseph Smith Papers*, ed. Dean C. Jessee, Ronald K. Esplin, and Richard Lyman Bushman (Salt Lake City: Church Historian's Press, 2012), 214–17.

3. For more on the idea of *ought* and *actual* identities, see Armand L. Mauss, "Apostasy and the Management of Spoiled Identity," in *The Politics of Religious Apostasy: The Role of Apostates in the Transformation of Religious Movements*, ed. David G. Bromley (Westport, CT: Praeger, 1998), 60.

4. Susan Engel, *Context Is Everything: The Nature of Memory* (New York: W. H. Freeman, 1999), 31. See pp. 24–51 for more on *autobiography*.

5. Davidson et al., *Joseph Smith Histories*, 1:214–17.

6. Engel, *Context Is Everything*, 9, 18–33, 48.

7. According to Peter Bauder in 1834, Joseph Smith "could give me no Christian experience" in an October 1830 interview, meaning that Smith was then unwilling or unable to describe a conversion experience akin to other evangelical converts. See Bauder, *The Kingdom and the Gospel of Jesus Christ: Contrasted with That of Anti-Christ* (Canajoharie, NY: Calhoun, 1834), 36–38.

8. Davidson et al., *Joseph Smith Histories*, 1:214–17.

9. Davidson et al., *Joseph Smith Histories*, 1:214–17.

10. James B. Allen began to develop this point in "Eight Contemporary Accounts of Joseph Smith's First Vision—What Do We Learn From Them?," *Improvement Era* 73, no. 4 (April 1970): 4–13.

2

Past, Present, and Persecution

The 1838/39 Account

Owing to the many reports which have been put in circulation by evil disposed and designing persons in relation to the rise and progress of the Church of Jesus Christ of Latter day Saints, all of which have been designed by the authors thereof to militate against its character as a church, and its progress in the world; I have been induced to write this history so as to disabuse the publick mind, and put all enquirers after truth into possession of the facts as they have transpired in relation both to myself and the Church.

—Joseph Smith, 1838/39[1]

Eighteen years after his vision, Joseph Smith arrived in Far West, Missouri, after a taxing midwinter journey with his pregnant wife, Emma. The town was growing in a new county created by the Missouri legislature to segregate Latter-day Saints from other settlers.

Soon after arriving, Smith spent six days in the spring of 1838 writing, with Sidney Rigdon as adviser and George Robinson as clerk, the first pages of a history of the church he had founded eight years earlier, including an account of his first vision a decade before that.[2]

Joseph Smith did not want to write his history. He did not think himself literarily capable.[3] An 1831 revelation to Smith had identified John Whitmer, one of the witnesses who testified that Smith had shown him the text of the Book of Mormon inscribed on gold plates, as the man tasked with writing and keeping the history.[4] But the estranged and recently excommunicated Whitmer remained unresponsive to Smith's demand that he surrender his "notes on the history."[5] So with help from the more literate Rigdon and Robinson, Smith began anew. The document they composed apparently no longer exists, but its contents were "incorporated into the later surviving history manuscripts."[6]

As with autobiographical memory generally, this one was composed by Smith in and for the present; it is past that made sense in his present. Thus, the 1838/39 account of Smith's theophany—the one most published, quoted, and known—is evidence of the memory of events that made him the prophet of a persecuted people.

■ ■ ■

Every memory has a culture, an environment, in which it is consolidated. Consolidation is "the construction and continued reorganization of mental representations."[7] It results from the combination of complex neurological processes and acts of consciousness. Consolidation happens when a person attends to new information and associates it "meaningfully and systematically with knowledge already well-established in memory."[8] *Remembering*, then, becomes the process of putting pieces of the past and the present together—in a way, the opposite of *dismember*.

Up to 1838 and long after, Smith had remembered his first vision continually. Before, during, and after his experience in the woods, he made decisions that led his brain to form and re-form in ways that encoded some fragments of the experience but not others—choices that enabled him, when primed in some way or another, to recall some elements but not others. After his vision he gained subsequent experience that enlarged and shaped, as well as limited, his capacity to identify and ascribe meanings to the experience via a continual process of remembering it.[9]

Joseph Smith never simply retrieved static data about external stimuli he experienced—that is not how memory works. Like everyone else, he actively reconstructed his experience, using knowledge he already had to understand new experience and give it meaning consistent with his present purposes.[10] Daniel Schacter, a leading psychologist of memory, wrote, "the idea that there is a one-to-one correspondence between a bit of information stored away somewhere in our brain and the conscious experience of a memory that results from activating this bit of information is so intuitively compelling that it seems almost nonsensical to question it."[11] But Schacter and others questioned it and discovered that a memory is less stored artifact than present production.

Memories are not stored intact, like video recordings that can be replayed. Schacter wrote that "just as visual perception of the three-dimensional world depends on combining information from the two eyes, perception in time—remembering—depends on combining information from the present and the past."[12] "Merely to remember something is meaningless," Roger Shattuck added, "unless the remembered image is combined with a moment in the present affording a view of the same object or objects."[13] In sum, past experiences can leave traces in the brain that lie dormant until something in the present cues the creation of a memory.

What, then, in 1838 cued and so significantly shaped Joseph Smith's sense of his past? He lived in Kirtland, Ohio, when the year began. There, over the past seven years, a few thousand of the saints he led had gathered in response to his revelations, acquired hundreds of valuable acres, expanded a bustling industrial center, and erected an impressive temple, but their Zion and plans for gathering covenant Israel were undermined by local opponents, a national economic crisis, and internal dissent.

Smith had been accused (and acquitted) of a conspiracy to murder one of his arch antagonists.[14] More devastatingly, however, before and during the economic crisis, Smith's relationships with several of his closest counselors and associates were upset until a group of prominent dissenters rejected his religious authority and economic policy, and tried to replace him.[15] Threatened with lawsuits and violence, Smith fled Ohio overnight in an inglorious and discouraging end to an era recently so ripe with Pentecostal ecstasy and expectations.[16]

In spring 1838, followers in Far West, Missouri, gave Joseph Smith and his family a kind, hospitable reception, but conditions there were not much better, and they quickly grew worse.[17] Smith found that John Whitmer, his brother David, and William Phelps—the three-headed presidency of the church in Missouri—each resigned or had been excommunicated, along with Smith's assistant president over the entire church, Oliver Cowdery.

Previously one of Smith's ablest supporters, Cowdery had been a close associate since 1829, intimately involved in launching the church. Two weeks after Cowdery's resignation, Smith began writing the 1838 version of the church's history from the beginning, with Rigdon and Robinson assisting.[18] A year later Smith revised it, recording in late spring 1839 the best-known memory of his first vision.

That intervening year—characterized by violence, abandonment, and imprisonment—was the worst of Joseph Smith's life. In June 1838, Sidney Rigdon had delivered a pair of provocative sermons, insinuating that dissidents like Cowdery and the Whitmers were unwelcome, even in danger. Then on July 4, Rigdon excoriated external enemies, declaring independence from mobocracy and threatening a war of extermination against "that mob that comes upon us to disturb us."[19] The rhetoric resonated with Smith and other saints who were worn down with persecution.

When Daviess County settlers tried to bar saints from the polls on Election Day in August, hundreds of men responded by forming a paramilitary band that became known as the Danites. They, along with others, pressured prominent dissenters to leave Far West, fought at the election, and obliged a hostile justice of the peace to sign a statement that he would not be party to mobbing saints. Meanwhile, settlers laid siege to saints in Carroll County, who fled toward Far West while militia commanders reported blood lust and intensifying demand for saints' scalps.[20]

Missouri's governor was deaf to the saints' appeals for intervention on their behalf, turning them militant and defensive until they made preemptive strikes. Smith "was very plain and pointed in his remarks, and expressed a determination to put down the mob or die in the attempt."[21] "The Mormons have become desperate," one of their lawyers warned the governor, who responded with an executive order to the state militia to rid Missouri of Latter-day Saints.[22]

Within days of the October 27 order, Smith, along with his brother Hyrum, Sidney Rigdon, and a few other associates, went to negotiate terms of surrender and was captured, then bound for a preliminary hearing without due process, resulting in his incarceration in Liberty, Missouri, for "overt acts of treason."[23] Smith's wife, children, and remaining followers meanwhile left the state, their revealed land of promise, the site for New Jerusalem.

Smith fumed from his shared cell, furious at officials he regarded as impotent and at disciples who defected and testified against him.[24] Confined in that small, stinking space, he determined, if he was ever released, to tell the story of the saints' persecution, to wield history—memory—in his defense. Through letters from prison he called on his people to document their sufferings to "publish to all the world."[25]

In April 1839, Joseph Smith and his fellow prisoners were indicted for treason and lesser charges by a grand jury in Gallatin, Missouri, and granted a venue change. They brokered a deal with their guards and, as Hyrum put it, "took our change of venue to the state of Illinois." There they found their families and a few thousand other exiles scattered along the Mississippi around Quincy.[26]

Smith patched up the church, relocated to a new gathering place on a peninsula fifty miles to the north, and "began to study & prepare to dictate history" by June 10, 1839. The next day, an Irish convert named James Mulholland noted that Joseph Smith "commenced to dictate and I to write history."[27]

The memory Smith dictated that day was cued by the intentional, explicit act of composing autobiography. That act, in the context of the saints' 1838 war with Missouri, consolidated a defensive, resolute memory of the vision that would, over time, significantly shape the saints' shared story.

■ ■ ■

"Owing to the many reports which have been put in circulation by evil disposed and designing persons in relation to the rise and progress of the Church of Latter day Saints," Smith began, the words sounding as if he spat them out in defiance. "I have been induced to write this history." He had "to disabuse the publick mind, and put all enquirers after truth into possession of the facts."[28]

In a present rife with concerted opposition often led by ministers, Smith's mind was cued to search the past for the origins of persecution. He found it in the form of evangelicals from whom he had unsuccessfully sought solace in his youth. Smith's crisis in this memory was caused by clergymen who created a contest for souls and turned the Bible into a battleground. As he remembered it in the 1839 present, Smith's vision rescued him from disingenuous Protestant "Priests," as he repeatedly called them. When, in the wake of war with Missouri, he recalled his youthful rejection, it seemed to Smith that he had always been severely persecuted.

More than any of his other vision memories, the 1838/39 account emphasizes sectarian competition, asking "who of all these parties are right." Recalling fears about the status of his teenage soul and concerns that the Calvinists could be right, Joseph Smith remembered that he had favored Methodism but felt paralyzed by pluralism. He noted how Protestant clergymen zealously fought to redeem his soul, only to have their pretense exposed as sectarian strife. Then, in the vision, the Son of God told Smith that the churches "were all wrong . . . that all their creeds were an abomination in his sight, that those professors were all corrupt."

Reading James 1:5's invitation to ask God for wisdom is especially pronounced in his 1839 memory. The resulting epiphany enabled him to transcend the clergy because it led him to the woods where he learned from God directly that "they draw near to to me with their lips but their hearts are far from me, They teach for doctrines the commandments of men, having a form of Godliness but they deny the power thereof."[29]

Unique to and prominent in this memory is Smith's vivid recollection of rejection when he shared the experience with a Methodist minister. He dismissed Smith and expressed contempt for the vision, "saying it was all of the devil." As he dictated to James Mulholland, Smith told the story up through the Methodist minister's rejection. Then his mind shifted from a straightforward narration of the event into interpretive memory in which he started to muse about how it *felt* to be him, and what his experienced *seemed* like as he reflected on it "both then and since."

Aside from the specific, stinging rejection by the Methodist minister, there is no factual memory in this part of his 1839 narrative. His memory of persecution in childhood was vague and impersonal. He recounted his "serious reflection" that he had attracted so much unsolicited attention though "an obscure boy." He described his "great sorrow" vividly. An outward observer would not likely interpret these events as intensely as Smith subjectively did.

In the aftermath of Missouri, the vision meant the beginning of "a great deal of prejudice against me among professors of religion and . . . the cause of great persecution which continued to increase" until "all the sects united to persecute me." In Smith's interpretive memory, the preacher spoke specifically for everyone else.

In the process of assigning this meaning to his memory, Smith declared, as if responding to the preacher, that "it was nevertheless a fact, that I had seen a vision." Then he returned to his interpretive mode, telling candidly how, subsequent to the vision itself, as he braved "the bitterest persecution and reviling," he found meaning in it by comparing his experience to St. Paul's before Herod Agrippa.[30]

■ ■ ■

In Smith's 1839 present, persecution dominated his past. He had triumphed over mobs and militias, and now he made sense of his present position as the embattled president of a new church. This combination of Smith's past and present consolidated a defensive, resolute memory in which reporting his first vision catalyzed his lifetime of persecution. War with Missouri "poisoned Mormon memory," wrote Richard Bushman, Smith's best biographer.[31] War with Missouri at least shaped the way Joseph Smith and saints ever since remember his first vision and position it in their shared story.

The interpretive memory Smith dictated post-Missouri includes more than six hundred words describing how the vision led to persecution. This is the version of Smith's memory that was eventually canonized. Many saints have parts of it memorized. It shapes their identity as a people persecuted for transcending creedal Christianity and accessing God directly.

That outcome was not inevitable. Joseph Smith consolidated alternative memories of his vision. In 1832 he wrote one in his own hand. He or his followers could have chosen to select and relate it instead.

Notes

1. "History, 1838–1856, vol. A-1 [23 December 1805–30 August 1834]," 1, The Joseph Smith Papers, accessed February 25, 2019, https://www.josephsmithpapers.org/paper-summary/history-1838-1856-volume-a-1-23-december-1805-30-august-1834/1

2. Dean C. Jessee, Mark Ashurst-McGee, and Richard L. Jensen, eds., *Journals*, vol. 1, *1832–1839*, vol. 1 of the Journals series of *The Joseph Smith Papers*, ed. Dean C. Jessee, Ronald K. Esplin, and Richard Lyman Bushman (Salt Lake City: Church Historian's Press, 2008), 260–64.

3. See Joseph Smith to William W. Phelps, November 27, 1832, in Matthew C. Godfrey, Mark Ashurst-McGee, Grant Underwood, Robert J. Woodford, and William G. Hartley, eds., *Documents*, vol. 2, *July 1831–January 1833*, vol. 2 in the Documents series of *The Joseph Smith Papers*, ed. Dean C. Jessee, Ronald K. Esplin, Richard Lyman Bushman, and Matthew J. Grow (Salt Lake City: Church Historian's Press, 2013), 315–21.

4. Robin Scott Jensen, Robert J. Woodford, and Steven C. Harper, eds., *Revelations and Translations*, vol. 1 *Manuscript Revelation Books*, ed. Dean C. Jessee, Ronald K. Esplin, and Richard Lyman Bushman (Salt Lake City: Church Historian's Press, 2011), 102, 329; Karen Lynn Davidson, Richard L. Jensen, and David J. Whittaker, eds., *Assigned Histories, 1831–1847*, vol. 2 in the Histories series of *The Joseph Smith Papers*, ed. Dean C. Jessee, Ronald K. Esplin, and Richard Lyman Bushman (Salt Lake City: Church Historian's Press, 2012), 3–110.

5. Dean C. Jessee, Mark Ashurst-McGee, and Richard L. Jensen, eds., *Journals*, vol. 1, *1832–1839*, vol. 1 of the Journals series of *The Joseph Smith Papers*, ed. Dean C. Jessee, Ronald K. Esplin, and Richard Lyman Bushman (Salt Lake City: Church Historian's Press, 2008), 249.

6. Dean C. Jessee, Mark Ashurst-McGee, and Richard L. Jensen, eds., *Journals*, vol. 1, *1832–1839*, vol. 1 of the Journals series of *The Joseph Smith Papers*, ed. Dean C. Jessee,

Ronald K. Esplin, and Richard Lyman Bushman (Salt Lake City: Church Historian's Press, 2008), xxiii.

7. Thomas J. Anastasio, Kristen Ann Ehrenberger, Patrick Watson, and Wenyi Zhang, *Individual and Collective Memory Consolidation: Analogous Processes on Different Levels* (Cambridge, MA: MIT Press, 2012), 17.

8. Eric R. Kandel, *In Search of Memory: The Emergence of a New Science of Mind* (New York: Norton, 2006), 210.

9. David C. Rubin, ed., *Autobiographical Memory* (New York: Cambridge University Press, 1986), 4; also Richard Lyman Bushman, *Joseph Smith: Rough Stone Rolling* (New York: Alfred A. Knopf, 2005), 389–90.

10. Chris Westbury and Daniel C. Dennett, "Mining the Past to Construct the Future: Memory and Belief as Forms of Knowledge," in *Memory, Brain, and Belief*, ed. Daniel L. Schacter and Elaine Scarry (Cambridge, MA: Harvard University Press, 2000), 19.

11. Daniel L. Schacter, *Searching for Memory: The Brain, the Mind, and the Past* (New York: Basic Books, 1996), 71.

12. Schacter, *Searching for Memory*, 28.

13. Roger Shattuck, *Proust's Binoculars* (Princeton, NJ: Princeton University Press, 1983), 46–47.

14. Dale W. Adams, "Grandison Newell's Obsession," *Journal of Mormon History* 30, no. 1 (2004): 168–88.

15. Bushman, *Rough Stone Rolling*, 336–41; Jessee et al., *Journals*, 1:226–33.

16. Bushman, *Rough Stone Rolling*, 336–41.

17. Jessee et al., *Journals*, 1:237.

18. Jessee et al., *Journals*, 1:250–60.

19. Sydney Rigdon, *Oration Delivered on the 4th of July, 1838, at Far West, Caldwell County, Missouri* (Far West, MO: Journal Office, 1838), 12.

20. Bushman, *Rough Stone Rolling*, 360.

21. Warren Foote, Autobiography, 1817–1901, L. Tom Perry Special Collections, Harold B. Lee Library, Brigham Young University, Provo, Utah, p. 24.

22. David R. Atchison to Lilburn W. Boggs, October 22, 1838, as quoted in Bushman, *Rough Stone Rolling*, 362, and cited in footnote 27, p. 631.

23. Bushman, *Rough Stone Rolling*, 369.

24. Joseph Smith to The Church of Latter Day Saints in Caldwell County, December 16, 1838, Liberty, Missouri, Church History Library, Salt Lake City; also in *Times and Seasons* 1 (April 1840): 82–86; Bushman, *Rough Stone Rolling*, 376.

25. Dean C. Jessee, ed., *Personal Writings of Joseph Smith* (Salt Lake City: Deseret Book, 2002), 445.

26. Alexander L. Baugh, "'We Took Our Change of Venue to the State of Illinois': The Gallatin Hearing and the Escape of Joseph Smith and the Mormon Prisoners from Missouri, April 1839," *Mormon Historical Studies* 2, no. 1 (2001): 67.

27. Jessee et al., *Journals*, 1:340 and related notes 29–30.

28. Karen Lynn Davidson, David J. Whittaker, Mark Ashurst-McGee, and Richard L. Jensen, eds., *Joseph Smith Histories*, vol. 1, *1832–1844*, vol. 1 of the Histories series

of *The Joseph Smith Papers*, ed. Dean C. Jessee, Ronald K. Esplin, and Richard Lyman Bushman (Salt Lake City: Church Historian's Press, 2012), 204.

29. Davidson et al., *Joseph Smith Histories*, 1:204–20.
30. Davidson et al., *Joseph Smith Histories*, 1:216–19.
31. Bushman, *Rough Stone Rolling*, 372.

3

An Account of His Marvelous Experience

The 1832 Account

I cried unto the Lord for mercy for there was none else to whom
I could go and to obtain mercy and the Lord heard my cry in the
wilderness and while in <the> attitude of calling upon the Lord <in
the 16th year of my age> a piller of light above the brightness of the
sun at noon day come down from above and rested upon me and
I was filled with the spirit of god and the <Lord>opened the heavens
upon me and I saw the Lord and he spake unto me saying Joseph
<my son> thy sins are forgiven thee. go thy <way> walk in my stat-
utes and keep my commandments behold I am the Lord of glory
I was crucifyed for the world that all those who believe on my name
may have Eternal life <behold> the world lieth in sin and at this time
and none doeth good no not one they have turned asside from the
gospel and keep not <my> commandments they draw near to me
with their lips while their hearts are far from me and mine anger is
kindling against the inhabitants of the earth to visit them acording to
thir ungodliness and to bring to pass that which <hath> been spoken
by the mouth of the prophets and Ap[o]stles behold and lo I come
quickly as it [is?] written of me in the cloud <clothed> in the glory of
my Father and my soul was filled with love and for many days I could
rejoice with great Joy and the Lord was with me but could find none
that would believe the hevnly vision.

—Joseph Smith, 1832[1]

The minister's rejection immediately and permanently affected the consolidation of Joseph Smith's memories. All available evidence indicates that he
kept the experience to himself for years after that first telling. Inwardly he
felt conflicted—fractured between what his culture told him he ought to
be and what his experience told him he actually was.[2] This conflict later
combined with whatever present circumstances he was experiencing to

shape his memories of the vision. In 1839 his vision led to persecution, but long before that it was about forgiveness, authority, a soft answer to the Methodist minister, and more—all at once.

The earliest known recorded reference Smith made to his vision was in the prologue to a constitution created at the organization of the Church of Christ in 1830 (renamed The Church of Jesus Christ of Latter-day Saints in 1838). This document begins by emphasizing Smith's revelations, including being "called of God an Apostle of Jesus Christ," receiving direction from "an Holy Angel," and having the power to miraculously translate the Book of Mormon.

These credentials overshadow the first item in the list: God's first manifestation to Smith, obscured simply with these words: "it truly was manifested unto the first elder that he had received remission of his sins."[3] The only reason to conclude that this refers to Smith's first vision is that he composed a narrative of the experience more than two years later in which he emphasized how he became convicted of his sins and received forgiveness while praying in the wilderness.[4]

By the fall of 1832, then, Smith was able to narrate his experience again. It took heaven and earth to convince him to record it. A revelation from God on April 6, 1830, had told him to record the events that made him a prophet and apostle, but he was slow to follow it.[5]

He began recording some revelations possibly as early as 1828, and some revisions to the Bible by the summer of 1830. By then, too, Cowdery had made both an original and a printer's manuscript of the Book of Mormon. Early in 1831 Smith announced a revelation appointing a church historian to document his ministry.[6] Until late 1832, however, he apparently did not document his own past.[7]

By the summer of 1832, Joseph Smith was president of the Church of Christ, which he had organized in 1830. He led the church (along with counselors Sidney Rigdon and Frederick Williams) by the authority of his revelations. Rigdon was erratic and unstable after the March 1832 beating, tarring, and feathering he endured with Smith at the hands of hostile neighbors in Hiram, Ohio. That July, Rigdon declared among the saints in Kirtland, Ohio, that keys of authority had been taken from the church and vested solely in him.[8] Days later, Smith confiscated Rigdon's preaching license and asserted, "I myself hold the Keys of this last dispensation and I forever will hold them in time and in eternity."[9]

Smith had spent several weeks earlier that summer meditating in Greenville, Indiana, where he stayed with Newel Whitney as he recovered from a stagecoach accident that occurred as they and Rigdon returned to Ohio after visiting saints in Missouri. From Greenville, Smith wrote to his wife about remembering "all the past moments of my life." He told Emma he had wept about his sins and felt relieved by receiving God's forgiveness. When he recorded his first known narration of his vision later that year, worrying about his sins and receiving God's forgiveness dominated the story.[10]

Smith also began articulating a theology of historical memory at about the same time as he recorded the 1832 account of the first vision.[11] With Frederick Williams, who had replaced Rigdon as scribe, Smith wrote from his Ohio headquarters to followers who were struggling on Missouri's Jacksonian frontier to establish a countercultural, premillennial Zion according to his revelations.[12] He emphasized the duty of the church's historian "to keep a hystory and a general church receord of all things that transpire in Zion . . . and also there manner of life and the[ir] faith and works."[13]

His revealed rationale for recording history linked it with divine judgment, spelling out eventual rewards for those who consecrated their lives and property to the cause and regrets for those who did not. He penned his prayer for deliverance "from the little narrow prison almost as it were totel darkness of paper pen and ink and a crooked broken scattered and imperfect language."[14] In 1832, in other words, Joseph Smith knew that God had commanded him to record his history, and that alone he was inadequate to the task.

In that present Smith consolidated and, with Frederick Williams, composed "A History of the life of Joseph Smith Jr. an account of his marvilous experience and of all the mighty acts which he doeth in the name of Jesus Ch[r]ist the son of the living God."[15]

▨ ▨ ▨

The rough, six-page autobiography states grand themes expressed by a man of limited education. At age twenty-six, Smith remembered vivid feelings, images, and words associated with his vulnerable, introspective, teenage self in an evangelical culture and employed them to affirm his present position. In language echoing religious revivals, he described consciousness of his sins and his frustrated efforts to find forgiveness in a church that matched the New Testament model. He emphasized the personal redemption Christ offered him as an anxious young man.[16]

This is the memory that consolidated when Joseph Smith remembered the original event to satisfy cultural prescriptions while he was trying, counterculturally, to gather Old Testament Israel into a New Testament Zion out of a Jacksonian culture by the power of his revelations. It was shaped by his late 1832 preoccupation to record history, his sense of inadequacy as a writer, and rivalry with Rigdon.

Its stately opening emphasizes Smith as apostle, visited by angels, a holder of the high priesthood. The first words in his own hand, referring to himself in third person, echo his earlier response to Rigdon in affirming divine bestowal of the "Kees of the Kingdom of God" on him, emphasizing, contra Rigdon's claim, that those keys remain with Joseph Smith. In the next line he shifts to a first-person disclaimer, strikingly demure in contrast, implying that the unrefined composition owes to his meager education.

This 1832 autobiography was ultimately unsatisfying to Joseph Smith. He felt conflicted about its contents. Literarily, it is "a traditional form of spiritual autobiography familiar to him and those around him."[17] He remembered his experience in terms of acceptable spiritual discourse, mimicking a generic style and tone that emphasized personal sinfulness and redemption by Christ. By following the script, he sought consensus with cultural mediators—with the Methodist minister. There is no evidence that Smith did so conspiratorially or even consciously. Since his ability to form memories depended on what he already knew, he may not have had the power to remember otherwise. Sociocultural mores limited the ways he could frame his original experience.[18]

That explains in part why his 1832 account of the vision sounds like the memory of a Methodist convert aspiring to convince his minister of his legitimate conversion experience. The memory consolidated that way. Yet, even as he wrote the memory in 1832, Smith was no longer that person. He seems to have still nursed the psychological wounds of being rejected, but his revelations had tended away from evangelical Protestantism toward nearly universal salvation in degrees of heavenly glory and temple rituals mediated by priesthoods.[19]

Joseph Smith's 1832 present included resources for remembering that were unavailable to him at the time of his vision. Therefore, remembering to resolve dissonance after a dozen years created a dilemma. His 1832 identity was far removed from the anxious teen who hoped for a minister's validation that he was indeed born again. In other words, Smith tried in his 1832 memory to conform to the cultural script, but as a result the memory did not resonate well with his present, and subjectively speaking, "a memory is true if it resonates with oneself."[20]

Joseph Smith probably intended the 1832 document to serve as source material for his church's historians, who began their histories where his autobiography ends.[21] Neither Oliver Cowdery nor John Whitmer, however, seemed to know that the 1832 document existed. Their histories reveal no dependence on it, not even awareness of it. Joseph Smith never published it. He apparently regarded it as an unusable draft. Perhaps he thought it too marred by his being "deprived of the bennifit of an education." Maybe the perspective he gained with subsequent experiences made this memory unsatisfying.[22]

Why would Joseph Smith record an unsatisfying memory? Why compose a record of all the marvelous events that made him a prophet and then keep it from his people? In light of his later memories of the same event, his 1832 autobiography is best understood as a conflicted consolidation—an unsuccessful attempt to reconcile his experience with a socially safe identity. In 1832 he tried to describe the experience "as if it were primarily a vision granted to assure him of his personal redemption."[23]

For these or other reasons, the 1832 memory did not shape the saints' story. In fact, for more than a century it remained outside the buffer, the collection of items available for consolidating collective memory. For Joseph Smith's individual memory, however, the 1832 consolidation fixed one point from which he never turned: he prayed to God in the woods, and his ministry began when God answered.[24]

Notes

1. "History, circa Summer 1832," 3, The Joseph Smith Papers, accessed February 25, 2019, https://www.josephsmithpapers.org/paper-summary/history-circa-summer-1832/3

2. For more on ought and actual identities see Armand L. Mauss, "Apostasy and the Management of Spoiled Identity," in *The Politics of Religious Apostasy: The Role of Apostates in the Transformation of Religious Movements*, ed. David G. Bromley (Westport, CT: Praeger, 1998), 60.

3. Karen Lynn Davidson, David J. Whittaker, Mark Ashurst-McGee, and Richard L. Jensen, eds., *Joseph Smith Histories, 1832–1844*, vol. 1 of the Histories series of *The Joseph Smith Papers*, ed. Dean C. Jessee, Ronald K. Esplin, and Richard Lyman Bushman (Salt Lake City: Church Historian's Press, 2012), xv–xivv; Robin Scott Jensen, Robert J. Woodford, and Steven C. Harper, eds., *Revelations and Translations*, vol. 1, *Manuscript Revelation Books*, vol. 1 of the Revelations and Translations series of *The Joseph Smith Papers*, ed. Dean C. Jessee, Ronald K. Esplin, and Richard Lyman Bushman (Salt Lake City: Church Historian's Press, 2011), 75–77.

4. Davidson et al., *Joseph Smith Histories*, 1:10–16.

5. Michael Hubbard MacKay, Gerrit J. Dirkmaat, Grant Underwood, Robert J. Woodford, and William G. Hartley, eds., *Documents*, vol. 1, *July 1828–June 1831*, vol. 1 of the Documents series of *The Joseph Smith Papers*, ed. Dean C. Jessee, Ronald K. Esplin, Richard Lyman Bushman, and Matthew J. Grow (Salt Lake City: Church Historian's Press, 2013), 126–30. Available online at "Revelation, 6 April 1830 [D&C 21]," p. 28, *The Joseph Smith Papers*, accessed June 28, 2018, http://www.josephsmithpapers.org/paper-summary/revelation-6-april-1830-dc-21/1.

6. Jensen et al., eds., *Revelations and Translations*, 1:27–29, 131–33; Jessee et al., eds., *Journals*, 1:xxxv–xxxviii; Michael Hubbard MacKay, Gerrit J. Dirkmaat, Grand Underwood, Robert J. Woodford, and William G. Hartley, eds., *Documents*, vol. 1, *July 1828–June 1831*, vol. 1 of the Documents series of *The Joseph Smith Papers*, ed. Dean C. Jessee, Ronald K. Esplin, and Richard Lyman Bushman (Salt Lake City: Church Historian's Press, 2013), 284–86.

7. Karen Lynn Davidson, David J. Whittaker, Mark Ashurst-McGee, and Richard L. Jensen, eds., *Joseph Smith Histories, 1832–1844*, vol. 1 of the Histories series of *The Joseph Smith Papers*, ed. Dean C. Jessee, Ronald K. Esplin, and Richard Lyman Bushman (Salt Lake City: Church Historian's Press, 2012), 6.

8. On Rigdon's claim, see Lucy Mack Smith, *Lucy's Book: A Critical Edition of Lucy Mack Smith's Family Memoir*, ed. Lavina Fielding Anderson (Salt Lake City: Signature Books, 2001), 560–64; Philo Dibble, "Early Scenes in Church History," in *Four Faith Promoting Classics* (Salt Lake City: Bookcraft, 1968), 74–96; and see the following at the Church History Library in Salt Lake City: Reynolds Cahoon Diary, July 5–17, 1832; Charles C. Rich, "History Charles Coulson Rich," MS 3–4.

9. Smith, *Lucy's Book*, 560–64.

10. Joseph Smith, Letter to Emma Smith, June 6, 1832, in Matthew C. Godfrey, Mark Ashurst-McGee, Grant Underwood, Robert J. Woodford, and William G. Hartley, eds., *Documents*, vol. 2, *July 1831–January 1833*, vol. 2 of the Documents series of *The Joseph Smith Papers*, ed. Dean C. Jessee, Ronald K. Esplin, Richard Lyman Bushman, and Matthew J. Grow (Salt Lake City: Church Historian's Press, 2013), 246–57.

11. Joseph Smith, Letter to William W. Phelps, November 27, 1832, in Matthew C. Godfrey, Mark Ashurst-McGee, Grant Underwood, Robert J. Woodford, and William G. Hartley, eds., *Documents*, vol. 2, *July 1831–January 1833*, vol. 2 of the Documents series of *The Joseph Smith Papers*, ed. Dean C. Jessee, Ronald K. Esplin, Richard Lyman Bushman, and Matthew J. Grow (Salt Lake City: Church Historian's Press, 2013), 315–21.

12. Frederick G. Williams Papers 1834–1842, MS 782, folder 1, item 6, Church History Library, Salt Lake City. Joseph Smith began his July 31, 1832, letter to William Phelps, "I sit down to dictate for Broth Frederick to write." Retained copy in handwriting of Frederick G. Williams, in Robin Scott Jensen, Robert J. Woodford, and Steven C. Harper, eds., *Manuscript Revelation Books*, facsimile edition, vol. 1 of the Revelations and Translations series of *The Joseph Smith Papers*, ed. Dean C. Jessee, Ronald K. Esplin, and Richard Lyman Bushman (Salt Lake City: Church Historian's Press, 2009), 453.

13. Smith, Letter to Phelps, in Godfrey et al., *Documents*, 2:315–21.

14. Smith, Letter to Phelps, in Godfrey et al., *Documents*, 2:315–21; "Let Every Man Learn His Duty," *Evening and the Morning Star* 1, no. 8 (January 1833): 121–22.

15. The historical introduction in Davidson et al., *Joseph Smith Histories*, 1:5–10, is the best-informed assessment of when and how Smith and Williams composed this document.

16. Karen Lynn Davidson, David J. Whittaker, Mark Ashurst-McGee, and Richard L. Jensen, eds., *Joseph Smith Histories, 1832–1844*, vol. 1 of the Histories series of *The Joseph Smith Papers*, ed. Dean C. Jessee, Ronald K. Esplin, and Richard Lyman Bushman (Salt Lake City: Church Historian's Press, 2012), 10–16.

17. Neal A. Lambert and Richard H. Cracroft, "Literary Form and Historical Understanding: Joseph Smith's First Vision," *Journal of Mormon History* 7 (1980): 33.

18. Maurice Halbwachs and others have argued that all individual memory is in some sense collective, since it is socially mediated. See Thomas J. Anastasio, Kristen Ann Ehrenberger, Patrick Watson, and Wenyi Zhang, *Individual and Collective Memory Consolidation: Analogous Processes on Different Levels* (Cambridge, MA: MIT Press, 2012), 45–48.

19. See D&C 76 and 84, "Doctrine and Covenants, 1844," *The Joseph Smith Papers*, accessed May 31, 2015, http://josephsmithpapers.org/paperSummary/doctrine-and-covenants-1844. Ann Taves challenged and refined my thinking on this point, for which I am grateful. See Ann Taves and Steven C. Harper, "Joseph Smith's First Vision: New Methods for the Analysis of Experience-Related Texts," *Mormon Studies Review* 3 (2016): 53–84.

20. Engel, *Context Is Everything*, 13.

21. Davidson et al., *Joseph Smith Histories*, 1:5n11.

22. Karen Lynn Davidson, David J. Whittaker, Mark Ashurst-McGee, and Richard L. Jensen, eds., *Joseph Smith Histories, 1832–1844*, vol. 1 of the Histories series of *The Joseph Smith Papers*, ed. Dean C. Jessee, Ronald K. Esplin, and Richard Lyman Bushman (Salt Lake City: Church Historian's Press, 2012), 10–16.

23. Lambert and Cracroft, "Literary Form," 36–37.

24. Karen Lynn Davidson, David J. Whittaker, Mark Ashurst-McGee, and Richard L. Jensen, eds., *Joseph Smith Histories, 1832–1844*, vol. 1 of the Histories series of *The Joseph Smith Papers*, ed. Dean C. Jessee, Ronald K. Esplin, and Richard Lyman Bushman (Salt Lake City: Church Historian's Press, 2012), 10–16; Richard Lyman Bushman, *Joseph Smith: Rough Stone Rolling* (New York: Knopf, 2005), 69.

4

First Communication

The 1835 Account

Being wrought up in my mind, respecting the subject of religion and looking ~~upon~~ <at> the different systems taught the children of men, I knew not who was right or who was wrong and concidering it of the first importance that I should be right, in matters that involve eternal consequences; being thus perplexed in mind I retired to the silent grove and bowd down before the Lord, under a realising sense that he had said (if the bible be true) ask and you shall receive knock and it shall be opened seek and you shall find and again, if any man lack wisdom let him ask of God who giveth to all men libarally and upbradeth not; information was what I most desired at this time, and with a fixed determination ~~I~~ to obtain it, I called upon the Lord for the first time, in the place above stated or in other words I made a fruitless attempt to pray, my toung seemed to be swolen in my mouth, so that I could not utter, I heard a noise behind me like some person walking towards me, <I> strove again to pray, but could not, the noise of walking seemed to draw nearer, I sprung up on my feet, ~~and~~ and looked around, but saw no person or thing that was calculated to produce the noise of walking, I kneeled again my mouth was opened and my toung liberated, and I called on the Lord in mighty prayer, a pillar of fire appeared above my head, it presently rested down upon ~~my~~ <me> ~~head~~, and filled me with joy unspeakable, a personage appeard in the midst, of this pillar of flame which was spread all around, and yet nothing consumed, another personage soon appeard like unto the first, he said unto me thy sins are forgiven thee, he testifyed unto me that Jesus Christ is the son of God; <and I saw many angels in this vision> I was about 14. years old when I received this first communication.

—Joseph Smith, 1835[1]

The long shadow cast by the minister's rejection explains why Smith's memory formed and re-formed as it did in the context of later experiences. Biographer Richard Bushman observed how the 1832 and 1838/39 memories share the story "of a lonely adolescent, occupied with spiritual agonies, trying to account for his fabulous experiences," noting how the later document "has a more confident public tone. Joseph, still the perplexed youth, is also the prophet about to usher in the last dispensation."[2]

Both the 1832 and 1838/39 memories are best read as responses to the Methodist minister. In 1832 Smith remembered to please him and the authority he represented. In 1838/39 he remembered to reject and replace the minister and the authority represented. Smith's 1838/39 perspective is enlarged and institutional. From that point of view the vision was not simply another manifestation of Christ to a born-again soul. It was an indictment of apostate churches and their creeds—not simply the marvelous acts of Joseph Smith but the story of "the rise and progress of the Church of Jesus Christ of Latter-day Saints."[3]

In both 1832 and 1838/39, Smith adapted a familiar cultural script to respond to the rejection he experienced. In 1832, he used a script common to Methodist converts to remember himself as one of many. But that memory dissatisfied Smith. Christopher Jones showed that the 1838/39 document shares at least as much with contemporary evangelical (especially Methodist) conversion narratives as the 1832 document does.[4] By 1838/39, a mixture of psychological pain and an established prophetic stature positioned Smith to adapt the same script to a different end, remembering that he alone had accessed the power of God, not merely the form of godliness.

Methodist conversion narratives had long since asserted their superiority over others who had a form of godliness but lacked the power that Methodist converts accessed by dramatic, divine experience. Joseph Smith told the same story to turn the Methodist argument on itself.[5] Change just a few words the Son of God says to Smith and the 1838/39 document is entirely generic, except that it uncharacteristically, unflinchingly, adamantly affirms the literal reality of the experience compared to contemporary conversion narratives.[6]

Joseph Smith flipped the cultural script. As a result, in his 1838/39 memory he triumphed over the minister, over persecution. The document's relationship to evangelical conversion narratives mirrors the restored church's relationship to historical Christianity, sharing themes while severing ties.[7]

Given the right context and cues, however, Joseph Smith could produce a memory of his first vision that did not need to respond to the minister. The memory cue made all the difference. Smith's 1832 and 1838/39 accounts of his vision were cued by intentional, explicit remembering. The resulting memory was composed by a systematic search or strategic retrieval. But in between those memories, in 1835, he told the story spontaneously. The resulting memory was cued by an extemporaneous association of experiences that made him a prophet.

■ ■ ■

On November 9, 1835, Robert Matthews arrived at Smith's Ohio home and introduced himself as Joshua, a Jewish minister. He was the head of a crumbling "kingdom" and recently acquitted of murder in New York. Curious, Smith scrutinized the stranger, tried unsuccessfully to learn his real name, and engaged in a religious dialogue. Matthews meanwhile observed Smith and tried to assess his intentions. During their visits, Smith told an unplanned account of his theophany to the rival prophet, resulting in a memory formed automatically by an unsolicited cue rather than by a systematic search.[8]

Smith recited his story to Matthews, and a scribe recorded it as Smith's "relation of the circumstances connected with the coming forth of the book of Mormon," beginning with his first vision. He said he was "wrought up" about which doctrine was right. He had to be "right in matters that involve eternal consequences," and being "perplexed" about it, he went to the woods to pray, hoping the Bible's promises about asking and receiving were true.[9]

For the first time in the historical record, Smith remembered that he felt tongue-tied and feared that a person was coming after him. He tried again, and this time "mighty prayer" evoked a fiery pillar, feelings of intense joy, and a personage who introduced another who said Joseph was forgiven and "Jesus Christ is the Son of God."[10]

Spontaneous cues activated different pieces of the past stored in different parts of Smith's brain, resulting in this memory in which Smith is not confined by the identity of an evangelical convert and not worried even subconsciously about the approval of the minister. He is a prophet among prophets with increased "capacity for expressing the uniqueness of his experience."[11] In reciting his prophetic resume, Smith told the story of how he produced the Book of Mormon and associated his vision with that project as his "first" revelation.

Comparing credentials with Matthews enabled Joseph Smith to consolidate a memory of his vision he could not have produced before he published the Book of Mormon in 1830. Nor would it have been the same if it consolidated in a different context. The spontaneous memory is sans persecution. It shows that, given the right cues and context, he could make a memory that did not need to respond to the Methodist minister, whether to please him or to rebuke him.

After telling his story, Smith hosted Matthews for dinner, and then the guest described his prophetic credentials by interpreting biblical apocalypses. Their exchange went on for parts of three days until Smith dismissed Matthews on the authority of a superior revelation. "I told him," Smith's journal says, "that my God told me that his God is the Devil, and I could not keep him any longer, and he must depart."[12]

Notes

1. "Journal, 1835–1836," 23–24, in Dean C. Jessee, Mark Ashurst-McGee, and Richard L. Jensen, eds., *Journals*, vol. 1, *1832–1839*, vol. 1 of the Journals series of *The Joseph Smith Papers*, ed. Dean C. Jessee, Ronald K. Esplin, and Richard Lyman Bushman (Salt Lake City: Church Historian's Press, 2008), 53–223.

2. Richard Lyman Bushman, *Joseph Smith: Rough Stone Rolling* (New York: Knopf, 2005), 389. See Richard H. Cracroft and Neal E. Lambert, "Literary Form and Historical Understanding: Joseph Smith's First Vision," *Journal of Mormon History* 7 (1980): 31–42.

3. Karen Lynn Davidson, David J. Whittaker, Mark Ashurst-McGee, and Richard L. Jensen, eds., *Joseph Smith Histories, 1832–1844*, vol. 1 of the Histories series of *The Joseph Smith Papers*, ed. Dean C. Jessee, Ronald K. Esplin, and Richard Lyman Bushman (Salt Lake City: Church Historian's Press, 2012), 204–19. Cracroft and Lambert, "Literary Form and Historical Understanding," 39.

4. See Christopher C. Jones, "The Power and Form of Godliness: Methodist Conversion Narratives and Joseph Smith's First Vision," *Journal of Mormon History* 37, no. 2 (Spring 2011): 88–114.

5. Jones, "The Power and Form of Godliness," 88–114.

6. Ann Kirschner, "Tending to Edify, Astonish, and Instruct: Published Narratives of Spiritual Dreams and Visions in the Early Republic," *Early American Studies* 1, no. 1 (Spring 2003): 198–229.

7. See Marvin Hill, "A Note on Joseph Smith's First Vision and Its Import in the Shaping of Early Mormonism," *Dialogue* 12 (Spring 1979): 90–99.

8. Daniel L. Schacter, *Searching for Memory: The Brain, the Mind, and the Past* (New York: Basic Books, 1996), 39–71, 120–21.

9. Dean C. Jessee, Mark Ashurst-McGee, and Richard L. Jensen, eds., *Journals*, vol. 1, *1832–1839*, vol. 1 of the Journals series of *The Joseph Smith Papers*, ed. Dean C. Jessee, Ronald K. Esplin, and Richard Lyman Bushman (Salt Lake City: Church Historian's Press, 2008), 87–88.

10. Jessee et al., *Journals*, 1:87–88.

11. Lambert and Cracroft, "Literary Form," 37.

12. Jessee et al., *Journals*, 1:95.

5

Consolidation

When about fourteen years of age I began to reflect upon the importance of being prepared for a future state, and upon enquiring the plan of salvation I found that there was a great clash in religious sentiment; if I went to one society they referred me to one plan, and another to another; each one pointing to his own particular creed as the summum bonum of perfection: considering that all could not be right, and that God could not be the author of so much confusion I determined to investigate the subject more fully, believing that if God had a church it would not be split up into factions, and that if he taught one society to worship one way, and administer in one set of ordinances, he would not teach another principles which were diametrically opposed. Believing the word of God I had confidence in the declaration of James; "If any man lack wisdom let him ask of God who giveth to all men liberally and upbraideth not and it shall be given him," I retired to a secret place in a grove and began to call upon the Lord, while fervently engaged in supplication my mind was taken away from the objects with which I was surrounded, and I was enwrapped in a heavenly vision and saw two glorious personages who exactly resembled each other in features, and likeness, surrounded with a brilliant light which eclipsed the sun at noon-day. They told me that all religious denominations were believing in incorrect doctrines, and that none of them was acknowledged of God as his church and kingdom. And I was expressly commanded to "go not after them," at the same time receiving a promise that the fulness of the gospel should at some future time be made known unto me.

—Joseph Smith, 1842[1]

Leading theorists compare the process of memory consolidation to water being poured from a leaky bucket into a much less leaky bucket. In this sense, Joseph Smith lost much information in the pouring but still retained a durable, consolidated memory. This durability is seen through the similarities among his vision accounts, including the final extant account from Smith himself in 1842.

Memory consolidates in both buckets, but the process and the products differ. The short-term consolidation of memory "occurs on the level of neurons and synapses."[2] It typically takes seconds to minutes and produces memory that is easily disrupted and manipulated, unless it is like the water that gets poured into and then remains in the second bucket. Long-term consolidation requires the cooperation of various brain regions "over time periods of months, years, and even decades."[3] The memory that consolidates, like the water that makes it into the less leaky bucket, is remarkably stable over time. No one knows exactly why, but repeatedly rehearsed personal narratives resist erosion over time, and some actually strengthen.

One explanation holds that autobiographical memories include a variety of kinds of information—sights, sounds, spaces, and language—each of which is managed by a different region of the brain. Other brain regions are thought to be "convergence zones" in which sensory perceptions are linked and bound to previous knowledge. So remembering, neurologically speaking, happens when signals from convergence zones activate stored fragments of related sensory perceptions.

As Joseph Smith processed his vision experience, in part by recuperating and re-forming stored information, fragments of old memories combined with current experiences to produce memories that could be vivid or vague. The degree of clarity depended mainly on how deeply he consciously processed any given detail of the experience at the time, and how frequently and consciously he later recalled it. Each time he recalled the event, he reoriented himself relative to it. Frequent rehearsal of an event over time forges long-term links between related perceptions and previous knowledge.[4] This theory and the evidence that supports it explain why some autobiographical memories become more precise and complete over time.[5]

The short- and long-term processes of consolidation include both forgetting and remembering. Like the water that leaked out of the metaphorical buckets, forgetting was as important as remembering in creating the coherence of Joseph Smith's autobiographical narratives. The memory that remains after forgetting is the meaningful past. Rare individuals who cannot forget facts struggle to find coherence and lack the ability to conceptualize.[6]

Joseph Smith remembered or forgot elements of his vision based on what he knew at the time and how often and how deeply he recalled it. In 1835, he vividly described aspects he processed deeply, then added as an afterthought his approximate age as best his vague memory could recover. Likewise, in 1839 he remembered that an unusual religious excitement occurred in his region only "sometime in the second year after our removal to Manchester," but he felt sure that it began with the Methodists. He remembered that the vision occurred in the "morning of a beautiful clear day early in the spring of eighteen hundred and twenty," but apparently he could not recall which day. He noted that after the vision he was "between fourteen and fifteen years of age," which his scribe later qualified further by inserting "or thereabouts."[7]

The ideas he consolidated best, and thus remembered most vividly, were the ones he associated most meaningfully with the resolution to his problem of finding how to be saved. These were points at which emotion and cognition combined, as in his 1832 description, "my mind become exceedingly distressed," or his 1838/39 welding of "serious reflection and great uneasiness" and "laboring under the extreme difficulties caused" by competing preachers and doctrines. In 1835 Smith said that he was "wrought up in [his] mind" and "perplexed in mind" and describes his increasing consciousness of the possibility of a divine answer and his "fixed determination to obtain" one.[8]

His 1832 account says that his mind became "seriously imprest with regard to the all important concerns for the welfare of my immortal soul," that denominational strife made him grieve and "marvel exceedingly," and that as he "pondered" in distress he "felt to mourn" and finally "cried unto the Lord for mercy" and experienced a theophany that filled his soul with love for days and led him to "rejoice with great Joy."[9] Intense emotion and repeated reflection combined to create Joseph Smith's most vivid and enduring memories. By remembering these elements and forgetting others, he became aware of what was meaningful about his experience.

Neuroscience has shown that "memory is not fixed at the time of learning but takes time to develop its permanent form." So some leading psychologists consider it "a mistake to assume that interpretation of recalled knowledge happens only at the preloading, perceptual stage—to assume that once knowledge 'enters memory' (through the front door), it is happily stored away, to be 'retrieved' intact at later times of 'recollection.'"[10] Joseph Smith's earliest memories of his vision were based on factual, sensory, and emotional elements. Those facts accumulated more and more meaning in light of subsequent experience. For example, he interpreted his vision as "first"—the "first vision" as Mormons widely know it today—only after subsequent visions.

Interpretive memory—the kind that becomes possible with the passage of time and experience—is unsurprisingly most substantial in a late account, 1838/39. It shows how he continued to consciously interpret the experience over the years. In 1842 he added amendments to the 1838/39 document, including this interpretive memory:

> It seems as though the adversary was aware at a very early period of my life that I was destined to prove a disturber & annoyer of his kingdom, or else why should the powers of Darkness combine against me, why the oppression & persecution that arose against me, almost in my infancy?[11]

To the thirty-four-year-old Smith, embroiled at the time of the redaction in efforts to extradite him from Illinois to Missouri, oppression and persecution *seemed* to have begun in infancy and lasted for a lifetime.

■ ■ ■

Historians often assume that an experience recorded at or shortly after the event will be accurate and that later memories are less accurate in proportion to the historical distance between them and the event. These assumptions are understandable but misguided attempts to impose predictability on memories, as if they were reducible to an equation. Time may be an enemy to memory, but it is also its most significant ally.[12] Both distortion and accuracy in remembered events have been proven by experiments and observations and are to be expected. One way this occurs is when semantic memories (cultural knowledge and information known simply from frequent exposure) blend with autobiographical memory. Joseph Smith probably unconsciously conflated semantic memories (information he simply knew from frequent exposure in his youth in an evangelical and visionary culture) with what he knew from his own experience.

To put it simply, memories are both accurate and inaccurate. They are both distorted and true perceptions of the past as seen from the present. It is not wise to take for granted that Joseph Smith's memory was accurate at the time of his experience but increasingly inaccurate in proportion to the passage of time. Nor is it wise to assume that his memories were inaccurate because they contain discrepancies. He undoubtedly experienced a vision, whatever that means.

In her 1945 biography, Fawn Brodie characterized Joseph Smith's 1838/39 narrative as the "elaboration of some half-remembered dream stimulated by the early revival excitement and reinforced by the rich folklore of visions circulating in his neighborhood."[13] She thought it was a late production to shore up his authority amid dissent. When Brodie wrote in the mid-twentieth century, much less was known about the complex processes we call memory, but she accurately sensed that the culture and occasion of remembering in 1838/39 required Smith to recover a past episode and fit it to present purposes.

Brodie interpreted both Smith's past and present more skeptically than he did. But her interpretation created space for his autobiographical memory (a half-remembered dream), semantic memory (the rich folklore), and working memory's role in refashioning these into an interpretive memory for practical, present purposes (to solidify authority amid dissent). Brodie dismissed this process and its results too casually.

Joseph Smith's memory of his experience was in some senses both more and less than Brodie allowed. His accounts show awareness that he was aware during the original experience. The documents are richly descriptive of his mental world, saturated with cognitive words and deeply emotional clauses. Clearly Smith's accounts evidence explicit memory—consciousness of his consciousness. His memories are nothing like a half-remembered dream. They are narrative descriptions of his experience, journeys inside of his *mind*, a word he used frequently when recounting it. As a result, Smith's accounts of his theophany are representative of the dynamic memory processes psychologists have observed. He likely drew unconsciously on his semantic memory to fill in the gaps of his autobiographical memory, but he also left some gaps, acknowledging uncertainty of some elements.

Joseph Smith's memories reflect his growing awareness of the vision's meaning as he transformed sensory impressions into subjective meanings. He consciously experienced the vision as it occurred, but he also re-experienced and interpreted it over time. That process continued throughout his life.

■ ■ ■

In the summer of 1839, Joseph Smith settled his family in what would become Nauvoo, Illinois, and by the end of the next year it was filling with
converts protected by the empowering and pacifying charter granted by the
state legislature. For nearly three years, Smith and the saints enjoyed a comparatively peaceful lull, but then in 1842 he was charged as an accessory
in the attempted murder of a former Missouri governor. In the meantime,
during the mid-1839–1842 calm, Smith, this time with help from Howard
Coray, redacted his history again and softened it significantly in the process.

The resulting circa-1840 version was nearly identical to the 1838/39 account, yet the differences reflect a change in Smith's present circumstances.
The circa-1840 account begins simply, "I was born in the town of Sharon,"
eliding completely the 1839 document's opening salvo aimed at "evil disposed and designing persons." Smith also excised some of the earlier
version's contempt for denominational competition. Most tellingly, he
simply cut nearly all of the interpretive memory that followed the story of
rejection by a Methodist minister, in which he defends himself against prejudice and persecution.[14] Less embattled present circumstances correlate
with Smith's de-emphasis on early and unyielding persecution.

Then, responding in 1842 to the request of *Chicago Democrat* editor
John Wentworth, Smith softened even further.[15] Compared to his 1838/
39 memory (cued by war with Missouri) that Christianity was corrupt
and its creeds abominable to God, in 1842 he remembered, with an eye to
public relations, the divine message "that all religious denominations were
believing in incorrect doctrines."[16]

Smith had his gentler account—the one written for Wentworth—
published on March 1, 1842, in the *Times and Seasons* newspaper. Two
weeks later the same paper featured the 1839 first vision account—not
the less embattled redaction but the one that exists, it says, to combat
persecutors, that pronounces the Christian creeds abominable, and that
calls the Christian clergy formalists. There is nothing in the historical record explaining why Smith published some accounts of his vision and not
others, but clearly the decisions were not inevitable.

■ ■ ■

Joseph Smith's memories show both cognitive sophistication and a rich
mixture of emotions. They reveal both forgetting and enduring, vivid memories of elements of the experience that deeply impressed him—anxious

uncertainty prior to the vision, the epiphany that resulted from reading and reflecting on James 1:5, the feeling of love and redemption resulting from the theophany, and the reality of the vision itself. Interpretive and introspective memories are present as well, since Smith's retellings both imply and explicitly identify meanings he later gave to factual memories. Indeed, the accounts reveal that he consciously interpreted the experience and discovered meanings in it later that were not available to him when it occurred. The accounts are not, by Smith's acknowledgment, a flawless recreation of the event, nor are they likely "a complete fabrication of life events."[17] Rather, they are products of Smith's subjective, constructive process of remembering. They evidence short- and long-term memory consolidation.

The evitable decision to publish the 1838/39 memory, the product of a painful past and a persecuted present, shaped the saints' narrative. In that memory, God's power became the antidote to Christian confusion. The choice to relate to the past that way linked the declaration that Christianity had apostatized to the saints' sense of being persecuted people. It placed both apostate Christianity and persecution at the beginning, giving the *restored* Church of Jesus Christ of Latter-day Saints its story, its reason for being.

Notes

1. "Church History," March 1, 1842, pp. 706–707, in Karen Lynn Davidson, David J. Whittaker, Mark Ashurst-McGee, and Richard L. Jensen, eds., *Joseph Smith Histories, 1832–1844*, vol. 1 of the Histories series of *The Joseph Smith Papers* (Salt Lake City: Church Historian's Press, 2012), 489–501.*The Joseph Smith Papers*, accessed August 23, 2018, http://www.josephsmithpapers.org/paper-summary/church-history-1-march-1842/2.

2. Thomas J. Anastasio, Kristen Ann Ehrenberger, Patrick Watson, and Wenyi Zhang, *Individual and Collective Memory Consolidation: Analogous Processes on Different Levels* (Cambridge, MA: MIT Press, 2012), 29.

3. Daniel L. Schacter, *Searching for Memory: The Brain, the Mind, and the Past* (New York: Basic Books, 1996), 83.

4. A. R. Damasio, "Time-Locked Multiregional Retroactivation: A Systems-Level Proposal for the Neural Substrates of Recall and Recognition," *Cognition* 33 (1989): 25–62.

5. Schacter, *Searching for Memory*, 88.

6. See A. R. Luria, *The Mind of a Mnemonist: A Little Book About a Vast Memory*, translated by Lynn Solataroff (New York: Basic Books, 1968).

7. "History, 1838–1856, volume A-1 [23 December 1805–30 August 1834]," 4, The Joseph Smith Papers, accessed February 26, 2019, https://www.josephsmithpapers.org/paper-summary/history-1838-1856-volume-a-1-23-december-1805-30-august-1834/4.

8. Dean C. Jessee, Mark Ashurst-McGee, and Richard L. Jensen, eds., *Journals,* vol. 1, *1832–1839* (Salt Lake City: Church Historian's Press, 2008), 1:87–88.

9. Karen Lynn Davidson, David J. Whittaker, Mark Ashurst-McGee, and Richard L. Jensen, eds., *Joseph Smith Histories, 1832–1844,* vol. 1 of the Histories series of *The Joseph Smith Papers* (Salt Lake City: Church Historian's Press, 2012), 10–16.

10. Larry R. Squire, "Biological Foundations of Accuracy and Inaccuracy in Memory," in *Memory Distortion: How Minds, Brains, and Societies Reconstruct the Past,* ed. Daniel L. Schacter (Cambridge, MA: Harvard University Press, 1995), 211.

11. Karen Lynn Davidson, David J. Whittaker, Mark Ashurst-McGee, and Richard L. Jensen, eds., *Joseph Smith Histories, 1832–1844,* vol. 1 of the Histories series of *The Joseph Smith Papers,* ed. Dean C. Jessee, Ronald K. Esplin, and Richard Lyman Bushman (Salt Lake City: Church Historian's Press, 2012), 214–15. The insertion is in the handwriting of Willard Richards in Manuscript History, book A1, pp. 132–33, accessed October 4, 2013, http://josephsmithpapers.org/paperSummary/history-1838-1856-volume-a-1?dm=image-and-text&zm=zoom-inner&tm=expanded&p=138&s=undefined&sm=none. According to his diary, Richards wrote this redaction on December 2, 1842. The diary is at the Church History Library, Salt Lake City.

12. Schacter, *Searching for Memory,* 81–82.

13. Fawn M. Brodie, *No Man Knows My History: The Life of Joseph Smith,* 2nd ed., rev & enl. (New York: Vintage, 1995), 24, 25.

14. Critical editions of these versions of Smith's history are conveniently published in parallel columns in Davidson et al., *Joseph Smith Histories,* 1:204–21.

15. "No manuscript copy has been located, and it is not known how much of the history was originally written or dictated by J[oseph] S[mith]. . . . Whatever his debt to Phelps, Pratt, or others, JS took responsibility for 'Church History' when it was published in the *Times and Seasons.* His name appears as author, and a note below his name further confirms his approval." See the Historical Introduction to "Church History," March 1, 1842, p. 707, *The Joseph Smith Papers,* accessed August 23, 2018, http://www.josephsmithpapers.org/paper-summary/church-history-1-march-1842/2.

16. Joseph Smith, "Church History," *Times and Seasons* 3 (March 1, 1842): 706–10.

17. C. R. Barclay, "Schematization of Autobiographical Memory," in *Autobiographical Memory,* ed. D. C. Rubin (Cambridge: Cambridge University Press, 1986), 97.

PART II
COLLECTIVE MEMORY

6

Extract from His History

If something happened that morning in 1820 it passed totally unnoticed in Joseph's home town, and apparently did not even fix itself in
the minds of members of his own family.
— Fawn Brodie, *No Man Knows My History,* 1945[1]

In April 1841, more than a year after Joseph Smith consolidated his most
enduring memory of the vision and recorded it, and at about the time that
version was redacted to be less defensive, his younger brother William,
one of the twelve apostles since 1835, steamed down the Ohio River. He
was aboard the same boat as Yale-educated minister James Murdock, who
interviewed the thirty-year-old William after learning he was Joseph Smith's
brother.

"I then retired and committed to writing the substance of his statements,"
Murdock reported. "The next day, I read to him what I had written. He
pointed out one or two slight mistakes, added some things not before mentioned, which I noted down, and he then pronounced the whole correct."
Murdock published the revised entry from his journal in the *Congregational
Observer* of June 19, 1841, "with some enlargement to render it more
intelligible."[2]

William Smith's process of remembering—aided and shaped by
Murdock's questioning, recording, reporting, and finally publishing—
resulted in a memory that conflated into a single experience visions that
Joseph Smith, at least by 1832, remembered as separate and distinct.[3]
Smith's 1832 autobiography puts about two years between his first vision
and his second. In 1835 he approximated three years between these events.
By 1838/39, remembering much more explicitly, Smith separated the
visions temporally by nearly three-and-a-half years.[4]

William Smith, however, restated his conflated memory of these same
events repeatedly, at least into his seventies, always compressing his brother's
temporal sequence. This was true even in memories that were clearly
shaped by later published accounts that preserve Joseph Smith's distinction

between his first vision and subsequent ones in which he learned about the Book of Mormon plates.[5]

William Smith left no evidence that his brother told family members of a vision in 1820, though he recorded vivid memories of Joseph Smith telling the family of an angel revealing the Book of Mormon plates a few years later.[6]

The persistence of William's memory is interesting. As he aged, his version of events more nearly matched his brother's, but never fully. In 1841 William thought his brother's first vision occurred indoors. By 1883 he was telling the story more like his brother did, of an experience in the woods. William was nine in spring 1820 and about twelve when, according to Joseph Smith, an angel revealed the Book of Mormon plates to him. Given William's young age, it is unsurprising that he conflated events that his brother remembered differently.

William's indistinct memory of the first vision is one of many. Other people who were close to Joseph Smith, including his mother and Oliver Cowdery, left no personal memory of hearing him talk about his 1820 theophany. Joseph Smith biographer Fawn Brodie concluded, "if something happened that morning in 1820 it passed totally unnoticed in Joseph's home town, and apparently did not even fix itself in the minds of members of his own family."[7] Or, more likely, no one but Joseph Smith and one Methodist minister knew about it.

■ ■ ■

Many modern saints easily recall that, when Joseph Smith returned from the woods after his vision, he told his concerned mother, "I have learned for myself that Presbyterianism is not true."[8] This is part of an 1842 redaction to the 1838/39 account, so it was not likely part of the original consolidation. The redaction says only that Smith told his mother what he learned, not how. So there is no evidence that he told anyone but the minister for a decade or so. In 1832, Smith remembered and wrote in his own hand that after his vision he could find no one who believed him.[9] There is no known evidence of him relating his experience to family members or others—nothing like his mother's memory of the family listening to Joseph rehearse other visions.

Her memoir is full of her unique memory of events, but to depict Joseph's first vision, she simply quoted her son's 1838/39 account of the vision, which was published before she wrote. She situated her son's memory, an "extract from his history," in the midst of her vivid and personal recollections.[10] Notes used to draft Lucy Mack Smith's memoir include the 1820 vision as an afterthought.[11] And in her 1845 sermon to the saints, delivered about the same time she was dictating her memoirs, she said that she began to receive the gospel in 1827 when her son received the Book of Mormon plates, making no mention of an earlier vision.[12]

Though offering no evidence that Joseph Smith told his family of his vision shortly after it occurred, his mother's memoir shows the Smiths to be a visionary family, one of many in the visionary culture that historian Richard Bushman and others have described.[13] Smith's father experienced vivid dreams or visions. Lucy dictated her memories of her husband's dreams and of her own.

She remembered that, two or three years before her son Joseph was born in 1805, her "mind became deeply impressed with the subject of religion." She began attending Methodist meetings, which frustrated her in-laws. Her husband's demand that she stop attending hurt her feelings. "I retired to a grove not far distant," she said, "where I prayed to the Lord." That night she dreamed and learned as a result that her husband would wholeheartedly receive the gospel later in life. According to her memory of it, the experience resolved her crisis.[14]

This visionary family culture, and the larger world to which it belonged, shaped Smith's experience in the woods and his memories of it. The historical record is silent about whether Smith's mother or father told their vision memories to their children, but, given Lucy Mack Smith's obvious penchant for remembering and recording visions on behalf of her family, she likely shaped the way her son learned to seek resolution to spiritual crises and to construct autobiographical narratives.[15]

The historical record's silence in this sense is not likely the result of unconsolidated memory, as if Smith told the story in intimate settings but those who heard failed to remember. Nor, with the possible exception of Cowdery, does it seem likely that family members or close associates remembered but failed to record the memory. Several of them recorded memories of Smith's other experiences in detail. It seems much more likely that they had nothing to remember, that they were not told of the vision at the time or for years afterward.

More curious is Oliver Cowdery's memory, which, if the historical record is an accurate representation, consolidated much like William Smith's. Oliver Cowdery was twenty-one when he met Joseph Smith early in 1828 and became his scribe. Cowdery later told the story officially, as the church's second elder and record keeper. He published eight letters in the church's newspaper during the year beginning in October 1834.

"That our narrative may be correct," Cowdery's first letter began, Joseph Smith "has offered to assist us. Indeed, there are many items connected with the fore part of this subject that render his labor indispensable." But with Smith's help, Cowdery assured readers, "and with authentic documents now in our possession," he could compose "a pleasing and agreeable narrative."[16]

Few modern readers would agree that he did so. He started with a compelling narrative based on his own memory, but interrupted with long digressions. He promised "a full history of the rise of this church," of Smith's life and character, but never delivered. He obfuscated instead, as if the source material needed to tell the story never materialized or, as Roger Nicholson concluded, he "knew more than he was allowed to write at that time."[17]

Finally in his third letter, published in December 1834, Cowdery began to tell the story of Smith's early life. He referred readers to Smith's own version of his youth, as published on a preceding page from a letter to Cowdery that was intended to furnish the desired information. But Smith did not supply it, showing his reticence to publish an account of his vision, though he had written the unpublished 1832 account in his own hand more than two years earlier. Instead, in his 1834 letter Smith simply told how his family moved from Vermont to New York, and then spent the rest of the letter defending his character, likely conscious of Eber Howe's exposé *Mormonism Unvailed*, published in Painesville, Ohio, earlier that year.[18]

Having referred readers to a story that Smith did not provide, Cowdery told instead of a great awakening involving Methodist minister George Lane. Cowdery introduced his characters and situated them amid the conflict of sectarian strife, but just when Joseph was about to find resolution in the woods, Cowdery wandered to make a point about legitimate priesthood authority. Then the story ended abruptly before it resolved. When the next installment appeared in print two months later, Cowdery reminded readers "that I mentioned the time of a religious excitement, in Palmyra and vicinity to have been in the 15th year of our brother J. Smith jr's age—that was an error in the type—it should have been in the 17th."[19]

With this change, Cowdery either was complicit in leaving the vision out or never knew it, resulting in a history that elided Smith's original vision while asserting the second vision that resulted in the Book of Mormon. As a result, like William Smith's memories but unlike Joseph's, Cowdery's history blurs the two visionary experiences and situates them in 1823.[20] So readers of the saints' newspaper never learned of Smith's first vision from that source.

■ ■ ■

In 1980, James Allen, the foremost scholar of Smith's theophany, asked "when and why the vision as a descriptive report began to assume its present role in Mormon thought."[21] Certainly not in the 1820s. The historical record shows no evidence of a shared memory; none of Smith's family members left known original memories of hearing him give a first-hand account of his vision, nor did Oliver Cowdery, his closest associate in restoring the church. When telling the story later, they and others like them simply repeated Smith's by-then-published version or blurred multiple stories, or some of each. These accounts lack the intimacy and emotion that characterize the records of the several people who wrote of hearing Smith tell the story in the 1830s.

Aside from confiding in the Methodist minister, Smith appears not to have shared the vision until the 1830s, when he did so privately among small groups of followers, and especially the 1840s, when he allowed the vision to be published in various venues and forms.

Notes

1. Fawn M. Brodie, *No Man Knows My History: The Life of Joseph Smith*, 2nd ed., rev. & enl. (New York: Vintage, 1995), 25.
2. Dan Vogel, ed., *Early Mormon Documents* (Salt Lake City: Signature, 1996), 1:477–78.
3. Vogel, ed., *Early Mormon Documents*, 1:478, 490–91.
4. Karen Lynn Davidson, David J. Whittaker, Mark Ashurst-McGee, and Richard L. Jensen, eds., *Joseph Smith Histories, 1832–1844*, vol. 1 of the Histories series of *The Joseph Smith Papers*, ed. Dean C. Jessee, Ronald K. Esplin, and Richard Lyman Bushman (Salt Lake City: Church Historian's Press, 2012), 88.
5. Vogel, ed., *Early Mormon Documents*, 1:493–96, 503–6.

6. Remembering in 1883, William said that Joseph told him (though it's unclear when) that "he did not know which way to go," and so went to the woods to pray and there saw a divine personage. "After he had received this vision, he called his father's family together and told them what he had seen," William remembered, suggesting that Joseph learned of the golden plates from this experience. Vogel, ed., *Early Mormon Documents*, 1:478, 490.

7. Brodie, *No Man Knows My History*, 25.

8. Karen Lynn Davidson, David J. Whittaker, Mark Ashurst-McGee, and Richard L. Jensen, eds., *Joseph Smith Histories, 1832–1844*, vol. 1 of the Histories series of *The Joseph Smith Papers*, ed. Dean C. Jessee, Ronald K. Esplin, and Richard Lyman Bushman (Salt Lake City: Church Historian's Press, 2012), 215.

9. "History, circa Summer 1832," p. 3, in Davidson et al., *Joseph Smith Histories*, 1:2–23.

10. Lucy Mack Smith, History, 1845, p. 73, Church History Library, Salt Lake City, and at josephsmithpapers.org, accessed February 24, 2014, http://josephsmithpapers.org/paperSummary/lucy-mack-smith-history-1845.

11. See Lucy Mack Smith, notebook in handwriting of Martha Jane Knowlton Coray, L. Tom Perry Special Collections, Harold B. Lee Library, Brigham Young University, 23. See Lucy Mack Smith, *Lucy's Book: A Critical Edition of Lucy Mack Smith's Family Memoir*, ed. Lavina Fielding Anderson (Salt Lake City: Signature, 2001), 140–41.

12. Smith, *Lucy's Book*, 141n40.

13. Richard L. Bushman, "The Visionary World of Joseph Smith," *BYU Studies* 37, no. 1 (1997–98): 183–204; Christopher C. Jones, "The Power and Form of Godliness: Methodist Conversion Narratives and Joseph Smith's First Vision," *Journal of Mormon History* 37, no. 2 (Spring 2011): 88–114; Elden J. Watson, "The 'Prognostication' of Asa Wild," *BYU Studies* 37, no. 3 (1997–98): 223–30.

14. Lucy Mack Smith, History, 1845, p. 50, Church History Library, Salt Lake City, and at josephsmithpapers.org, accessed February 24, 2014, http://josephsmithpapers.org/paperSummary/lucy-mack-smith-history-1845?dm=image-and-text&zm=zoom-inner&tm=expanded&p=57&s=undefined&sm=none.

15. Susan Engel, *Context Is Everything: The Nature of Memory* (New York: W. H. Freeman, 1999), 32.

16. Davidson et al., *Joseph Smith Histories*, 1:39–40.

17. Roger Nicholson, "The Cowdery Conundrum: Oliver's Aborted Attempt to Describe Joseph Smith's First Vision in 1834 and 1835," *Interpreter: A Journal of Mormon Scripture* 8 (2014): 27–44. Quote is from p. 44.

18. Joseph Smith to Oliver Cowdery, December 1834, Kirtland, Ohio, *Latter Day Saints' Messenger and Advocate* 1 (December 1834): 40.

19. Davidson et al., *Joseph Smith Histories*, 1:54–56.

20. Davidson et al., *Joseph Smith Histories*, 1:52–56, see esp. footnote79; James B. Allen, "Emergence of a Fundamental: The Expanding Role of Joseph Smith's First Vision in Mormon Religious Thought," *Journal of Mormon History* 7 (1980): 51.

21. Allen, "Emergence of a Fundamental," 44.

7

I Heard Him Relate His First Vision

President Smith preached last Sabbath, and I gave him the text: "This is my belovd Son; hear ye him!"

—William W. Phelps, 1835[1]

I heard him relate his first vision, when the Father and Son appeared to him.

—Mary Isabella Hales Horne[2]

Joseph Smith's reluctance to tell of his first vision apparently ended in the early to mid-1830s. At about the same time Cowdery's history began circulating, Smith told private gatherings of followers about his vision, perhaps because he had already put it down on paper in 1832. Or perhaps Cowdery's conflation of events that Smith separated motivated him to clarify. The record is too thin to prove cause and effect, but correlation is clear.

Until recently, the known historical record contained little evidence of Smith talking about his first vision. However, recent research related to *The Joseph Smith Papers* shows that as early as 1833, Smith remembered the vision with believers, who then communicated it to others. These tellings and retellings formed a transactive memory, "a set of individual memory systems in combination with the communication that takes place between [the] individuals."[3] In other words, a transactive memory is the result of people sharing a memory, meaning not just one person relaying memory to another, but two or more people doing memory work together.

While preaching in Salt Lake City in 1853, Milo Andrus remembered that, at age nineteen, about 1833, he listened to "the testimony of that man Joseph Smith"—how Smith envisioned a glorious angel in the woods "and trees seemed to be consumed in blaze" as he learned that "darkness covered the earth" and the Christian creeds were "universally wrong."[4]

In late 1839 Joseph Curtis wrote, "In the spring of 1835 Joseph Smith ... came to Michigan & paid us a visit." While there, Smith explained to believers "the reason why he preached the doctrine he did." Curtis remembered Smith telling the story of sectarian revival, how members of his family joined in the excitement, and how he felt anxious and found guidance in James 1:5. "Believing it," Curtis wrote, "he went with a determination to obtain to enquire of the lord himself after some struggle the Lord manifested to him that the different sects were rong."[5]

Curtis was likely describing the same meeting that Edward Stevenson attended in an old log school house. Stevenson's memory was of Smith's manners more than his words, and of his own response. "The Prophet stood at a table for the pulpit," he remembered, "whare he began relateing his vision and before he got through he was in the midst of the congregation with uplifted hand." Stevenson was sure that everyone present was "convicted of the truth of his vision, of an Angle to him." To Stevenson at least, Smith seemed "to assume a heavenly whiteness and his voice was so peirseing and forcible." The memory was "indelibly imprinted in my mind," he reported.[6]

William Phelps asked Smith to preach on the vision in June 1835, showing that he already had some sense of Smith's story by then and was excited to hear more. He soon had a memorable, emotional reaction to Smith's personal telling and shared the memory with others. Shortly after Smith returned from Michigan to his Kirtland, Ohio, headquarters, Phelps wrote to his wife in Missouri, "President Smith preached last Sabbath, and I gave him the text: 'This is my belovd Son; hear ye him!'" Having heard Smith's story before and delighted to hear it again, Phelps wrote Sally that Smith "preached one of the greatest sermons I ever heard."[7]

By telling memories of his vision, Smith shared it in several ways, making those who heard co-owners in a sense, and giving them some power over how the story was told, remembered, and communicated. Gaining confidence as he shared the story with believers, Smith told it not only to Matthews in the midst of his friends as he had been doing but also to an inquiring believer a week later.[8] Then he told it again a year later to a "vast concourse" of saints packed in the pews of their recently completed Kirtland temple, with others standing in the aisles. He related "many Particulars of the manner of his first visions," bringing some to tears. Apostle Parley Pratt then wrote rapturously about the experience to converts he and others had made in Canada.[9]

Mary Horne, one of those converts, heard the story, perhaps repeatedly, from Joseph Smith himself in Toronto in the summer of 1837. She was among the few who accompanied her prophet as he visited each congregation. "I heard him relate his first vision when the Father and Son appeared to him," she remembered. And, like others who are on record, she noted the emotional power of the telling, an element that helped the memory endure and increased her desire and ability to communicate it later.[10] Smith's telling of the story to Robert Matthews in November 1835 no longer seems anomalous, only in that a record of that telling was captured in Smith's journal while other tellings in 1833, 1835, 1836, and 1837 occurred during gaps in his journal keeping.

This period of transactive memory making produced the earliest record that Smith was visited by two divine, corporeal beings. In November 1835 Smith emphasized how "a personage appeard in the midst of this pillar of flame which was spread all around, and yet nothing consumed, another personage soon appeard like unto the first."[11] The record of this telling does not identify the personages, but Phelps's request that Smith elaborate on the idea, "This is my belovd Son; hear ye him!" identifies the personages as a divine Father and Son.[12] By August 1836 the Presbyterian minister of Kirtland's Old South Church reported his own observations of the saints headquartered in his town. "The fundamental principle of Mormonism," he wrote, "is that God continues to hold intercourse with the saints on earth by visions and revelations." Reverend Coe continued, "They believe that the true God is a material being, composed of body and parts."[13] Twenty-first-century saints associate Coe's distinctive features of the faith—continuing revelation from a corporeal God—with Smith's first vision.

It has been argued and is now widely assumed in academic circles that Joseph Smith's theology began with a Trinitarian concept that transformed later into emphasis on the separate, embodied natures of God and Christ. If that is true, the supporting idea—that Smith's first vision story was employed only after 1840 and especially emphasized late in the nineteenth century to effect that transformation—is not true.[14] Smith and others were telling of the vision in the 1830s, and its implications for the trinity and materiality of God were asserted that early.

About the same time that Reverend Coe commented on the "fundamental principle of Mormonism," a boy named John Alger heard Smith saying that God "touched his eyes with his finger and said, 'Joseph, this is my Beloved Son, hear Him.' As soon as the Lord had touched his eyes with his finger he immediately saw the Savior." The experience endured in Alger's memory, and he passed it on to others.[15]

Similarly, Samuel Bennett, who published a defense of the restored church in 1840 in Philadelphia, where Smith had lately been discussing the vision with Orson Pratt and possibly others, argued that God had revealed his corporeality often, "and especially in these last days hath his bodily presence been manifested."[16]

Historians have long wondered why Smith "withheld the vision from the public until 1840," but the newly discovered evidence shows that he shared it, at least with some believers. He may have delayed publication, but he told the vision story repeatedly, perhaps often, in private settings, earlier and more frequently than has been previously thought.[17]

These tellings created a transactive memory—the beginnings of the saints' collective memory of the vision—in which several of Smith's followers shared a detailed story with rich emotional reactions. These experiences created intimacy between Smith and the believers who heard him and those who heard them. But such selective telling, especially in the face of Cowdery's published history, meant that many saints had no awareness of the vision, while others experienced it via a transactive bond with Smith that they never forgot.

Notes

1. William W. Phelps to Sally Phelps, June 2, 1835, MS, Church History Library, Salt Lake City.
2. Observation, M. Isabella Horne, "Testimony of Sister M. Isabella Horne," *Woman's Exponent* 39, no. 1 (June 1910): 6.
3. Daniel M. Wegner, "Transactive Memory: A Contemporary Analysis of the Group Mind," in *Theories of Group Behavior*, ed. Brian Mullen and George R. Goethals (New York: Springer-Verlag, 1987), 186.
4. Milo Andrus, July 17, 1853, Papers of George D. Watt, MS 4534, box 2, disk 1. May 1853–July 1853 images 231–256. Partial transcript in CR 100 317, box 2, folder 15. Transcribed by LaJean Purcell Carruth, October 3, 2012, corrected October 2013.
5. Joseph Curtis, "History of Joseph Curtis," MS 1654, Church History Library, Salt Lake City, 5.
6. Edward Stevenson, "The Life and History of Edward Stevenson," MS 21, Church History Library, Salt Lake City.
7. William W. Phelps to Sally Phelps, June 2, 1835, MS, Church History Library, Salt Lake City.
8. "Journal, 1835–1836," p. 36, in Dean C. Jessee, Mark Ashurst-McGee, and Richard L. Jensen, eds., *Journals*, vol. 1, *1832–1839* (Salt Lake City: Church Historian's Press, 2008), 53–223.
9. Parley P. Pratt to Latter-day Saints in Canada, November 27, 1836, MS, Church History Library, Salt Lake City.

10. M. Isabella Horne, "The Prophet Joseph Smith, Testimony of Sister M. Isabella Horne," *Relief Society Magazine,* March 1951, 158–60.

11. Jessee et al., *Journals,* 1:87–88.

12. William W. Phelps to Sally Phelps, June 2, 1835, MS, Church History Library, Salt Lake City.

13. Milton V. Backman Jr., ed., "Truman Coe's 1836 Description of Mormonism," *BYU Studies* 17, no. 3 (1977): 347–55. An early assertion of anthropomorphism is Parley P. Pratt, *Mormonism Unveiled: Zion's Watchman Unmasked, and Its Editor, Mr. L.R. Sunderland, Exposed: Truth Vindicated: The Devil and Priestcraft in Danger!* (New York: Parley P. Pratt, 1838), 29; see also Samuel Bennett, *A Few Remarks by Way of Reply to an Anonymous Scribbler, Calling Himself a Philanthropist: Disabusing the Church of Jesus Christ of Latter-day Saints of the Slanders and Falsehoods Which He Has Attempted to Fasten upon It* (Philadelphia: Brown, Bicking & Guilpert, 1840), 11.

14. See Thomas G. Alexander, "The Reconstruction of Mormon Doctrine: From Joseph Smith to Progressive Theology," *Sunstone* 5 (July–August 1980): 32–39; see also James B. Allen, "Emergence of a Fundamental: The Expanding Role of Joseph Smith's First Vision in Mormon Religious Thought," *Journal of Mormon History* 7 (1980): 43–61.

15. A. Karl Larson and Katherine Miles Larson, eds., *The Diary of Charles Lowell Walker* (Logan: Utah State University Press, 1980), 1:755–56. According to Walker, Alger "told us at the bottom of the meeting house steps that he was in the House of Father Smith in Kirtland when Joseph made this declaration, and that Joseph while speaking of it put his finger to his right eye, suiting the action with the words so as to illustrate and at the same time impress the occurrence on the minds of those unto whom He was speaking." Wilford Woodruff preached in 1837 that God was embodied. See Thomas G. Alexander, *Things in Heaven and Earth: The Life and Times of Wilford Woodruff* (Salt Lake City: Signature, 1993), 58.

16. Bennett, *A Few Remarks by Way of Reply to an Anonymous Scribbler,* 11.

17. See Allen, "Emergence," 51–52.

8

Interesting Account

[Joseph Smith] **retired to a secret place, in a grove,** but a short distance from his father's house, and knelt down, and **began to call upon the Lord.** At first, he was severely tempted by the powers of darkness, which endeavoured to overcome him; but he continued to seek for deliverance, until darkness gave way from his mind; and he was enabled to pray, in fervency of the spirit, and in faith. And, while thus pouring out his soul, anxiously desiring an answer from God, he, at length, saw a very bright and glorious light in the heavens above; which, at first, seemed to be at a considerable distance. He continued praying, while the light appeared to be gradually descending towards him; and, as it drew nearer, it increased in brightness, and magnitude, so that, by the time that it reached the tops of the trees, the whole wilderness, for some distance around, was illuminated in a most glorious and brilliant manner. He expected to have seen the leaves and boughs of the trees consumed, as soon as the light came in contact with them; but, perceiving that it did not produce that effect, he was encouraged with the hopes of being able to endure its presence. It continued descending, slowly, until it rested upon the earth, and he was enveloped in the midst of it. When it first came upon him, it produced a peculiar sensation throughout his whole system; and, immediately, **his mind was caught away, from the natural objects with which he was surrounded; and he was enwrapped in a heavenly vision, and saw two glorious personages, who exactly resembled each other in their features or likeness.** He was informed, that his sins were forgiven. He was also informed upon the subjects, which had for some time previously agitated his mind, viz.—**that all the religious denominations were believing in incorrect doctrines; and, consequently, that none of them was acknowledged of God, as his church and kingdom. And he was expressly commanded, to go not after them; and he received a promise that the true doctrine—the fulness of the gospel, should, at some future time, be made known to him.**

—Orson Pratt, 1840[1]

Joseph Smith was traveling between Washington, DC, and the Delaware River Valley in 1839 when he crossed paths with Orson Pratt, an apostle in his late twenties, on his way to a mission in the British Isles. As they traveled together, Pratt listened to his prophet's memories. In Scotland early in fall 1840, he published a thirty-one-page tract titled *Interesting Account of Several Remarkable Visions*, which is the most significant, far-reaching manifestation of transactive memory—"individual memory systems in combination with the communication that takes place between individuals"—related to Joseph Smith's first vision.[2]

Joseph Smith had developed a narrative and confidence by telling his vision story to intimate groups of believers in the 1830s. Then he began in the 1840s to publish it, first through followers like Pratt, and then by telling it to journalists and historians, hoping—perhaps knowing—that they would circulate it in print.

Smith apparently did not share his 1832 autobiography with the church's historians at the time, but he must have shown it to Orson Pratt or told him what it said, at least in part. Smith's 1832 account and Pratt's *Interesting Account* have an intertextual relationship, seen especially in the way Pratt elaborates on Smith's religious crisis and its resolution. *Interesting Account* also has an intertextual connection with Smith's later tellings, especially his 1842 answer to Chicago editor John Wentworth. Either Pratt captured elements of Smith's oral story that were not recorded anywhere else before 1840 but were recorded in later tellings and/or Smith liked Pratt's version so much that he began to borrow lines and ideas from it when he retold the story, including in writing it for an inquiring public in 1842.[3]

Pratt's acquisition of Smith's memory and Smith's willingness to let Pratt publish his version of it represent memory as a transaction. In fact, all of the records of Smith's retellings suggest that his accounts are not his memories alone. There was always a cooperative quality to what might be too simply regarded as individual memories. Smith remembered in and for a social context, and he always recruited an ally or two to assist in his compositions even before sharing them with others, making them more than his own memories.[4] Pratt's full, literate effort to communicate the story in print captured and communicated the most complete transactive memory of the first vision.

■ ■ ■

As the first published account of Smith's first vision, Pratt's *Interesting Account* marks the end of any reticence remaining from Smith's rejection after his first teenage telling. Having told the story to friendly audiences throughout the 1830s and finding approval there, Smith grew comfortable with the memory that consolidated as he collaborated with his followers.

Soon that memory was spanning the globe. Pratt wrote to fellow apostle George Smith that he would "bring about 2000 pamphlets with [him]" to London in October 1840.[5] It was published in two editions in New York beginning in 1841, and editions were published in Germany in 1842. In 1844 a missionary in the South Pacific gave a copy to members of the London Missionary Society.[6] Versions were published in Paris in 1850, Sydney in 1851, Copenhagen in 1851 and 1860, and Holland around 1865.[7]

In March 1842, Joseph Smith published in the saints' Nauvoo newspaper his letter to Chicago editor John Wentworth, including his bold but non-combative account of the vision.[8] A year later, again pleased by the invitation to tell his own story, Smith repurposed that account for publication by a Philadelphia historian named Israel Daniel Rupp.[9]

Joseph Smith continued to share the story with gatherings of saints until his death in June 1844. Levi Richards wrote shortly after hearing Smith say in 1843 "that when he was a youth he . . . could not find out which of all the sects were right—he went into the grove &, enquired of the Lord which of all the sects were right—he received for answer that none of them were right, that they were all wrong, & that the Everlasting covenant was broken."[10]

In May 1844, a month before Smith was murdered in Illinois, he told Alexander Neibaur and others an emotional story of not knowing, or being able to feel, which church was right, then opening the Bible to "the first Passage that struck him," and then acting on the scripture's directive to ask God. Smith "went into the woods to pray." Neibaur recorded that Smith knelt but was overcome before he recovered enough to see a fire descend from heaven with a personage, followed by another, who answered his question about whether he should become a Methodist by saying, "No, they are not my People . . . but this is my Beloved son harken ye him."[11]

Smith's early 1840s tellings are confident consolidations of memories narrated in his own voice, far less beholden to a cultural script than his earliest effort to put the story in writing. The editor of the *Pittsburgh Weekly Gazette* interviewed Smith in the summer of 1843 and two days later published the prophet's story as follows:

The Lord does reveal himself to me. I know it. He revealed himself first to me when I was about fourteen years old, a mere boy. I will tell you about it. There was a reformation among the different religious denominations in the neighborhood where I lived, and I became serious, and was desirous to know what Church to join. While thinking of this matter, I opened the [New] Testament promiscuously on these words, in James, "Ask of the Lord who giveth to all men liberally and upbraideth not." I just determined I'd ask him. I immediately went out into the woods where my father had a clearing, and went to the stump where I had stuck my axe when I had quit work, and I kneeled down, and prayed, saying, "O Lord, what Church shall I join?" Directly I saw a light, and then a glorious personage in the light, and then another personage, and the first personage said to the second, "Behold my beloved Son, hear him." I then, addressed this second person, saying, "O Lord, what Church shall I join." He replied, "don't join any of them, they are all corrupt." The vision then vanished, and when I come to myself, I was sprawling on my back; and it was some time before my strength returned. When I went home and told the people that I had a revelation, and that all the churches were corrupt, they persecuted me, and they have persecuted me ever since.[12]

It is impossible to tell how much the editor shaped Smith's memory, but that's really the point: by telling the story of his first vision, Smith shared it in several senses. It became a kind of common property, shaped and reshaped not only by the dynamics of individual memory but also by its communication and recommunication. In this process, the answer to James Allen's inquiry posed earlier becomes clear. He wondered "when and why the vision as a descriptive report began to assume its present role in Mormon thought." It was undoubtedly through memory sharing, well before Smith's death.[13]

The known historical record indicates that Smith began to tell the story cautiously, only among friends, while suppressing an effort to print the story. The selective telling seems to have increased the intimate, emotional quality of the sharing, but it also left many saints unaware of Smith's experience. By the 1840s the story made its way into print several times in a variety of venues, all apparently with Smith's support. These published memories did not burst into existence in their developed state in the 1840s, however, nor did they guarantee that all saints shared a memory of the vision.

If Smith had continued to suppress his story, it may have died with him. By sharing it, he ensured that published accounts of the 1840s consolidated via transaction. Individuals remembered and communicated memories, like Smith telling Orson Pratt, who remembered and communicated in *Interesting Account*. These published memories were now in the saints' memory buffer, available to be selected, related to other items, and repeated until they became common knowledge. Just because Smith's memories survived him, however, and *could* be consolidated as a collective memory, it was by no means inevitable that one or more of them *would*.

Notes

1. "Appendix: Orson Pratt, A[n] Interesting Account of Several Remarkable Visions, 1840," p. 5, in Karen Lynn Davidson, David J. Whittaker, Mark Ashurst-McGee, and Richard L. Jensen, editors., *Joseph Smith Histories, 1832–1844*, vol. 1 of the Histories series of *The Joseph Smith Papers*, ed. Dean C. Jessee, Ronald K. Esplin, and Richard Lyman Bushman (Salt Lake City: Church Historian's Press, 2012), 517–546. The highlighted text also appears in "Church History," 1 March 1, 1842, pp. 706–710, in Davidson et al., *Joseph Smith Histories*, Volume 1: 489–501. Bold typeface indicates passages that were later used word for word or closely paraphrased in "Church History," March 1, 1842, pp. 706–7 and "Latter Day Saints," 1844, pp. 404–5, both available via *The Joseph Smith Papers*, accessed November 1, 2018. See "Appendix: Orson Pratt, A[n] Interesting Account of Several Remarkable Visions, 1840," 4, The Joseph Smith Papers, accessed February 28, 2019.
2. Daniel M. Wegner, "Transactive Memory: A Contemporary Analysis of the Group Mind," chap. 9 in *Theories of Group Behavior*, ed. Brian Mullen and George R. Goethals (New York: Springer-Verlag, 1987), 186; Orson Pratt, *A Interesting Account of Several Remarkable Visions, and of the Late Discovery of Ancient American Records* (Edinburgh, Scotland: Ballantyne and Hughes, 1840).
3. Karen Lynn Davidson, David J. Whittaker, Mark Ashurst-McGee, and Richard L. Jensen, eds., *Joseph Smith Histories, 1832–1844*, vol. 1 of the Histories series of *The Joseph Smith Papers*, ed. Dean C. Jessee, Ronald K. Esplin, and Richard Lyman Bushman (Salt Lake City: Church Historian's Press, 2012), 517–24.
4. Davidson et al., *Joseph Smith Histories,* 1:201–2.
5. Orson Pratt, Edinburgh, Scotland, to George A. Smith, London, England, September 24, 1840, George Albert Smith, Papers, Church History Library, Salt Lake City.
6. See Addison Pratt's journal entry for September 17, 1844. S. George Ellsworth, ed., *The Journals of Addison Pratt* (Salt Lake City: University of Utah Press, 1990), 197.
7. Davidson et al., *Joseph Smith Histories*, 1:519nn7–9. See Erastus Snow report of Danish mission: https://dcms.lds.org/delivery/DeliveryManagerServlet?dps_pid=IE561751.

8. Davidson et al., *Joseph Smith Histories*, 1:489–501.

9. Davidson et al., *Joseph Smith Histories*, 1:502–16.

10. Levi Richards, Journal, June 11, 1843, Church History Library: "At 6 P.M. heard Eld. G J Adams upon the book of Mormon proved from the 24th, 28th & 29 of Isaiah that the everlasting covenant which was set up by Christ & the apostles had been broken . . . —Pres. J. Smith bore testimony to the same—saying that when he was a youth he began to think about these things but could not find out which of all the sects were right—he went into the grove &, enquired of the Lord which of all the sects were right—he received for answer that none of them were right, that they were all wrong, & that the Everlasting covenant was broken—he said he understood the fulness of the Gospel from beginning to end—& could Teach it & also the order of the priesthood in all its ramifications—Earth & hell had opposed him & tryed to destroy him—but they had not done it & they <never would.>"

11. Alexander Neibaur, Journal, May 24, 1844, Church History Library, Salt Lake City: "Br Joseph tolt us the first call he had a Revival meeting his mother & Br & Sist got Religion, he wanted to get Religion too wanted to feel & sho shout like the Rest but could feel nothing, opened his Bible f the first Passage that struck him was if any man lack wisdom let him ask of God who giveth to all men liberallity & upbraidat[h] not went into the Wood to pray kneelt himself down his tongue was closet cleavet to his roof – could utter not a word, felt easier after a while = saw a fire towards heaven came near & nearer saw a personage in the fire light complexion blue eyes a piece of white cloth drawn over his shoulders his right arm bear after a wile a other person came to the side of the first Mr Smith then asked must I join the Methodist Church = No = they are not my People, all have gone astray there is none that doeth good no not one, but this is my Beloved son harken ye him, the fire drew nigher Rested upon the tree enveloped him [*page torn*] comforted Indeavoured to arise but felt uncomen feeble = got into the house told the Methodist priest, [who] said this was not a age for God to Reveal himself in Vision Revelation has ceased with the New Testament."

12. "The Prairies, Nauvoo, Joe Smith, the Temple, the Mormons, &c.," *Pittsburgh Weekly Gazette* 58 (September 15, 1843): 3. In Erick B. Welch and John W. Carlson, eds., *Opening the Heavens* (Salt Lake City: Brigham Young University Press and Deseret Book, 2005), 24–25.

13. James B. Allen, "Emergence of a Fundamental: The Expanding Role of Joseph Smith's First Vision in Mormon Religious Thought," *Journal of Mormon History* 7 (1980): 44.

9

Addition, Subtraction, and Canonization

> The Prophet was to furnish all the materials; and our business was not only to combine and arrange in chronological order, but to spread out or amplify not a little, in as good historical style as may be.
>
> —Howard Coray[1]

In spring 1841, Willard Richards arrived in Nauvoo, Illinois, after serving for four years as a missionary in Britain. In December, Joseph Smith made Richards his secretary. A year later Richards also became church historian. These roles positioned him next to Smith as the saints' primary decision maker about what memories of the vision would be available to them and how.

Richards kept Smith's diary and spent most days turning his earlier diaries and other disparate records into his Manuscript History, the project Smith had begun with help from others in 1838, beginning with his most embattled account of the vision.[2] Howard Coray, who preceded Richards on the project, described the transactive process of their work: "The Prophet was to furnish all the materials; and our business was not only to combine and arrange in chronological order, but to spread out or amplify not a little, in as good historical style as may be."[3]

By March 1842, when the history began to be published serially in the *Times and Seasons*, Smith's associates had penned 157 pages. Richards wrote nearly 400 pages in six months after Smith appointed him to the task later that year. The history opens with the story of Smith's vision, long since written by James Mulholland, but in the process of revising it—perhaps at Smith's dictation—Richards made a redaction with long-term implications. The 1838/39 account shifts from the end of the vision, with Smith lying on his back, looking into heaven, to Smith telling the Methodist minister about the vision a few days later. In 1842, Richards inserted the following text between the end of the vision and telling the preacher:

When the light had departed, I had no strength, but soon recovering in some degree I went home. And as I leaned up to the fire piece Mother enquired what the matter was. I replied never mind all is well— I am well enough— off. I then told my mother I have learned for myself that Presbyterianism is not True.— It seems as though the adversary was aware at a very early period of my life that I was destined to prove a disturbere & an annoyer of his kingdom, or else why should the powers of Darkness combine against me. why the oppression & persecution that arose against me, almost in my infancy?[4]

This redaction came a little too late to be published with the rest of the story in the *Times and Seasons* in 1842.[5]

About a year after he redacted Smith's 1838/39 vision memory, Richards included Smith's November 9, 1835, journal entry in the history. In the process he included Smith's story of telling his vision to Robert Matthews, but Richards elided more than 340 words about the vision itself and replaced them simply with "as recorded in the former part of this history."[6]

That elision limited the resources from which Latter-day Saints could consolidate collective memory of Smith's vision. So did Smith's apparent suppression of his 1832 autobiography. His 1844 death ended his ability to consolidate or record new memory items that his followers might use to consolidate collective memory. In 1846 Richards packed up Smith's 1832 autobiography, his 1835 journal, and the multiplying volumes of his Manuscript History and followed Brigham Young to the Salt Lake Valley, where the records remained packed until June 1853, and where the 1832 and 1835 accounts of Smith's vision would remain generally unknown for over a century.

■ ▩ ▪

If Latter-day Saints were going to consolidate a shared memory of Smith's first vision, they would need at least one of his stable recorded memories, and they would need at least one authoritative figure to select it and relate it meaningfully to what they knew and how they perceived of themselves. They would need to have it repeated until it became common knowledge.

Individual minds hold consolidated and unconsolidated components from which more memory can be constructed. Choices people make about how to attend to these components, however subtle or subconscious, enable them to identify and manage relationships between them. The function of relating happens in the brain region known as the hippocampus. By analogy, groups consolidate collective memories via a social hippocampus—a person or group who selects, relates, and repeats the memory until it is common knowledge.

Clearly, Joseph Smith's memories and choices exerted the most influence over how his followers could and would form a collective memory of his vision, but after him several key players functioned as selectors, relaters, and repeaters. They made choices that determined what components were available to the Latter-day Saints so they could consolidate new memory, they decided how to relate those components together, and they either neglected or rehearsed the story among the saints often enough for it to become lost from or consolidated as memory.

In 1842, as Smith published his 1838/39 memory in the *Times and Seasons* at Nauvoo, Illinois, a Yale graduate and Protestant professor named Jonathan Turner published an alternate version more than a hundred miles away in Jacksonville. Concerned that Latter-day Saints were "the most dangerous and virulent enemies to our political and religious purity," Turner drew not on the history Smith was publishing but on Oliver Cowdery's earlier *Messenger and Advocate* articles, preserving and exaggerating Cowdery's conflation of Smith's first and subsequent visions.[7] This way of remembering Smith's vision thus remained a live if not likely possibility for collective consolidation.

Willard Richards died early in 1854, leaving the role of church historian—of selecting and relating records—to Joseph Smith's cousin, George A. Smith.[8] He was busy pioneering and was not given to meticulous record keeping. When he did relate his cousin's vision, George Smith told it similarly to Turner. His tenure as church historian would likely have yielded both a diminished and different memory of Smith's vision among the saints if other selectors, relaters, and repeaters had not countered that trajectory.

Two key resources Joseph Smith left for consolidating a collective memory included his premeditated 1832 autobiography and his spontaneously remembered account recorded in his 1835 journal. But they were unpublished. The originals were locked in a trunk; Richards had not selected them for consolidation by the saints, not related them meaningfully to their shared story, and not repeated them so they could become common knowledge. George Smith did not include them in the social hippocampus to be buffered, selected, related to other pieces of knowledge, or finally become part of the saints' generalized understanding of Smith's vision.

That these sources could have informed a collective memory shows us that nothing about its consolidation was foregone or fixed. Everything hung on the unpredictable and unplanned combination of influences that led Smith to remember and privilege some memories above others as he did, and his followers to select from and relate to those memories as they did.

■ ■ ■

Early in the spring of 1850, thirty-year-old Franklin Richards, an apostle for a little over a year, arrived in Britain to lead more than thirty thousand British Mormons in their relentless effort to convert others. He brought with him an idea for a new "collection of revelations." Unlike previous pamphlets aimed at making converts, Richards envisioned something "for the use of the Elders and Saints to arm and better qualify them for their service in our great war."[9] Published in 1851 as the *Pearl of Great Price*, the salmon-colored booklet included revelations Smith had published in periodicals but had not canonized or put in a book. These included the 1838/39 account of his first vision.[10]

Nearly three decades later, at the church's semiannual conference, George Q. Cannon, just named as a counselor to new president John Taylor, successor to Brigham Young, stood at the pulpit overlooking the pews of the egg-shaped tabernacle in the shadow of the rising Salt Lake Temple and held up a copy of the *Pearl of Great Price* along with a collection of Smith's revelations. "It has been deemed wise to submit these books with their contents to the Conference," Cannon said, "to see whether the Conference will vote to accept the books and their contents as from God."[11]

Smith's nephew and Cannon's fellow counselor to John Taylor, Joseph F. Smith, proposed that the books be canonized by what the saints had long called common consent, and the assembly unanimously affirmed it by raising their right hands. Thus, Joseph Smith's 1838/39 account became scripture. Canonization requires a community.[12] "Scripture is scripture," wrote Stephen Stein, "only insofar as it is recognized and understood as such by a given community."[13] Making Joseph Smith's first vision story scripture reflected its consolidation as collective knowledge and ensured that it would continue to be so.

Between the relatively widespread circulation of Joseph Smith's first vision story beginning in the 1840s, its 1851 publication in the *Pearl of Great Price*, and its canonization in 1880, a consolidation process occurred on a collective level that is analogous to the way Smith's individual memory consolidated. Smith's individual consolidation moved his memory from inside him to a text, and the collective consolidation then took that text from a modest circulation among some saints to a much wider circulation to, finally, canon.

Collective consolidation follows a reciprocal pattern. Individuals construct their past based on understandings they share with their culture. Smith's memory formed as he articulated it with and for audiences from a combination of his experience and cultural resources. Middleton and Edwards emphasized that the cultural context is not simply the background against which someone like Joseph Smith remembered, but "the substance of collective memory itself, contestively established in talk."[14] Smith's followers then reversed the process Smith had undergone by internalizing the memory and using it to shape their shared culture.

This process—culture shaping memory and memory shaping culture—created a stable (though never static) collective memory that saints have used ever since to form and reform their identity, since "collective remembering is essential to the identity and integrity of a community."[15] The precarious process described previously, together with the contingent consolidation of collective memory described in what follows, created the Latter-day Saints.

Notes

1. Howard Coray, "Autobiography," Church History Library, Salt Lake City.
2. Davis Bitton and Leonard J. Arrington, *Mormons and Their Historians* (Salt Lake City: University of Utah Press, 1988), 3–14.
3. Coray, "Autobiography."
4. Joseph Smith, History, 1838–1856, vol. A-1, p. 132, Church History Library, Salt Lake City, http://josephsmithpapers.org/paperSummary/history-1838-1856-volume-a-1-23-december-1805-30-august-1834?locale=eng&p=138.
5. "History of Joseph Smith Continued," *Times and Seasons* 4 (April 1, 1842): 748
6. Joseph Smith, History, 1838–1856, vol. B-1, p. 637, Church History Library, Salt Lake City. The elided words are essentially the epigraph to chap. 4.

7. "In the year 1823," Turner wrote, "when our prophet was about seventeen years of age, his mind became, for the first time, deeply excited on the subject of religion, by Mr. Lane, a devoted and talented elder of the Methodist church, under whose preaching there was 'a great awakening,' and numbers, among whom were our prophet and several members of his family, were 'professedly added to the kingdom of the Lord.' After the revival ceased, the usual strife for proselytes between the several sects commenced; this resulted, so far as the Smiths were concerned, in bringing the mother, one sister, and two brothers into the Presbyterian church but leaving Joseph, as he states, in disgust with all the sects, and almost in despair of ever coming to the knowledge of the truth, amid so many contradictory and conflicting claims. He resorted to prayer for 'a full manifestation of Divine approbation,' and 'for the assurance that he was accepted of him.' This occurred some time in the winter of 1823." J. B. Turner, *Mormonism in All Ages: Or the Rise, Progress, and Causes of Mormonism with the Biography of Its Author and Founder, Joseph Smith Junior* (New York: Platt & Peters, 1842), 3, 14, accessed May 29, 2014, http://books.google.com/books?id=blIm AQAAIAAJ&printsec=frontcover&source=gbs_ge_summary_r&cad=0#v=onepag e&q&f=false.

8. Davis Bitton and Leonard J. Arrington, *The Mormons and Their Historians* (Salt Lake City: University of Utah Press, 1988), 14–15.

9. Franklin D. Richards to Dr. Levi Richards, February 1, 1851, excerpted in Rodney Turner, "Franklin D. Richards and the Pearl of Great Price," in *Regional Studies in Latter-day Saint Church History: British Isles,* ed. Donald Q. Cannon (Provo, UT: Department of Church History and Doctrine, Brigham Young University, 1990), 180.

10. *The Pearl of Great Price: Being a Choice Selection from the Revelations, Translations, and Narrations of Joseph Smith* (Liverpool: F. G. Richards, 1851).

11. Journal History of the Church of Jesus Christ of Latter-day Saints, October 10, 1880.

12. Wilfred Cantwell Smith, *What Is Scripture?: A Comparative Approach* (Minneapolis: Fortress, 1993), ix. Conference Report, October 10, 1880; Journal History, October 10, 1880.

13. Stephen J. Stein, "America's Bibles: Canon, Commentary, and Community," *Church History* 64, no. 2 (June 1995): 171.

14. David Middleton and Derek Edwards, eds., *Collective Remembering* (London: Sage, 1990), 11.

15. Middleton and Edwards, eds., *Collective Remembering*, 10.

10

Collective Consolidation Begins

In the first vision which Joseph Smith received in the spring of the
year 1820, he being between fourteen and fifteen years of age, both
the Father and the Son, while he was praying, appeared unto him.
—Orson Pratt, 1849[1]

Emotion modulates the selection and relation of specific memory
items, and subsequent activation of those memory items arouses
emotion.
—Thomas J. Anastasio et al.[2]

In the fall of 1840, with the publication of *Interesting Account*, Orson Pratt
had become the first person to publish a description of the first vision meant
for the public. Forty years later, on October 10, 1880, sixty-nine-year-old
Orson Pratt, with his snow-white hair and beard, watched with great satisfaction as Latter-day Saints assembled in a general conference raised their
hands in support of a proposal to add Smith's first vision to their canon.[3]
Pratt, now the longest tenured apostle, withstood the effects of diabetes long
enough to witness the event.[4]

No one had worked harder or more effectively to construct the collective
memory of what Latter-day Saints would come to regard as their founding
event.[5] More than thirty years earlier, in 1849, Orson Pratt (pictured in
figure 10.1) apparently coined the term *first vision*, and by 1880 he would
ensure that a mere mention of that pair of words evoked a shared meaning
in the minds of most saints.

In 1849, Pratt was replying via the saints' British periodical *Millennial Star*
to a pamphlet titled *The Materialism of the Mormons or Latter-day Saints,
Examined and Exposed*. Along with a series of articles (also published as
a pamphlet) on the *Absurdities of Immaterialism*, Pratt published a shorter
essay asking, "Are the Father and the Son Two Distinct Personages?"[6]
His answer was yes, as "all revelation, both ancient and modern, that has
said any thing on this subject, has represented the Father and Son as two

Figure 10.1 Orson Pratt (1811–81) was the Latter-day Saints' most important nineteenth-century selector, relater, and repeater of Joseph Smith's first vision.
Photo by Savage and Ottinger, Salt Lake City. Courtesy Church History Library.

distinct persons." Turning to the Johanine logos hymn and then to Genesis, Pratt argued for the distinctiveness of God and Christ from the beginning, evoking his basic knowledge of Hebrew to argue, as Joseph Smith had, that the Hebrew Bible assumed a plurality of gods. When he continued the article a month later, Pratt turned to the New Testament, citing a heavenly voice claiming Jesus as "my beloved Son" after his baptism by John, Jesus praying to a father from the cross, and Stephen seeing God and Christ as recorded in the Book of Acts.

Then he made the earliest known reference in the historical record to "the first vision":[7]

In the first vision which Joseph Smith received in the spring of the year 1820, he being between fourteen and fifteen years of age, both the Father and the Son, while he was praying, appeared unto him. He said, "When the light rested upon me, I saw two personages, whose brightness and glory defy all description, standing above me in the air. One of them spake unto me, calling me by name, and said—(*pointing to the other*)—This is my beloved, Son, hear him." Thus we find that the visions both of the ancient and modern prophets agree, and clearly demonstrate the existence of two distinct persons—the Father and Son.[8]

Orson Pratt had internalized Smith's 1838/39 account. It appears from the available evidence that Pratt branded the event "the first vision."

By choosing this passage for this argument about distinct deities, Pratt continued a discussion about the nature of God and Christ in which saints had been engaged since at least the late 1830s as part of constructing and maintaining theological boundaries between themselves and other, especially evangelical, Christians. He also prefigured the way later saints regarded the vision as clear proof that God and Christ were distinct and embodied.

Orson Pratt's essay is one of many illustrations between 1840 and 1880 of how key individuals can influence the process of collective memory consolidation. He was the most significant person in the process of making Smith's vision shared knowledge among Latter-day Saints.

■ ■ ■

Collective memories form and finally consolidate from a multitude of items, each with many possible meanings, that make up a collective memory buffer. This collection of memories is the social working memory composed of all unconsolidated memory items and some consolidated memories.[9]

From these variable components within the collective memory buffer, any number of meanings, combinations, or permutations *could* consolidate into a collective memory, but relatively few actually do. The items that do end up consolidating collectively are ones that have been selected and related by one or more group members. When group members pay sufficient attention to the items in the collective buffer, they make choices about which ones to select and how to relate them to each other and to other group members.

These choices ultimately bind bits of memories together so that they have shared meanings and significance. The significance of the memories is also heavily influenced by emotion, again in a reciprocal manner; according to

Anastasio and his colleagues, "emotion modulates the selection and relation of specific memory items, and subsequent activation of those memory items arouses emotion."[10]

As group members attend and relate emotionally to the choices made by the selector(s) and relater(s), stable narratives form out of the variable parts of the social working memory. These narratives undergo a process of becoming both generalized and specific; that is, in time, much of the narrative becomes common, unattributed knowledge, while some of it becomes specific, attributed detail. What gets tagged for specific recall and what becomes generalized is modulated by how the selectors/relaters choose to direct their attention, and the emotions associated with doing so.

The consolidation process is effortful and slow and can involve a great deal of contest and negotiation. Should the process be disrupted, selected but not-yet-consolidated items will not consolidate. That said, the memories that make it through this process are incredibly durable. Once created, consolidated memories can be efficiently and quickly accessed by the remembering entity.[11]

■　■　■

Orson Pratt was the foremost relater in the process of consolidating a collective memory of the first vision. Like Joseph Smith and everyone else, Pratt inescapably remembered in a sociocultural context, and in his case that memory environment was shaped by Smith's own memories of his vision. Indeed, the earlier stabilization of Joseph Smith's first vision story in both Pratt's mind and in the *Pearl of Great Price* was the most significant determinant of what became the collective memory of the event, since "existing stable memories, by modulating the attention paid to certain events in the collective memory buffer, recur to influence the process of collective memory consolidation."[12]

That may seem obvious, but it would be unwise to assume that Latter-day Saints' collective memory of Smith's first vision inevitably echoed their founding prophet's narrative. It was not inevitable that Smith's own memory would consolidate as it did and result in a written, and thus easily transmissible, form. And once it did, there was no guarantee that saints generally would come to share that memory in that form.

Neither of Smith's immediate successors as prophet/presidents of The Church of Jesus Christ of Latter-day Saints simply assumed his 1838/39 narrative. The generalization and widespread sharing of that memory consolidated only around 1880. The fact that it consolidated as it did does not diminish the contingent variables that could have changed the course of history.

Consolidation of a collective memory of Joseph Smith's first vision was effortful and long, featuring both prominent players and the laity in a negotiable, undetermined outcome that could have taken many different turns than it did, each of which would have resulted in a different collective memory of Smith's vision, or none at all.[13]

After Joseph Smith, Orson Pratt made the most significant and substantial choices about how the vision would be remembered and rendered meaningful. This role can hardly be overstated, since "the content of a stable memory is not just a collection of isolated facts," the vast array of information and multiple meanings Pratt could have evoked. "Rather, the products of the consolidation process are efficiently organized webs of associations and generalized knowledge constructs that are derived from the systems of relationships the selector/relater establishes."[14] Pratt helped some elements of the first vision become generalized, and he created a network of ideas that associated with the first vision.

Pratt knew a vast array of information from which he could select and form associations, including not only his experience listening to Smith relate his vision and the 1842 publication of it in the *Times and Seasons* but also the Judeo-Christian scriptures and tradition, some Hebrew, and a substantial knowledge of math and science. Together with present concerns, current events, and ideas shared by Latter-day Saints, this cache of ideas old and new, stable and labile, made Orson Pratt's mind a collective memory buffer, a warehouse and workshop for deciding how to remember the vision story.

Pratt was influenced in his selection and presentation by his argument about the materiality of God.[15] In 1849, Pratt was, moreover, guided by his role of leading British saints, who were then more numerous and generally younger in the faith than their American counterparts. As time went on (as will be shown subsequently), Pratt continually selected, related, and repeated Smith's 1838/39 account, often all by himself and even when fellow apostles and presidents Brigham Young and John Taylor were either unconcerned with the vision or selecting and relating it in other ways.

By choosing to attend to Joseph Smith's first vision as he did, Orson Pratt taught the Latter-day Saints to pay attention to it. He tagged the vision story in the saints' memory in a way that made it the specific referent in the otherwise general narrative of apostasy and restoration. Orson Pratt arranged the vision story meaningfully for Latter-day Saints, relating new and old components to create a stable, generalized, collective memory that became common knowledge over time.

Notes

1. Orson Pratt, "Are the Father and the Son Two Distinct Persons?" *Latter-Day Saints' Millennial Star*, 11, no. 20 (October 15, 1849): 310.
2. Thomas J. Anastasio Kristen Ann Ehrenberger, Patrick Watson, and Wenyi Zhang, *Individual and Collective Memory Consolidation: Analagous Processes on Different Levels* (Cambridge, Massachusetts: MIT Press, 2012), 107.
3. Orson Pratt had substantially revised Latter-day Saint scriptures into new editions in anticipation of the proposal.
4. Breck England, *The Life and Thought of Orson Pratt* (Salt Lake City: University of Utah Press, 1985), 247–86.
5. Milton V. Backman Jr., "Defender of the First Vision," in *Regional Studies in Church History: New York*, ed. Larry C. Porter, Milton V. Backman Jr., and Susan Easton Black (Provo, UT: Brigham Young University Department of Church History and Doctrine, 1992), 33–48.
6. Orson Pratt, "Are the Father and the Son Two Distinct Persons?" *Latter-Day Saints' Millennial Star* 11, no. 18 (September 15, 1849), 281–84, continued in 11, no. 20 (October 15, 1849): 309–12.
7. Orson Pratt, "Are the Father and the Son Two Distinct Persons?" *Latter-Day Saints' Millennial Star* 11, no. 20 (October 15, 1849): 309–12. Continued from 11, no. 18 (September 15, 1849), 281–84.
8. Pratt, "Are the Father and the Son Two Distinct Persons?," 310.
9. Anastasio, et al., *Individual and Collective Memory Consolidation*, 96.
10. Anastasio et al., *Individual and Collective Memory Consolidation*, 107.
11. Anastasio et al., *Individual and Collective Memory Consolidation*, 157.
12. Anastasio et al., *Individual and Collective Memory Consolidation*, 99.
13. Anastasio et al., *Individual and Collective Memory Consolidation*, 157.
14. Anastasio et al., *Individual and Collective Memory Consolidation*, 106.
15. Anastasio et al., *Individual and Collective Memory Consolidation*, 92–93.

11

An Interview with Joseph Smith in 1859

When, where, and how were you, Joseph Smith, first called? How old
were you? And what were your qualifications?

—Orson Pratt, 1859[1]

Orson Pratt continued in the roles of selector and relater and repeater
throughout his life. As far as the historical record shows, he wrote and
spoke more on the topic of Smith's first vision than any of his contemporaries.[2] He shaped the Latter-day Saints' collective memory of the vision by
paying attention to it often in particular ways and in present contexts that
shaped the memory.

Ten years after Pratt coined the term *first vision* in 1849, Latter-day Saints
were wrapped up in a period of intense paranoia. They were threatened with
annihilation that, to them, seemed due in large part to internal sinfulness.
First there was a disastrous end to the immigration season in 1856, leaving
hundreds of converts starved and frozen to death short of their Utah des-
tination. Then came news that a federal army was on the way to subdue
and subject them, then the reactionary massacre of a California-bound emigrant company, and, in the midst of it all, the most intense preaching the
saints ever heard from their leaders. It felt like they were coming apart as
a people, and "when a group feels physically, economically, or otherwise
threatened, it often turns to the discursive realm" to remember in ways that
facilitate survival.[3]

In this context, Orson Pratt preached an 1859 sermon in which he imagined a conversation with Joseph Smith.[4] He wanted to show that mankind
had apostatized from being governed by God through prophets, so God
had called Smith. Pratt acted as a kind of medium between the saints and
their departed prophet:

When, where, and how were you, Joseph Smith, first called? How old were
you? And what were your qualifications? I was between fourteen and fifteen years of age. Had you been to college? No. Had you studied in any

seminary of learning? No. Did you know how to read? Yes. How to write? Yes. Did you understand much about arithmetic? No. About grammar? No. Did you understand all the branches of education which are generally taught in our common schools? No. But yet you say the Lord called you when you were but fourteen or fifteen years of age? How did he call you? I will give you a brief history as it came from his own mouth. I have often heard him relate it.[5]

He was wrought upon by the Spirit of God, and felt the necessity of repenting of his sins and serving God. He retired from his father's house a little way, and bowed himself down in the wilderness, and called upon the name of the Lord. He was inexperienced, and in great anxiety and trouble of mind in regard to what church he should join. He had been solicited by many churches to join with them, and he was in great anxiety to know which was right. He pleaded with the Lord to give him wisdom on the subject; and while he was thus praying, he beheld a vision, and saw a light approaching him from the heavens; and as it came down and rested on the tops of the trees, it became more glorious; and as it surrounded him, his mind was immediately caught away from beholding surrounding objects. In this cloud of light he saw two glorious personages; and one, pointing to the other, said, "Behold My Beloved Son. Hear ye Him!" Then he was instructed and informed in regard to many things pertaining to his own welfare, and commanded not to unite himself to any of those churches. He was also informed that at some future time the fulness of the Gospel should be made manifest to him, and he should be an instrument in the hands of God of laying the foundation of the kingdom of God.[6]

Orson Pratt could (and in fact did) speak to the saints on hundreds of topics. But more frequently than any of his contemporaries he selected Smith's first vision as his text and related it in meaningful ways.

The setting, delivery, and experience of such sermons created environments that gradually consolidated collective memory. Pratt took the pulpit as the primary arbiter of the saints' shared past and shaped it in ways similar to what happens when parents remember with young children as they sort through family photographs, guiding them to conclusions about the significance of past events, cuing memories, providing descriptions, and elaborating contextual information in ways that shape how the memories consolidate.

In the embattled and uncertain present, Orson Pratt made Smith and his vision familiar, memorable, and reassuring. His imagined conversation with Smith formed an environment where the saints who participated with him were particularly likely to process and remember the event as Pratt presented it, making his memory their memory.

It helped very much that Pratt's audience recognized him and the setting as authoritative. He stood before them as an apostle, a scholar, and a witness, emphasizing that he often heard Joseph Smith relate the vision. In that role he set the scene and provided cues and prompts about the experience and its meanings. This is similar to the kind of memory work teachers do in classrooms. In such "reconstructive recaps," shards of memory are "tidied up" as teacher and pupils cooperate in the creation of collective memory making.[7]

■ ■ ■

At about the same time that Orson Pratt preached this sermon, the talented British writer and convert Edward Tullidge put his version of Smith's vision into the saints' collective buffer as well. Tullidge's epic poem, "The Prophet of the Nineteenth-Century," appeared in three installments in the pages of the *Millennial Star* in the early months of 1858. The ponderous text took a month to get to Smith's first vision.

When it did, the story combined elements of Smith's 1838/39 account with Tullidge's romantic imagination. What is missing is the narrative drama—tension and resolution—inherent in Smith's memory and Orson Pratt's retellings. Just as Tullidge slowed the pace and raised the tension Smith experienced due to "sectarian strife" and fruitless searching among contending Christians, just as Joseph "turned the pages of the sacred book" to discover that God will give wisdom to those who ask, Tullidge sent Smith to bed and promised readers the poem would continue in a month. When it did, Tullidge had Joseph sitting with his siblings at home as his parents led the family in the evening devotions, and the vision, presumably in the past, was only hinted at.[8]

Tullidge sent the first part of the poem to Brigham Young, seeking his approval to publish more—fifteen thousand lines in all. Young was preoccupied and likely did not read the whole sample Tullidge sent, nor did he encourage that it be selected for consolidation. Rather, Young sent word across the Atlantic that, given the times, the *Millennial Star*'s paper and ink may be more valuable sold separately, as raw supplies to other publishers.[9]

■ ■ ■

As Tullidge's poem shows, there were alternative ways to select and relate the parts of memory Latter-day Saints had at their disposal. Tullidge did not noticeably influence memory of Smith's vision when he published his poem, but other writers persistently told Smith's story the same way. Tullidge's weakness as a selector and relater contrasted with Pratt's strength. Pratt's narrative choices drew more specifically and repeatedly on Joseph Smith's 1838/39 account in ways that evoked emotional response and therefore consolidated collective memory.

The "discursive frame" Pratt employed in 1859 to help hearers understand, and relate to, Smith's story is remarkably faithful to Smith's recorded memories. Pratt's sentences are short, descriptive, and factual. Yet he revised in the process of his performance "such that the nature of the remembering was significantly a function of the style of the discourse which constituted it."[10] He trained the Saints to recall Joseph Smith as a young, innocent, ignorant seeker whose sincerity got the attention of God and his Beloved Son, who promised Joseph a key role in their future plans.

Just as parents and teachers shape the memories of young children and students, Pratt helped saints consolidate memory of Smith's vision, turning Smith's 1838/39 memory into generally shared knowledge with a few specialized cues for evoking the story: Smith read James 1:5, went to a grove to pray, and saw two personages, and one introduced the other as his Beloved Son.

Like Smith himself, Pratt recalled the vision repeatedly over time and in different historical environments, and the remaining records of these recountings make it possible to analyze his work as a consolidating agent of collective memory. "Accounts are always designed to accomplish particular pragmatic actions," so analysis of the written record of Pratt's memory-making work "means that versions of events cannot be taken merely as windows upon individuals' mental representations, but have to be studied in their social, conversational context."[11] In 1859, for example, the saints' fears provide a backdrop against which Pratt's interview format was likely comforting and grounding for a people otherwise in upheaval.

Pratt's many recitals of the first vision were memorable, whereas others', such as Tullidge's poem, did not endure. Pratt enjoyed status and authority among the saints, but that alone hardly accounts for his success. His discursive choices brought Joseph Smith back to life and evoked his vision as reassurance that God still favored the Latter-day Saints. All that meant that Pratt was more able than others to reach people emotionally and thus memorably.

Notes

1. "Theocracy," Discourse by Elder Orson Pratt, Tabernacle, Great Salt Lake City, Sunday, August 14, 1859, reported by G. D. Watt, *Journal of Discourses* 7 (1860): 210–27. Compare LaJean Carruth, translator of George Watt's shorthand record of this sermon, MS 4534, Church History Library, Salt Lake City. Carruth translation in author's possession. Used by permission.

2. According to Milton V. Backman, and my research reveals nothing but confirmation of this assessment. See Milton V. Backman Jr., "Defender of the First Vision," in *Regional Studies in Church History: New York,* ed. Larry C. Porter, Milton V. Backman Jr., and Susan Easton Black (Provo, UT: Brigham Young University Department of Church History and Doctrine, 1992), 42, 45.

3. Thomas J. Anastasio, Kristen Ann Ehrenberger, Patrick Watson, and Wenyi Zhang, *Individual and Collective Memory Consolidation: Analogous Processes on Different Levels* (Cambridge, MA, and London: MIT Press, 2012), 152.

4. Michael W. Homer, "Spiritualism and Mormonism: Some Thoughts on Similarities and Differences," *Dialogue: A Journal of Mormon Thought* 27, no. 1 (Spring 1994): 171–90.

5. "Theocracy," Discourse by Elder Orson Pratt, Tabernacle, Great Salt Lake City, Sunday, August 14, 1859, reported by G. D. Watt, *Journal of Discourses* 7 (1860): 210–27. Compare LaJean Carruth, translator of George Watt's shorthand record of this sermon, MS 4534, Church History Library, Salt Lake City. Carruth translation in author's possession. Used by permission.

6. "Theocracy," Discourse by Elder Orson Pratt, Tabernacle, Great Salt Lake City, Sunday, August 14, 1859, reported by G. D. Watt, *Journal of Discourses* 7 (1860): 220–21.

7. David Middleton and Derek Edwards, eds., *Collective Remembering* (London: Sage, 1990), 28, 38–39.

8. "A Chapter from the Prophet of the Nineteenth Century," *Latter-Day Saints' Millennial Star* 20, no. 1 (January 2, 1858): 14–15; "First Book of the Prophet of the Nineteenth Century," *Latter-Day Saints Millennial Star* 20, no. 8 (February 20, 1858): 126–27, and 20, no. 9 (February 27, 1858): 142–43. Thanks to Chad Foulger for bringing these sources to my attention.

9. Brigham Young to Asa Calkins, March 5, 1858, Brigham Young letterbooks, CR 12354 1, box 4, vol. 4, pp. 77–79. Thanks to Chad Foulger for bringing this letter to my attention.
10. Middleton and Edwards, eds., *Collective Remembering*, 35.
11. Middleton and Edwards, eds., *Collective Remembering*, 36.

12

Our History, 1869–74

When he was thus encircled about with this pillar of fire his mind was caught away from every object that surrounded him, and he was filled with the visions of the Almighty, and he saw, in the midst of this glorious pillar of fire, two glorious personages, whose countenances shone with an exceeding great luster. One of them spoke to him, saying, while pointing to the other, "This is My Beloved Son in whom I am well pleased. Hear ye Him."

Now here was a certainty; here was something that he saw and heard; here were personages capable of instructing him, and of telling him which was the true religion. How different this from going to an uninspired man professing to be a minister! One minute's instruction from personages clothed with the glory of God coming down from the eternal worlds is worth more than all the volumes that ever were written by uninspired men.

Mr. Smith, this young man, in the simplicity of his heart, continued saying to these personages, "which church shall I join, which is the true church?"

He then and there was commanded, in the most strict manner, to go not after them, for they had all gone out of the way; he was told there was no Christian church on the face of the earth according to the ancient pattern, as recorded in the New Testament; but they had all strayed from the ancient faith and had lost the gifts and power of the Holy Ghost; they had lost the spirit of revelation and prophecy, the power to heal the sick, and every other gift and blessing possessed and enjoyed by the ancient Church. "Go not after them," was the command given to this young man; and he was told that if he would be faithful in serving the true and living God, it should be made manifest to him, in a time to come, the true church that God intended to establish.

—Orson Pratt, 1869[1]

> Why should they feel such concern and anxiety in relation to his testimony as to persecute him, a boy not quite fifteen years of age? The reason was obvious—if that testimony was true, not one of their churches was the true Church of Christ.
>
> —Orson Pratt, 1874[2]

The transcontinental railroad neared completion in 1869. With it the Protestant establishment in the United States seemed to chug with increasing momentum toward a collision with Latter-day Saint hegemony over Utah Territory.[3] Predictably, Orson Pratt evoked Joseph Smith's memory of a persecuted past to consolidate group memory and solidify identity in what Latter-day Saints considered a persecuted present.

A decade after his hypothetical interview with Joseph Smith, Orson Pratt delivered another sermon on the first vision as tensions were rising in the early weeks of 1869. The inauguration of Ulysses Grant lay only two weeks away, shortly after which he would dispatch his secretary of war to Utah Territory.

Ready to rid the nation of polygamy, the second relic of barbarism, Republicans in Congress had contemplated a series of bills aimed at undermining the saints' stronghold. Closer to home the tenuous political landscape was about to fracture with most Latter-day Saints on one side but a growing number of gentiles (as the saints called everyone else) and economically powerful dissenters on the other.[4]

As Brigham Young galvanized the saints to cooperate economically in their hostile environment, Pratt shaped their shared memory and prepped for conflict that seemed "more like a fight between Methodism and Mormonism than any other thing."[5] In this setting Pratt highlighted Smith's defensive disdain for antagonistic Christianity.

Speaking to an audience composed mainly of saints who had not known their founding prophet, Orson Pratt again assumed the role of relater and rehearsed a "sense-making narrative" by choosing to tell the story of Smith's first vision with notably less harmonization of information unique to Smith's various tellings and increasing congruence with Smith's 1838/39 story of being persecuted. Tellingly, by this point Pratt safely assumed that Smith's first vision story was the beginning of "our history." It was "in print" in the *Pearl of Great Price* and on its way to canonization and collective consolidation.[6]

Much more than in his sermon a decade earlier, in 1869 Pratt generalized the memory of Smith's vision, taking interpretive liberties with the recorded details, even evoking new dialogue between Smith and deity. Pratt's 1869 story of the vision is three times longer than his story from 1859.

Pratt's same emphases from 1859 are present: Smith's youth, innocence, ignorance, sincerity, and the reality of the revelation and resulting true church. But in this telling Pratt greatly elaborated his "inferential links that fill in the gaps," resulting in a thicker description of Smith's evangelical environment.[7] Pratt's 1869 interpretation of the vision was more overt, more didactic. Like Joseph Smith, Orson Pratt found more and more meaning in the facts of the vision over time.

There is no known record of how the sermon was received, but for several reasons it created an effective environment for shaping a shared memory. First, Pratt selected a few elements from numerous possible ones. He related and bound them to each other as a shared memory, "invoking context and using inference to work out and justify particular versions of events."[8] Second, through his relating choices, Pratt assigned meaning and significance to the vision that was suited to his audience's present concerns, which maximized the modulating effects of their emotions to process the vision memory then and to arouse emotions whenever that memory later cued in their minds.[9] Third, Pratt used narrative—as Smith did—perhaps "the richest form of generalized memory." Finally, Pratt clearly thought that the story needed repeating to solidify the saints' memory and, thus, identity. Collective memories consolidate when "the relater repeatedly presents interrelated items to the generalizer."[10] Like individual memories, collective ones must be repeated and rehearsed in order to endure.[11]

■ ■ ■

More than a year later, in August 1870, the newly completed transcontinental railroad delivered Reverend John Philip Newman, chaplain of the United States Senate and pastor of Metropolitan Church in Washington, DC, to Salt Lake City. Newman had preached to President Grant and others on the evils of polygamy. Orson Pratt responded, and Newman had come to debate the apostle in person. The audience swelled each day the debate wore on in the newly completed tabernacle. Each side declared victory.[12] The first vision was not the topic, but this event and its environment formed yet another present in which Pratt continued to tell the story of the saints' shared past.

In March 1871 he preached again in the same space where he and Newman had debated. He began by reading the Eighty-Fifth Psalm, asserting that it had accurately prophesied a future that was now a verifiable past. From there Pratt situated the saints in that sacred history. In it, Smith's first vision functioned as the renewal of revelation.

In this sermon Pratt drew on his knowledge of Smith's vision narrative, which was very specifically encoded in his mind. Like Pratt's 1869 recounting of the vision, this sermon is situated against the formal opposition of the Protestant establishment. This time Pratt related Smith's vision to Judeo-Christian history, forming a sacred narrative and identity for saints as persecuted heirs of renewed revelation, fulfilling a prophesied future against the antagonism of apostate Christendom.

It is telling that Pratt began by acknowledging that the saints "already understand" how Smith's first vision inaugurated the series of events that fulfilled the prophecy of Psalm 85. They already shared that memory, he reminded his audience, even as he repeated the story again. Repetition solidifies memory, and as groups remember together, "narratives will be rehashed, strengthened, and occasionally modified."[13]

As he repeated the story in 1871, Pratt chose a new point to emphasize: the true church. "This Church has an existence this day in consequence of the fulfillment" of prophecy, he declared. It is little wonder that in this memory Pratt told the story of revelation past and present being disrupted by "the apostate church that sprang up in the days of the Apostles; a church which denied the spirit of revelation and had the wickedness and audacity to proclaim in the face and eyes of the Bible that it needed no new revelation." Specifically, Pratt (dis)credited "the councils that were called towards the close of the third and fourth centuries of the Christian era" as the agents of apostasy, "worse than the heathen" for declaring the Almighty mute.[14]

In emphasizing the church itself as the fruit of Smith's vision and the fulfillment of biblical prophecy, Pratt seems to have been influenced by Smith's 1838/39 account, the one excerpted in the *Pearl of Great Price* that was circulating among the saints as a prelude to canonization in 1880, the one Latter-day Saints were coming to know, the one that emphasizes the quest for a true church and the abominable creeds of Christendom in a defensive tone. Pratt makes the same salient points as Smith did there about questing for a true church amid the apostasy of all others. Indeed, he has

Smith asking God, "Lord show me which is the true church" and God answering with a promise to reveal "what was necessary to the constitution of the true church."[15]

One reason this sermon almost certainly compelled Pratt's audience and helped consolidate their shared, general memory is that he told it not only as sacred history but also as narrative drama, with Joseph Smith as protagonist against antagonistic Catholicism and Protestantism combined, and the devil himself leading them. Young Joseph Smith triumphs over his opposition by the grace of God, as persecuted visionaries in the sacred drama had before him.

■ ■ ■

As political and cultural opposition to the church continued through the 1870s, Orson Pratt continued to preach Smith's first vision as God's manifestation of which side he was on. These sermons explicitly worked to shape the saints' memory. Pratt, who was aging along with the church, spoke about the vision more and more consciously as history. He continued to situate it as a supernal event of sacred history, the link between the upset sacred past and the renewed sacred present. He evoked it nostalgically. Speaking of Smith in an 1872 sermon delivered forty-five years to the day he reportedly obtained the Book of Mormon plates, Pratt declared:

> The first vision that he had was in answer to prayer. Being but a youth, and anxious for the salvation of his soul, he secretly prayed, in the wilderness, that the Lord would show unto him what he should do, what church he should join. The Lord heard and answered this prayer. Do not be astonished, good Christians, because the Lord hears prayer in the 19th century. I know it is very popular to pray to the Lord in Christendom; but, when you talk about the Lord answering prayers, by giving revelations, visions, or sending angels, it is very unpopular. But unpopular as it was, this youth ventured to go and ask the Lord for wisdom, having, in the first place, read a passage in the New Testament, which says, "If any man lack wisdom, let him ask of God, who giveth to all men liberally, and upbraideth not; and it shall be given unto him."
>
> Joseph Smith was not so full of tradition that he could not lay hold of this promise. I do not know that he had been taught long enough, the idea that the Lord would not hear prayer. At any rate, having read this

passage, he prayed, really believing in his heart that the Lord would answer him, for he wanted wisdom, he wanted to know which was the true
Christian Church, that he might be united with it; and while pleading with
and praying to the Lord for this information, which was a matter of great
concern to him, the heavens were opened, and two personages clothed in
light or fire descended and stood before him.

As soon as this light surrounded him, and he was enclosed or enveloped
in it, his mind was caught away from earthly objects and things, and he saw
these two glorious personages, their countenances shining with exceeding
great brilliancy. One of them, while pointing to the other, addressed him
in this language, "Behold My Beloved Son. Hear ye Him!"

All fear was taken from this boy during the progress of this wonderful
event, and he felt happy, but anxious to know concerning the things about
which he had been praying, and he repeated his request, that he might be
told which was the true Christian church.

He was informed that there was no true Christian church on the
earth, that there was no people established or organized according to the
Apostolic order; that all had gone out of the way and had departed from
the ancient order of things; that they had denied the power of Godliness,
the gifts, miracles, the spirit of revelation and prophecy, visions, that all
these things had been done away with by the unbelief of the children of
men, and that there were no prophets or inspired men on the earth, as
there always had been when there was a true Church upon the earth. He
was strictly commanded to join none of them.

The Lord also informed him that, at some future period of time, if
he would be faithful in giving heed to the instructions which were then
imparted to him, and in his prayers to the Lord, he would impart to him
his own doctrine in plainness and simplicity.[16]

Two years later in 1874, Orson Pratt became church historian, and again
evoked the vision as the fulfillment of Old Testament prophecy, consciously
marking again the anniversary of Smith receiving the Book of Mormon
plates with a recital of the vision that began the last dispensation and provided continuity between God's work past, present, and future.[17]

As Pratt rehearsed memory to shape the present, the saints' present
shaped Pratt's memory. He spoke from the pulpit in the Mormon tabernacle a few months after Episcopalians consecrated St. Mark's Cathedral
three blocks away and less than a month before the dedication of First

Presbyterian Church just a block beyond that. With the federally backed Protestant establishment encroaching on the saints' establishment, church historian Orson Pratt continued to function as the major narrator, repeating again and again the story of Joseph Smith's first vision in ways that consolidated as a usable past in the context of an embattled present.

"I will read the 3rd and 4th verses of the 29th chapter of Isaiah," he said, quoting, "'And I will camp against thee round about, and I will lay siege against thee with a mount, and I will raise forts against thee.'" With that, Pratt announced,

> It will be forty-seven years the day after tomorrow since the plates, from which the Book of Mormon was translated, were obtained by the Prophet Joseph Smith, and as there may be persons in this assembly who are unacquainted with the circumstances of the finding of this book, I will relate some circumstances in relation to the beginning of this great and marvelous work.

Pratt emphasized again that Joseph Smith "was a boy about fourteen years of age at the time the Lord first revealed himself in a very marvelous manner to him." He rehearsed again the revival context, the widespread anxiety for salvation. "I presume that many of you, at some period of your existence, have been wrought upon in the same manner, because you have been anxious to join yourselves to the true church of God, if you could only find which was God's church," Pratt said. Then, having made the problem personal, he emphasized Smith's dilemma:

> If he went to one denomination they would say, "We are right, and the others are wrong," and so said all the others. Like most boys of his age, Joseph had never read the Bible to any great extent, hence he was unable to decide in his own mind, as to which was the true church. When he saw several denominations contending one with the other, he naturally enough supposed that some of them must be wrong.

Pratt followed Joseph Smith's narrative through his epiphany.

> He began to search the Bible in his leisure time after his work was done upon the farm; and in perusing the New Testament, he came across a passage which is very familiar indeed to most of my hearers; the passage reads

thus—"If any of you lack wisdom, let him ask of God, who giveth to all men liberally, and upbraideth not; and it shall be given him." Mr. Smith really believed this passage. He did not read this as one would read a novel, thinking that it was all imaginary; but, from his heart, he believed that it meant what it said, and he said to himself—"I certainly lack wisdom in relation to my duty. I do not know which of these denominations is correct, and which is the church of Christ. I desire to know, with all my heart, and I will go before the Lord, and call upon his name, claiming his promise."

Pratt's story continued as Joseph Smith left his parents' home, walked

into a little grove of timber, and called upon the Lord, claiming this promise, desiring to know his duty and to be informed where the true Church of Christ was. While thus praying, with all his heart, he discovered in the heavens above him, a very bright and glorious light, which gradually descended towards the earth, and when it reached the tops of the trees which overshadowed him, the brightness was so great that he expected to see the leaves of the tree consumed by it; but when he saw that they were not consumed he received courage. Finally the light rested down upon and overwhelmed him in the midst of it, and his mind at the same time seemed to be caught away from surrounding objects, and he saw nothing excepting the light and two glorious personages standing before him in the midst of this light. One of these personages, pointing to the other, said—"Behold My Beloved Son. Hear ye Him!"

Here Pratt placed special emphasis on, even augmented, Smith's anticlerical 1838/39 memory of the answer to his prayer about which church he should join:

He was immediately told, that there was no true Church of Christ on the earth, that all had gone astray, and had framed doctrines, dogmas, and creeds by human wisdom, and that the authority to administer in the holy ordinances of the Gospel was not among men upon the earth, and he was strictly commanded to go not after any of them, but to keep aloof from the whole of them.

Pratt adapted the story to present purposes further. Where Joseph Smith remembered telling his experience to one Protestant minister who rejected it, Pratt made it many ministers who told Smith "that there was no such thing as the visitation of heavenly messengers, that God gave no new revelation, and that no visions could be given to the children of men in this age."

Pratt concluded by echoing Joseph Smith's response to the minister who denied his experience. "He knew positively to the contrary," Pratt said.

He knew that he had seen this light, that he had beheld these two personages, and that he had heard the voice of one of them; he also knew that he had received instruction from them, and therefore, to be told that there was no such thing as revelation or vision in these days, was like telling him that the sun did not shine in these days. He knew to the contrary, and he continued to testify that God had made himself manifest to him; and in consequence of this, the prejudices of the different denominations were aroused against him. Why should they feel such concern and anxiety in relation to his testimony as to persecute him, a boy not quite fifteen years of age? The reason was obvious—if that testimony was true, not one of their churches was the true Church of Christ.[18]

Notes

1. "Mormonism," Discourse delivered by Elder Orson Pratt, Tabernacle, Salt Lake City, February 24, 1869, reported by David W. Evans, *Journal of Discourses* 12 (1869): 352–62.

2. "Joseph Smith's First Visions, Etc.," Discourse by Orson Pratt, delivered in New Tabernacle, September 20, 1874, reported by David W. Evans, *Journal of Discourses* 17 (1875): 278–88.

3. For the early part of this story, see Brent M. Rogers, *Unpopular Sovereignty: Mormons and the Federal Management of Early Utah Territory* (Lincoln and London: University of Nebraska Press, 2017).

4. James B. Allen and Glen M. Leonard, *The Story of the Latter-day Saints* (Salt Lake City: Deseret, 1976), 342–43; Ronald W. Walker, *Wayward Saints: The Social and Religious Protests of the Godbeites against Brigham Young* (Provo and Salt Lake City: Brigham Young University Press and University of Utah Press, 2009).

5. "The Situation in Utah," Salt Lake City, *Deseret News*, March 17, 1875, p. 2, accessed February 28, 2014, http://news.google.com/newspapers?nid=336&dat=18750323&id=vgBZAAAAIBAJ&sjid=yEcDAAAAIBAJ&pg=1295,2995673.

6. "Mormonism," Discourse delivered by Elder Orson Pratt, Tabernacle, Salt Lake City, February 24, 1869, reported by David W. Evans, *Journal of Discourses*, 12 (1869): 352–62.

7. David Middleton and Derek Edwards, eds., *Collective Remembering* (London: Sage, 1990), 35.

8. Middleton and Edwards, eds., *Collective Remembering*, 41.

9. Thomas J. Anastasio, Kristen Ann Ehrenberger, Patrick Watson, and Wenyi Zhang, *Individual and Collective Memory Consolidation: Analogous Processes on Different Levels* (Cambridge, MA, and London: MIT Press, 2012), 107.

10. Anastasio et al., *Individual and Collective Memory Consolidation*, 152.

11. See P. Boyer and J. V. Wertsch, eds., *Memory in Mind and Culture* (Cambridge: Cambridge University Press, 2009), 138–70.

12. Breck England, *The Life and Thought of Orson Pratt* (Salt Lake City: University of Utah Press, 1985), 240–46.

13. Anastasio et al., *Individual and Collective Memory Consolidation*, 152.

14. "The Fulfillment of Prophecy, The Early History of the Church, The Book of Mormon," Discourse by Orson Pratt, delivered in the New Tabernacle, Salt Lake City, March 19, 1871, reported by David W. Evans, *Journal of Discourses*, 14 (1872): 137–47.

15. "The Fulfillment of Prophecy, The Early History of the Church, The Book of Mormon," Discourse by Orson Pratt, delivered in the New Tabernacle, Salt Lake City, March 19, 1871, reported by David W. Evans, *Journal of Discourses*, 14 (1872): 137–47.

16. "Review of God's Dealings with the Prophet Joseph—Coming Forth of the Book of Mormon—Gathering, Etc.," Discourse by Elder Orson Pratt, delivered in the New Tabernacle, Salt Lake City, September 22, 1872, reported by David W. Evans, *Journal of Discourses* 15 (1873): 178–91.

17. "Joseph Smith's First Visions, Etc.," Discourse by Orson Pratt, delivered in New Tabernacle, September 20, 1874, reported by David W. Evans, *Journal of Discourses* 17 (1875): 278–88. Orson Pratt was sustained as church historian and recorder on May 9, 1874, and served until his death on October 3, 1881.

18. "Joseph Smith's First Visions, Etc.," Discourse by Orson Pratt, delivered in New Tabernacle, September 20, 1874, reported by David W. Evans, *Journal of Discourses* 17 (1875): 278–88.

13

Collective Consolidation Culminates

The Lord has taken a great deal of pains to bring us where we are and to give us the information we have. He came himself, accompanied by his Son Jesus, to the Prophet Joseph Smith. He didn't send anybody but came himself, and introducing his Son, said: "This is My Beloved Son. Hear Him!"

—John Taylor, 1879[1]

Many contingent choices determined whether and how Latter-day Saints would remember Smith's vision. In 1864, in the middle of his tenure as church historian, George A. Smith, Joseph's cousin and an apostle, spoke to saints in Ogden, Utah. The shorthand record of this sermon suggests that he blurred together events that Joseph Smith thought of as separate and distinct. He conflated Smith's early vision experiences as Oliver Cowdery did, not as Joseph Smith and Orson Pratt narrated the vision. George A. Smith apparently spoke of "when the angels appeared to Joseph Smith [and] manifested unto him a knowledge pertaining to the coming forth of the Book of Mormon and the word of the Lord in the last day that Satan came also with his power."[2]

This sermon was redacted. When it was published it included an extensive direct quote from Joseph Smith's 1838/39 narrative, specifying plainly the appearance of two divine beings—Father and Son—who delivered Joseph Smith from his unseen enemy.[3] Even so, two years later in 1866, George A. Smith again told the story with obvious differences from his prophet cousin's memory, including, again, the generic angel as revelator.

The transition of George A. Smith's 1864 sermon from its oral version into its redacted, published form, and his retelling a story very similar to the original two years later are evidence that a collective memory had not yet consolidated, not even in the mind of church historian George A. Smith, along the lines Orson Pratt emphasized.

The memories shared some elements. They shared a pluralistic background of theological chaos that frustrated Joseph; they shared his epiphany resulting from reading a passage in James, prompting him to ask the Lord. And there were obvious present purposes for George A. Smith's memory as well. All told, George A. Smith's memory focused on which church "had the power and holy priesthood which of them had the power of salvation from God and to his astonishment the angel appeared to them and said not any of them they have all gone astray all corrupt like mad men wandering about in darkness you are not to join any of them."[4]

It has long been thought that Brigham Young alluded to Smith's vision only occasionally.[5] LaJean Carruth's recent translation of shorthand records reveals that Young talked about it more often and in more detail than previously thought. Young evoked Smith's vision, for instance, in an 1855 sermon:

> When Joseph first received revelation, the Lord could not tell him what he was going to do he didn't tell him he was going to call him to be a prophet seer revelator high priest and founder of kingdom of God on earth. Joseph would have said what just what does that mean you are talking that I can't understand. He could merely reveal to him that the Lord was pleased to bless him and forgive his sins and there was a work for him to perform on the earth and that was about all he could reveal.[6]

A decade later, Brigham Young delivered his only known narrative version of the vision story. His point of emphasis was

> the very principle of Joseph Smith asking the Father in the name of Jesus according to the exhortation of James the Apostle that was repeated to us this morning, the effect of his asking the Father to teach him the right way, to show which of all these churches are correct that he might attach himself to that individual church.

Young continued to make the case that Smith's experience proved the promise in James 1:5 that God gives to those who ask.

> He did ask he did receive and the heavens were opened to him and the angels said to him all those that you behold all those that you hear lo here lo there lo in there lo yonder lo in another place here is Christ in the wilderness shall I say in our camp meeting here is Christ in our protracted meeting upon the anxious bench and here is Christ in the silent chamber

where we say nothing and lo here is Christ and lo there the Lord said to him through that messenger he is not there he is with none of them you will have to commence entirely anew. Joseph Smith was only a little over 14 years old this time.[7]

Here Brigham Young evoked the vision to make a point about apostate Christianity, situating young Joseph Smith amid evangelical confusion. In Young's version, which is briefer than even the most terse Orson Pratt narrative, the Lord speaks to Joseph Smith through a vague messenger rather than Smith's 1838/39 two personages—Father and Son—consistently emphasized by Pratt.[8]

Brigham Young, George Smith, Erastus Snow, Orson Pratt, John Taylor, and presumably other leaders and laity shared some memory elements of Smith's story.[9] It was not inevitable that a collective memory would consolidate out of the contents of that social working memory, however, or that it would take the form that it did. The saints had to select which version of the story to remember, choose how they would relate the available elements to each other in meaningful ways, and generalize those meanings in ways that resonated with their present circumstances.

Orson Pratt appointed himself to the tasks early, but as late as the 1870s the saints were still considering other ways of relating the elements of the story and deciding how much to emphasize it and to what uses they might put it. Smith's 1838/39 account in the *Pearl of Great Price* was formative of the consolidating memory, but it was not yet a collective memory. Pratt's persistence eventually carried the consolidation process. His way of relating the story took hold, aided greatly by his own publications and sermons and especially by the *Pearl of Great Price*. The saints' repeated exposure to this narrative consolidated their collective memory in the context of their quest to maintain their identity against intense pressure.

The process of consolidating a collective memory of Smith's first vision is perhaps best observed via John Taylor, who became president of the church in 1880 at the same time Smith's 1838/39 account (excerpted in the *Pearl of Great Price* since 1851) was canonized. In the 1860s and early 1870s, Taylor spoke occasionally and briefly of the vision, as others had before him, blurring events and revelations Joseph Smith remembered in 1838/39 as distinct, and speaking vaguely of the revelation coming via "an angel."[10] Clearly, though Orson Pratt had already developed and repeated a narrative of the vision based largely on Smith's 1838/39 account, that memory was not yet consolidated collectively.

When Taylor came to lead the church after Brigham Young's death in 1877, he gave increasingly specific sermons that depended on Smith's 1838/39 account of the vision. Early in 1879, for instance, Taylor declared how "the Prophet Joseph asked the angel which of the sects was right that he might join it," drawing on the text of Smith's 1838/39 account even as he continued to attribute the revelation to a mere "angel" in a way that would jar twenty-first-century saints whose collective memory is emphatic about God and Christ appearing to Smith together.[11]

As the saints felt increasing pressure to relinquish polygamy, Taylor preached adamantly about his determination to obey God's law and located the origins of it in Smith's vision. By the end of 1879 he preached a more specific version of it, drawn on the account that would be canonized a year later:

> The Lord has taken a great deal of pains to bring us where we are and to give us the information we have. He came himself, accompanied by his Son Jesus, to the Prophet Joseph Smith. He didn't send anybody but came himself, and introducing his Son, said: "This is My Beloved Son. Hear Him!"[12]

Just a few days later Taylor preached at greater length and specificity based on what had evidently become the standard story. "I refer now to the time that Joseph Smith came among men," Taylor said and then continued:

> What was his position? And how was he situated? I can tell you what he told me about it. He said that he was very ignorant of the ways, designs and purposes of God, and knew nothing about them; he was a youth unacquainted with religious matters or the systems and theories of the day. He went to the Lord, having read James' statement, that, "If any of you lack wisdom, let him ask of God, that giveth to all men liberally, and upbraideth not; and it shall be given him." He believed that statement and went to the Lord and asked him, and the Lord revealed himself to him together with his Son Jesus, and, pointing to the latter, said: "This is My Beloved Son. Hear Him!" He then asked in regard to the various religions with which he was surrounded. He enquired which of them was right for he wanted to know the right way and to walk in

it. He was told that none of them was right, that they had all departed from the right way, that they had forsaken God the fountain of living waters, and hewed them out cisterns, broken cisterns, that could hold no water. Afterwards the Angel Moroni came to him and revealed to him the Book of Mormon, with the history of which you are generally familiar, and also with the statements that I am now making pertaining to these things.[13]

Less than a month later, John Taylor repeated Joseph Smith's first vision again with unmistakable emphasis on the appearance of both Father and Son to Joseph Smith as commencement of the restoration of gospel fullness. Drawing on the now widely shared memory of Smith's 1838/39 story, John Taylor told the story again:

The Father pointing to the Son said, "This is My Beloved Son in whom I am well pleased. Hear ye Him!" Here, then, was a communication from the heavens made known unto man on the earth, and he at that time came into possession of a fact that no man knew in the world but he, and that is that God lived, for he had seen him, and that his Son Jesus Christ lived, for he also had seen him.[14]

This, then, is the saints' collective memory, consolidated by about 1880 from many elements with a variety of possible meanings, but among those the stable, modulated memory of Smith's story as it was told by him in 1838/ 39, published in 1842, excerpted in the *Pearl of Great Price* in 1851, and finally canonized by the saints in 1880, as interpreted and repeated over and over in that process by Orson Pratt (see Figure 13.1).[15]

The consolidation of this collective memory pleased Pratt very much. He said so when he rose to speak to the saints on September 19, 1880. It was his sixty-ninth birthday, and fifty years to the day since he became a Latter-day Saint. As the church's historian, its social hippocampus, Pratt had made the most significant choices about how Joseph Smith's first vision would be remembered and rendered meaningful. With the saints' cooperation, he stabilized their collective memory of apostate Christendom, renewed revelation, and restored authority, with Joseph Smith's first vision as the hinge of that history. That memory would never be static, but by 1880 it was stable and enduring.

Figure 13.1 Orson Pratt (1811–81) had been a Latter-day Saint for fifty years when, due in large part to his persistence, Joseph Smith's first vision became part of the Mormon canon in 1880.
Photo courtesy L. Tom Perry Special Collections, Harold B. Lee Library, Brigham Young University.

In the slow process of consolidation it had become generalized into common knowledge, condensed "and stored for the long term in a compact, efficient, accessible, and usable form."[16] But Pratt ensured that the generalized story included specific elements, deeply embedded details, as in two personages appearing to Joseph Smith and one of them saying to him, "This is My Beloved Son." By 1880 Orson Pratt had mediated the memory-making process, aiding the saints in their individual efforts to relate memory items together until their own brains represented those relationships automatically.[17]

It seemed right to Orson and the Latter-day Saints that on the memorable occasion of his jubilee, he rehearsed the narrative again. With one eye on the sacred past and another on the prophetic future, Pratt delivered a fluid discourse that captured the stable memory he had largely shaped. At its center he featured the vision.[18]

When Pratt finished, Wilford Woodruff rose and praised him as the person who had been a Latter-day Saint longer than any other living, an unmatched authority, a modern Paul. He turned Joseph Smith's individual memories into the memory of Latter-day Saints.[19]

A few weeks after celebrating his half a century as a Latter-day Saint, seventy-year-old Orson Pratt rose to speak again to saints assembled in their Salt Lake City tabernacle for general conference. It was October 1880, the setting in which the saints canonized Joseph Smith's 1838/39 account of his first vision. Pratt presented John Taylor (who now fully shared the memory Pratt had been rehearsing for four decades) to the saints and invited them to sustain him as their new prophet and president. Then Taylor asked Pratt to speak "on a particular subject," as he put it, "in which we are all interested, namely, the divine authority of the Priesthood, divine callings, ordinances, etc."[20]

Unsurprisingly, Joseph Smith's first vision was the heart of Pratt's discourse. There was a new twist, however. With increased consciousness of Smith's 1838/39 account came a puzzle, a priesthood puzzle. Pratt explained it. A September 1832 revelation to Joseph Smith said "no man could see the face of God the Father and live" unless he had priesthood. But, Pratt testified, Joseph Smith had seen God and Christ and lived. "This has troubled the minds of some of the Latter-day Saints," he acknowledged. "'How is it,' (say they) 'that Joseph lived, after having seen the face of the Father, after having heard the words of His mouth, after the Father had said unto him, 'He is My Beloved Son. Hear ye Him!'"[21]

Pratt found an answer in the Book of Mormon. It taught that men ordained to the priesthood on Earth were also ordained premortally.[22] Thus, Pratt declared, Smith had seen God as a boy and been ordained to priesthood premortally before he did. By reconciling Joseph Smith's September 1832 revelation and the newly canonized account of his first vision, Orson Prat facilitated memory recursion—mixing a consolidated memory with new items to form new memory. Even stable memory would change over time.

Orson Pratt was the saints' foremost relater and repeater of Smith's first vision, making their shared memory usable, a past for the present. On his deathbed in October 1881, he told Joseph F. Smith, "my body sleeps for a moment, but my testimony lives and shall endure forever."[23] With that Pratt captured his contribution and passed the baton.

Notes

1. Discourse by President John Taylor, delivered at American Fork, Friday, November 28, 1879, reported by Geo. F. Gibbs, *Journal of Discourses* 21 (1881): 116–17.

2. George A. Smith, November 15, 1864, Ogden Tabernacle. Papers of George D. Watt. Transcribed by LaJean Purcell Carruth, May 13, 2009. Compare to sermon in *Journal of Discourses* 11 (1867): 1, which was heavily edited and infused with extensive quotes that are not in the shorthand.

3. Historical Discourse, delivered by Elder George A. Smith, in the Tabernacle, Ogden City, on Tuesday, November 15, 1864, reported by G. D. Watt, *Journal of Discourses* 11 (1867): 1.

4. George A. Smith, July 8, 1866; Carruth transcription of Watt shorthand, MS 4534, Church History Library, Salt Lake City.

5. Compare "Articles and Covenants," circa April 1830 (http://josephsmithpapers. org/paperSummary/articles-and-covenants-circa-april-1830-dc-20)   with Joseph Smith, History, circa Summer 1832 (http://josephsmithpapers.org/paperSummary?target=x6547). For Brigham Young references, see Brigham Young, July 24, 1853, LaJean Purcell Carruth transcription of George Watt's shorthand of sermon redacted at *Journal of Discourses* 1 (1854): 244–45.

6. Brigham Young, March 25, 1855. Papers of George D. Watt, MS 4534, box 3, disk 1, images 142–53, Church History Library, Salt Lake City. Transcribed by LaJean Purcell Carruth, July 2009. Used by permission.

7. Brigham Young, July 8, 1866, Papers of George D. Watt. Transcribed by LaJean Purcell Carruth, December 10, 2008; corrected April 13, 2012.

8. "Mormonism," a Discourse delivered by Elder Orson Pratt, Tabernacle, Salt Lake City, February 24, 1869, reported by David W. Evans, *Journal of Discourses* 12 (1869): 352–62.

9. On October 7, 1866, Erastus Snow preached, "it was the influence of this spirit that led all the first elders of this church to it was the same that worked in the heart of Joseph when a boy and when he went to meeting to hear the Methodists and Presbyterians Baptist preach and at the time they were getting up a revival and trying to raise an excitement and bring about conversion to their churches he listened to their preaching and gave his heart to read the scriptures that spirit that was upon him led him that he could not be satisfied with what he saw and heard and his spirit was led to seek unto the Lord rather than into these sects and clergymen and when he read the words of Apostle James where in the Lord says unto the people if any man seek wisdom let him ask of God etc. he straightway seized upon this promise of the Lord and when he went to himself alone in the wilderness and bowed in the forest and bowed down his soul to the Lord to ask him for wisdom concerning these sects preaching and the religion they taught and the truth of the gospel and who had it and where it was the Lord sent unto him his messengers he was enveloped in the glory of God that rested down upon him to envelop him in it and the glory there of was like the brightness of the sun at noon day and exceeding anything that his eyes had seen before and he heard the voice of the Lord speaking unto him and bearing witness unto him and telling him

COLLECTIVE CONSOLIDATION CULMINATES 101

that those whom he had heard in the sectarian world was not the gospel in its ancient purity that those sects of the day were in error that many of their doctrines and
[—/fnds?] were incorrect that their organizations were not organization of heaven as
church and kingdom of God that he should not follow them but in the due time the
Lord God would reveal unto him the fullness of the gospel and establish his church
and kingdom upon the earth." LaJean Carruth translation of George Watt shorthand,
MS 4534, Church History Library, Salt Lake City.

10. For example, in 1863 Taylor reportedly preached, "How did this state of things
    called Mormonism originate? We read that an angel came down and revealed
    himself to Joseph Smith and manifested unto him in vision the true position of the
    world in a religious point of view. He was surrounded with light and glory while
    the heavenly messenger communicated these things unto him." See Discourse
    by Elder John Taylor, delivered in the Tabernacle, Great Salt Lake City, March 1,
    1863, reported by G. D. Watt, *Journal of Discourses* 10 (1865): 127. In 1872 Taylor
    reportedly preached, "Joseph Smith came forward telling us that an angel had
    administered to him, and had revealed unto him the principles of the Gospel as
    they existed in former days, and that God was going to set his hand to work in
    these last days to accomplish his purposes and build up his kingdom, to intro-
    duce correct principles, to overturn error, evil, and corruption, and to establish
    his Church and kingdom upon the earth. I have heard him talk about these things
    myself." Discourse by Elder John Taylor, delivered in the Tabernacle, Salt Lake
    City, Sunday, March 17, 1872, reported by David W. Evans, *Journal of Discourses*
    14 (1872): 365.

11. Discourse by President John Taylor, Delivered at Kaysville on Sunday afternoon,
    March 2, 1879, reported by George F. Gibbs, *Journal of Discourses* 20 (1880): 167.

12. Discourse by President John Taylor, delivered at American Fork, Friday, November
    28, 1879, reported by Geo. F. Gibbs, *Journal of Discourses* 21 (1881): 116–17.

13. Discourse by President John Taylor, delivered in the Fourteenth Ward Meetinghouse,
    Sunday evening, December 7, 1879, reported by John Irvine, *Journal of Discourses* 21
    (1881): 161.

14. Discourse by President John Taylor, delivered in the Salt Lake Assembly Hall, at the
    Quarterly Conference, Sunday afternoon, January 4, 1880, reported by John Irvine,
    Journal of Discourses 21 (1881): 65.

15. Thomas J. Anastasio, Kristen Ann Ehrenberger, Patrick Watson, and Wenyi Zhang,
    *Individual and Collective Memory Consolidation: Analogous Processes on Different
    Levels* (Cambridge, MA, and London: MIT Press, 2012), 11, 107, 109, 114.

16. Anastasio et al., *Individual and Collective Memory Consolidation*, 128.

17. Anastasio et al., *Individual and Collective Memory Consolidation*, 133.

18. "A Double Birthday—The Authority of the Priesthood, Etc.," Discourse by Elder
    Orson Pratt and Elder Wilford Woodruff, delivered in the Tabernacle, Salt Lake City,
    September 19, 1880, reported by John Irvine, *Journal of Discourses* 21 (1881): 303–16.

19. "A Double Birthday—The Authority of the Priesthood, Etc.," Discourse by Elder
    Orson Pratt and Elder Wilford Woodruff, delivered in the Tabernacle, Salt Lake City,
    September 19, 1880, reported by John Irvine, *Journal of Discourses* 21 (1881): 303–16.

20. "The Divine Authority of the Holy Priesthood, Etc.," Discourse by Elder Orson Pratt, delivered at General Conference, Salt Lake City, Sunday, October 10, 1880, reported by George F. Gibbs, *Journal of Discourses* 22 (1882): 27–38.
21. "The Divine Authority of the Holy Priesthood, Etc.," Discourse by Elder Orson Pratt, delivered at General Conference, Salt Lake City, Sunday, October 10, 1880, reported by George F. Gibbs, *Journal of Discourses* 22 (1882): 27–38.
22. "The Divine Authority of the Holy Priesthood, Etc.," Discourse by Elder Orson Pratt, delivered at General Conference, Salt Lake City, Sunday, October 10, 1880, reported by George F. Gibbs, *Journal of Discourses* 22 (1882): 27–38.
23. Breck England, *The Life and Thought of Orson Pratt* (Salt Lake City: University of Utah Press, 1985), 286.

14

The Inception of Mormonism and the Persecuted Present

What that Methodist preacher then said to Joseph, churches still say: "It is all of the devil." "There are no visions or revelations in these days; all such things ceased with the Apostles; there never will be any more of such." And this in the very face of revelation sweeping over the bosom of the age like a mighty ocean!

—Edward W. Tullidge, 1878[1]

Thomas Stenhouse was in his midtwenties in 1849. He was one of the thousands of British converts. He was helping convert others in the British Isles at the time that Orson Pratt published his article there naming Joseph Smith's experience his *first vision* and emphasizing how, at age fourteen, Smith beheld "both the Father and the Son, while he was praying."[2]

Not long before Smith's 1838/39 version of the vision was published in the *Pearl of Great Price* in 1851, Stenhouse married, then joined the saints' first mission to Italy, then was first to preach the restored gospel in Switzerland. By the mid-1850s, Stenhouse and his wife, Fanny, one of his converts, were bound for Utah Territory but detoured to spend several years leading saints in the eastern United States and helping to edit their periodical. Finally, in 1859, they arrived in Salt Lake City, pulling a handcart according to one account.[3]

By late 1869 Stenhouse had left the church. He felt pushed by economic hardship he thought Brigham Young's policies caused or at least complicated, and pulled by spiritualism, which seemed to him a more authentic way of experiencing revelation unfettered by prophets who meddled in temporal matters. In 1873 Stenhouse published the *Rocky Mountain Saints*, a history aimed primarily at gentile readers. Historian Ronald Walker called it the "first significant narrative history of the Mormon experience," and also "schizophrenic."[4]

Early in the book Stenhouse tells the story of Joseph Smith's first vision similar to how Orson Pratt was retelling the story during the same time period. That is, in terms of memory consolidation, he rehearsed Smith's widely published account, selecting and relating the items in it for readers to process either as general or specialized knowledge. Smith was a simple youth made spiritually anxious by competition among Protestants. He read from the New Testament "that Scripture which saith: 'If any of you lack wisdom, let him ask of God that giveth unto all men liberally and upbraideth not, and it shall be given him.'" Encouraged, Smith went to the woods to pray.

Stenhouse quotes Smith directly on his attempt to pray that was nearly ruined by an actual, though unseen, being before exerting himself and being delivered by a pillar of brilliant light in which were two glorious personages. "One of them spake unto me," Smith says through Stenhouse in the most specifically emphasized item in the consolidating group memory, "calling me by name, and said (pointing to the other), 'This is my beloved son hear Him!'" Stenhouse then paraphrases again before quoting, and thus selecting for specialized memory, Smith's statement about being told not to join any church, for all were wrong.[5]

Stenhouse also published an illustration titled "Inception of Mormonism—Joseph Smith's First Vision," in *Rocky Mountain Saints* (see figure 14.1). It shows a young Joseph Smith kneeling in the woods, looking up into the light emanating from two divine beings descending in flowing robes. Even with the title printed below the image, without the accompanying explanation, Stenhouse's target audience would probably have found little specific meaning in the image. But it would have made immediate sense to most saints even without a title.

That meaning, stable by about 1880, was their collective memory, their generalized knowledge of Smith's experience. It was shaped by the consolidation of his individual memories and, in turn, their selecting from those memories and relating them meaningfully to their present, resulting in a shared, usable past.

A less provocative response to the first vision that captured this way of remembering actually came from Edward Tullidge, an associate of Fanny and Thomas Stenhouse in dissent, though more ambivalent than they and clearly, in contrast to them, writing to the faithful rather than the antagonistic public. When in 1878 Tullidge published *Life of Joseph the Prophet*, his opening chapter primarily quoted Smith's soon-to-be canonized account of

INCEPTION OF MORMONISM—JOSEPH SMITH'S FIRST VISION.

Figure 14.1 One measure of the saints' consolidating collective memory is that many of them would have immediately interpreted this illustration with very specific, shared meanings.

Inception of Mormonism, page 1 of T. B. H. Stenhouse, *Rocky Mountain Saints: A Full and Complete History of the Mormons* (London: Ward, Loack and Tyler, 1873).

the vision, including the important 1842 redaction that defensively emphasized persecution.

Tullidge's readers heard Joseph Smith's story about rejection by a Methodist preacher who personified everyone else. The story culminated with Smith's own words: "men of high standing would take notice sufficient to excite the public mind against me and create a hot persecution; and this was common among all the sects—all united to persecute me."[6]

As Stenhouse and Tullidge captured the saints' consolidating memory of Smith's first vision in the 1870s, their respective books represented the present concerns in which that memory consolidated—enemies at home and abroad intent on undermining Zion. Among those enemies was Stenhouse's wife, Fanny, whose exposé *Tell It All*, along with her lectures, reached large audiences in England and the United States. In her husband's book, before and after the section that most saints presumably would have regarded as a fair statement of their founding prophet's original vision, Stenhouse called on his readers to oppose polygamy and Brigham Young's autocratic leadership.

For most saints this was simply one more attack on their faith, one more reason to respond in the defensive terms of that particular version of Smith's story—owing to the many reports circulated by "evil-disposed and designing" enemies.[7]

> To his quote from Joseph Smith about the vision evoking hot and widespread persecution, Tullidge added a concluding paragraph, a crescendo: What that Methodist preacher then said to Joseph, churches still say: "It is all of the devil." "There are no visions or revelations in these days; all such things ceased with the Apostles; there never will be any more of such." And this in the very face of revelation sweeping over the bosom of the age like a mighty ocean! Notwithstanding that since 1820, perhaps twenty-five million souls, outside of churches, and the majority of them from the intellectual classes, have accepted a dispensation of revelation in some form, churches stand today where they stood then. All Christendom, still remaining without a present revelation of Jesus, yet this Jesus the supreme revelator of his Father's kingdom![8]

Both Thomas Stenhouse and Edward Tullidge understood what resonated with Latter-day Saint readers—a persecuted past to make sense of a persecuted present. For both authors, the default starting point for that story was Joseph Smith's first vision as he remembered it in his persecuted present of 1838/39.

Notes

1. Edward W. Tullidge, *Life of Joseph the Prophet* (New York: Tullidge and Crandall, 1878), 5.
2. Orson Pratt, "Are the Father and the Son Two Distinct Persons," *Latter-Day Saints' Millennial Star* 11, no. 20 (October 15, 1849): 310.
3. Ronald W. Walker, *Wayward Saints: The Godbeites and Brigham Young* (Urbana and Chicago: University of Illinois Press, 1998); "The Stenhouses and the Making of a Mormon Image," *Journal of Mormon History* 1 (1974): 53. For Stenhouse's reflections

on his ministry in Europe, see T. B. H. Stenhouse, *The Rocky Mountain Saints* (New York: D. Appleton and Company, 1873), 9–12.

4. Direct quotes are from Walker, "The Stenhouses and the Making of a Mormon Image," 66–70. The same sentiments are expressed in Walker, *Wayward Saints*, 295–317.

5. Stenhouse, *The Rocky Mountain Saints*, 15–16.

6. Tullidge, *Life of Joseph the Prophet*, 5.

7. Karen Lynn Davidson, David J. Whittaker, Mark Ashurst-McGee, and Richard L. Jensen, eds., *Joseph Smith Histories, 1832–1844*, vol. 1 of the Histories series of *The Joseph Smith Papers*, ed. Dean C. Jessee, Ronald K. Esplin, and Richard Lyman Bushman (Salt Lake City: Church Historian's Press, 2012), 204.

8. Tullidge, *Life of Joseph the Prophet*, 5.

15

Recursion, Distortion, and
Source Amnesia

This scene represents the first vision of Joseph Smith, the Prophet. . . . In 1820 a revival takes place in the neighborhood—some of the Smith family joining various denominations. Joseph's revelations, reads the Bible—Epistle of St. James, Chapter 1, Verse 5—"If anyone lacketh wisdom, etc." resolves to go into the woods to pray. On a fine morning in the spring of 1820 he went to a secluded spot in the forest, commenced praying. The evil powers avail him. Almost in despair, he sees a glorious light in the heavens gradually descending, two glorious personages appear, the Father and the Son.

> —Carl Christian Anton Christensen[1]

Entities are more tolerant of memory inaccuracy than of incoherence.

> —Thomas J. Anastasio et al.[2]

In the late 1870s, as Orson Pratt's frequent rehearsals of Smith's vision were in the final stages of collective consolidation, Danish folk artist and convert Carl Christian Anton Christensen and others of his generation mediated the process of memory recursion: mixing consolidated memory with new items to form new memory.

Christensen toured settlements in Utah, Idaho, Arizona, and Wyoming, showing to interested audiences both young and old what became known as the "Mormon Panorama": a series of six-and-a-half-by-ten-foot paintings sewn and rolled together on a massive scroll. Each of the several paintings depicted a scene from church history.[3] Hanging the scroll from tripods with curtains on each side, Christensen staged an early version of a motion picture.

When Christensen stood to speak to audiences, he began with the first scene and said, according to his written lecture:

This scene represents the first vision of Joseph Smith, the Prophet. He was at that time a boy of between fourteen and fifteen years of age—born in the town of Sharon, State of Vermont, December 23, 1805. His parents moved into the state of New York when he was a bout ten years old, took up new land, Joseph helping his father as well as his age and strength would permit. Poor in means—Joseph had a very limited education.

In 1820 a revival takes place in the neighborhood—some of the Smith family joining various denominations. Joseph's revelations, reads the Bible—Epistle of St. James, Chapter 1, Verse 5—"If anyone lacketh wisdom, etc." resolves to go into the woods to pray. On a fine morning in the spring of 1820 he went to a secluded spot in the forest, commenced praying. The evil powers avail him. Almost in despair, he sees a glorious light in the heavens gradually descending, two glorious personages appear, the Father and the Son. Their appearance, their dress, power of motion UP AND DOWN, without the use of wings, their form, color of hair, dress, etc., IMAGE OF MAN, OR MAN IN THE IMAGE OF GOD. The Father calling Joseph by name, pointing to the other, saying "THIS IS MY BELOVED SON, HEAR YE HIM." Joseph directs question, "Which of all these sects or parties to join to please God?" Answer, "None of them, all in error. All departed from the true religion, serve God with their lips but their hearts are far from Him." The heavenly personages ascended again, the light follows them, Joseph finding himself as you here see, lying on his back gazing up towards heaven. A few days afterwards he meets one of those reverend divines that have been so energetic in the revival meetings, relates to him his vision. He treats Joseph with contempt, says, "It must have been from the devil, since God would not reveal Himself till the Last Day of Judgment, etc.", more willing to believe in revelations from the evil one than from God.[4]

Like Smith's narrative of his vision composed in his persecuted present, Christensen emphasized persecution in his scenes, both visually and orally, from the harassment Smith experienced as a result of his vision to his being tarred and feathered in Ohio to the Missouri persecutions to Smith's martyrdom to the saints' being driven from the United States. By so doing, he forged a coherent narrative characterized by chosen-ness and opposition. "History will preserve much," Christensen wrote, "but art alone can make the narrative of the suffering saints comprehensible for posterity."[5] Thus, his panorama is a pageant of persecution, the saints' suffering, and their relent-less onward drive.[6]

As the dramatic if primitive motion picture traveled throughout the West, Christensen's depiction of past persecutions would have resonated with Latter-day Saints who were dealing with a hostile government and Protestant establishment. The illustrated narration catalyzed memory re-cursion. The medium was especially good for transmitting the memory to another generation of Latter-day Saints.[7] "The success I have had every-where I have shown these scenes," Christensen reflected, "has far exceeded my expectations and has undoubtedly planted many a seed which, particu-larly in the hearts of children, will bear good fruit."

Many saints must have shared his view that they needed something like the paintings to create recursive memories, even if they did not think in those terms. "Now," Christensen said, because of the "Mormon Panorama," "the eye as well as the ear can receive correct ideas of the history of our church." Christensen fostered and observed the recursive process of collec-tive memory consolidation. "Since I began my work," he wrote,

> I myself have for the first time come to see the great significance of this, and many historical contributions from the fathers of our church pour in to me from every quarter. The old people are very interested in sharing and bearing their testimony of the past, and the youth seem completely lost in the contemplation of the great drama of our history.[8]

Christensen's son carried on the "Mormon Panorama" into the twentieth century. In time it included twenty-three scenes that highlight elements of the church's history and narrative to accompany the visual presen-tation. The only painting that no longer exists, sadly, is *The Vision*.[9] Still, Christensen's successful exhibit highlights one way that saints of three gen-erations showed desire to join in memory-making exercises to solidify their sense of a shared past, transmit it to the next generation, and in the process sustain their identity in an embattled present.

Between 1870 and 1900, the last Latter-day Saints who knew Joseph Smith gave way to generations that never did. Together these generations selected, related, and generalized knowledge from their environment and made it "consistent with their ongoing experience."[10] At points in that process, their collective memory prioritized coherence over accuracy, as collective memories usually do, and as Orson Pratt's October 1880 sermon suggests the saints' first vision memory did.

This process occurred at the individual level of selectors, relaters, and repeaters. It also occurred at the collective level as individuals told the first vision story using art, music, and the written word. The saints' major goal in this era was the survival of their distinctive faith amid escalating opposition from the larger culture and its institutions, especially the US government. Saints solidified their sense of exceptional, chosen, persecuted status and transmitted it to converts and especially to the next generation. One way they did so was by shaping and sharing the collective memory of Joseph Smith's first vision.

The cooperative and recursive process resulted in a shared memory that gave the saints of succeeding generations a coherent, shared past, but it inevitably distorted Smith's canonized account. Moreover, while it gave many of the saints power to recall their shared memory, it also resulted, for many, in what memory scholars call "source amnesia," the inability to attribute their knowledge to its original source. In the service of their goals, groups seeking to solidify and sustain their identities often sacrifice accuracy for coherence, and they experience both memory distortion and source amnesia, as what they know drifts from the original knowledge and they forget how they know what they know.

As a result, the first vision memory consolidation at the end of the nineteenth century depended on but was not the same as Joseph Smith's memory. It was coherent with the present. It was becoming strong, resilient, and enduring. In their first half century, Latter-day Saints forged a "generalized knowledge construct . . . shaped by the collective process of memory consolidation." In the next several decades, memory recursion shaped and reflected the way they thought, understood, and interpreted their past, present, and future.[11]

The saints' shared will to survive as a people, together with their related goals, desires, and emotions, has acted on their shared memory ever since it was consolidated. The combination of the stable memory and the saints' will to survive unitedly, to transmit their collective identity to a new generation, has been the most significant determinant of whether and how other knowledge has been selected and related to the existing memory.

■ ■ ■

Nothing illustrates these points as well as the beloved hymn now known as "Joseph Smith's First Prayer."[12]

George Manwaring, a British convert and self-taught composer, migrated to Utah in the early 1870s. Late that decade, in his early twenties, he was in Ephraim in central Utah on a sales call when C. C. A. Christensen invited him to his studio to see his newly completed painting, *The Vision*. Moved by the painting and inspired by Christensen's goal of transmitting memory and meaning, Manwaring composed the hymn:

> Oh, how lovely was the morning!
> Radiant beamed the sun above.
> Bees were humming, sweet birds singing
> Music ringing thru the grove,
> When within the shady woodland
> Joseph sought the God of love . . .
>
> Humbly kneeling, sweet appealing—
> 'Twas the boy's first uttered prayer—
> When the pow'rs of sin assailing
> Filled his soul with deep despair;
> But undaunted, still he trusted
> In his Heav'nly Father's care . . .
>
> Suddenly a light descended,
> Brighter far than noonday sun,
> And a shining, glorious pillar
> O'er him fell, around him shone,
> While appeared two heav'nly beings,
> God the Father and the Son . . .
>
> "Joseph, this is my Beloved;
> Hear him!" Oh, how sweet the word!
> Joseph's humble prayer was answered,
> And he listened to the Lord.
> Oh, what rapture filled his bosom,
> For he saw the living God . . .[13]

Besides Smith's canonized memory, Manwaring's hymn probably did more than any other single item to solidify a shared memory of the vision among the Latter-day Saints. Manwaring's admiring son wrote in 1902 about how prophets and preachers had told the vision "for years and years, but it was left to an English emigrant boy to put the story before the members of the church in music and in song."[14]

The proud son assessed the hymn's power to catalyze memory recursion among Latter-day Saints. The hymn both distorts and conveys Smith's memory. It also contributes to source amnesia. "Our species," wrote neuroscientist Larry Squire, "seems best adapted for accumulating knowledge—for inference, approximation, concept formation, and classification—not for the literal retention of the individual examplars that lead to and support general knowledge."[15]

Both Christensen's painting and Manwaring's hymn helped saints do what they were wired to do—store and recall general knowledge of Smith's vision without the ability or burden of knowing much, if anything, about how or where or when or why the knowledge originated. Squire observed that "autobiographical memory for the time and place when a particular event occurred is easily disconnected from the factual knowledge acquired during the event."[16]

Neurologically speaking, memory of an event, such as a hypothetical young woman watching C. C. A. Christensen's "Mormon Panorama" presentation in the Sanpete Valley of Central Utah in 1880 or singing Manwaring's hymn in Sunday school in 1884, recruits areas of the brain above and beyond those required for her to remember some of the facts she learned that day.[17] It is possible—likely, even, if she judged the experience especially engaging, dramatic, and emotionally evocative—that the hypothetical witness would remember the event, especially if she subsequently rehearsed it often in her mind and shared it with others.[18]

The young woman is hypothetical because, other than Manwaring's response to Christensen's painting, there are no other known autobiographical memories from this period of experiences relating to Smith's first vision. What remains is the factual memory she shared with other saints who listened to Christensen's lecture and Manwaring's hymn and many similar retellings, all blurring together. Later, she could have recalled and repeated general and specific facts about Smith's vision on cue without being able to specify how she knew what she knew.

Notes

1. Lectures as Written by C. C. A. Christensen, Scene One, L. Tom Perry Special Collections, Harold B. Lee Library, Brigham Young University, Provo, Utah.

2. Thomas J. Anastasio, Kristen Ann Ehrenberger, Patrick Watson, and Wenyi Zhang, *Individual and Collective Memory Consolidation: Analogous Processes on Different Levels* (Cambridge, MA, and London: MIT Press, 2012), 168.

3. Richard L. Jensen and Richard G. Oman, *C.C.A. Christensen 1831–1912: Mormon Immigrant Artist* (Salt Lake City: Church of Jesus Christ of Latter-day Saints, 1984), 18–19.

4. Lectures as Written by C. C. A. Christensen, Scene One, L. Tom Perry Special Collections, Harold B. Lee Library, Brigham Young University, Provo, Utah, box 8608, A1a no. 2440.

5. C. C. A. Christensen to A. W. Winburg, *Bibuken* [The Beehive], March 20, 1879. Quoted in Jensen and Oman, *C.C.A. Christensen 1831–1912*, 18.

6. The Mormon Panorama is accessible in Jensen and Oman, *C.C.A. Christensen 1831–1912*, 91–116, or Carl Carmer, "A Panorama of Mormon Life," *Art in America* 58 no. 3 (May–June 1970): 52–65.

7. Jensen and Oman, *C.C.A. Christensen 1831–1912*, 18–19.

8. C. C. A. Christensen to A. W. Winburg, *Bibuken* [The Beehive], March 20, 1879. Quoted in Jensen and Oman, *C.C.A. Christensen 1831–1912*, 18.

9. Jensen and Oman, *C.C.A. Christensen 1831–1912*, 91.

10. Anastasio et al., *Individual and Collective Memory Consolidation*, 6.

11. Anastasio et al., *Individual and Collective Memory Consolidation*, 174.

12. Hymns of The Church of Jesus Christ of Latter-day Saints (Salt Lake City: The Church of Jesus Christ of Latter-day Saints, 1985), no. 26. Also available at https://www.lds.org/music/library/hymns/joseph-smiths-first-prayer?lang=eng.

13. Hymns of The Church of Jesus Christ of Latter-day Saints (Salt Lake City: The Church of Jesus Christ of Latter-day Saints, 1985), no. 26. Also available at https://www.lds.org/music/library/hymns/joseph-smiths-first-prayer?lang=eng.

14. A biography of George Manwaring by his brother and his son is at http://freepages.genealogy.rootsweb.ancestry.com/~schick/manwaring/george.htm   (accessed November 7, 2014).

15. Larry R. Squire, "Biological Foundations of Accuracy and Inaccuracy in Memory," in *Memory Distortion: How Minds, Brains, and Societies Reconstruct the Past*, ed. Daniel L. Schacter (Cambridge, MA: Harvard University Press, 1995), 220.

16. Squire, "Biological Foundations of Accuracy and Inaccuracy in Memory," 219.

17. See George D. Pyper, *Stories of Latter-day Saint Hymns: Their Authors and Composers* (Salt Lake City: Deseret News Press, 1939), 33–38.

18. Squire, "Biological Foundations of Accuracy and Inaccuracy in Memory," 217–19.

16

Straightforward Recital

He must impart the glorious truth to them. His parents and his brethren listened and were lost in reverent awe at his straightforward recital.

—George Q. Cannon, 1888[1]

In view of the ease with which humans form concepts and generalize about specific experiences, perhaps the remarkable thing about declarative memory is that it can so often be accurate.

—Larry R. Squire[2]

George Q. Cannon was a major selector and relater and reteller, especially for young saints. Chosen as one of the apostles in 1860, he began in 1866 to publish the *Juvenile Instructor*—a periodical aptly named. Cannon intended by it to communicate the shared meanings of the restored church to its next generation. In 1867, worried about Protestants proselytizing in Utah, especially by providing education for children, Cannon urged his church to make its fledgling, scattered Sunday schools more robust, and was chosen to lead the effort. For the rest of the century he worked to get Sunday schools in every congregation and young saints into the Sunday schools, using the *Juvenile Instructor* to communicate his ideas widely.[3]

In October 1880, at the same time Joseph Smith's manuscript version of his first vision was canonized in the *Pearl of Great Price* and John Taylor formally became the church's president, George Cannon, Taylor's nephew, became his counselor. A few months earlier Cannon had written in the *Juvenile Instructor* that "Latter-day Saint children should know whom they worship," and used Joseph Smith's canonized vision account to assert a personal, approachable God and to undermine creedal Christianity's trinitarian God. "We are told by the Prophet Joseph, who saw the Father and the Son, that they were personages alike in form, substance and glory. Our Father and our God, then, is a Being whom we resemble in many things."[4]

The end for which Cannon evoked Smith's first vision as means was to persuade youth that the God of Joseph Smith would hear and answer them, and that "the children of the Latter-day Saints should seek unto God for themselves. Prayer and the exercise of faith will bring to them a knowledge that God is, and that he is a rewarder of all those who diligently seek Him." Cannon promised no visions to his readers but used Smith's vision to dismiss the God of creedal Christianity as impersonal on the one hand, and promised that the personal God of Joseph Smith would hear and answer them on the other hand.[5]

As federal opposition and the American people generally antagonized the saints, Cannon voiced their concern about losing their children to well-funded Protestant schools that offered Utah's youth a good education but, Cannon was sure, with sinister motives. "They are determined to capture the children," he declared in the *Juvenile Instructor* in June 1883.[6]

The same issue carried Cannon's article refuting both creedal Christianity and Darwinism, using Joseph Smith's first vision as the primary evidence against both. Paraphrasing Smith's account from the *Pearl of Great Price* and quoting the line "This is my beloved Son, hear Him," Cannon asserted that since God appeared to Joseph Smith and humans are created in his image, God cannot be "without body, parts and passions," nor can humans have evolved from "monkey tribes."[7]

Late in the 1880s Cannon published a dramatic biography of Joseph Smith. He intended to lionize Smith and did a good job of it, spending parts of two chapters on a vivid depiction of the vision. Cannon drew mainly from the canonized memory but clearly knew of other accounts. He inevitably morphed Smith's memory, noting that after the vision, Smith's "first thought was of his loved ones. He must impart the glorious truth to them. His parents and his brethren listened and were lost in reverent awe at his straightforward recital."[8] This scene is unsupported in the historical record. Smith's 1832 memory was that he could find no one who believed him. His 1838/39 memory was that he told a Methodist minister, who rebuffed him. His 1842 memory was that when his mother asked what was the matter, he said simply that he had learned that Presbyterianism was not true.

Another of the many first vision retellings among saints in the late nineteenth century belongs to Andrew Jenson, who became an assistant church historian in 1897. Prior to that, having been hired by the church to gather and publicize its history, Jenson wrote an 1886 article in which he adapted writings of George A. Smith and Orson Pratt to tell the familiar story and added that two glorious beings informed Smith "that all the religious sects of the present age had departed from the ancient Gospel of Jesus Christ and his Apostles, with its gifts and Priesthood, which should be made known to him in due season," a paraphrase of Smith's 1842 memory with an anachronistic addition about priesthood, which is not present in any of Smith's vision memories.[9]

The point here is not that Cannon and Jenson got the story wrong. Distortion is a given. As Squire observed, "in view of the ease with which humans form concepts and generalize about specific experiences, perhaps the remarkable thing about declarative memory is that it can so often be accurate."[10] The point here is that the remembering entity—whether an individual or a group—favors coherence over accuracy. Strict fidelity to the boundaries of Smith's recorded memories was not Cannon's priority, nor was it Jenson's, Christensen's, Manwaring's, or even Orson Pratt's.[11]

The importance of transmitting shared memory—shared meaning— to new converts and especially a new generation required retellings that were oral (like Orson Pratt's sermons and Manwaring's hymn), visual (like Christensen's painting), and printed (like Jenson's essay, Cannon's articles, or his biography of Smith). Regardless of the medium, these tellings were never epistemologically transparent. Those who heard, viewed, and sang may have assumed that Joseph Smith was the ultimate source of the knowledge. Many knew that his history was excerpted in the *Pearl of Great Price*, but they were unlikely to know the origins or circumstances of that composition and its subsequent history.

The selectors, relaters, and tellers worried about remembering the vision as a means to the end of conveying current meanings. They were not trying to recover the original experience as an end in itself. Their purpose was to apply Smith's vision to present priorities. So they thought little and communicated less about how they knew what they knew. They picked up on and emphasized the elements of persecution in Joseph Smith's accounts because they resonated so well with the present. They evoked imagination, emotion, and attention, all of which modulated each teller's and each hearer's capacity to remember.

This kind of remembering created both a shared memory and a multitude of individual ones, each inevitably distorted compared to Joseph Smith's own memories of the event. But for all that, the collective memory the saints forged became incredibly strong, resilient, recursive, and extremely well known to the saints.

Notes

1. George Q. Cannon, *The Life of Joseph Smith, The Prophet* (Salt Lake City: Juvenile Instructor Office, 1888), 37–38.
2. "Declarative memory is imperfect, subject to error and reconstruction, distortion, and dissociations between confidence and accuracy." Larry R. Squire, "Biological Foundations of Accuracy and Inaccuracy in Memory," in *Memory Distortion: How Minds, Brains, and Societies Reconstruct the Past,* ed. Daniel L. Schacter (Cambridge, MA: Harvard University Press, 1995), 220.
3. For Cannon's concern about Protestant schools, see the *Juvenile Instructor,* February 1, 1867. Davis Bitton, *George Q. Cannon: A Biography* (Salt Lake City: Deseret, 1999), 146–51.
4. George Q. Cannon, "Editorial Thoughts," *Juvenile Instructor* (Salt Lake City), July 15, 1880, 162.
5. Cannon, "Editorial Thoughts," 162.
6. Cannon, "Editorial Thoughts," 184.
7. George Q. Cannon, "Topics of the Times," *Juvenile Instructor* (Salt Lake City), June 15, 1883, 191.
8. Cannon, *Life of Joseph Smith,* 37–38.
9. Andrew Jenson, "Early Church History," *Historical Record* 5, no. 1 (January 1886): 1.
10. "Declarative memory is imperfect, subject to error and reconstruction, distortion, and dissociations between confidence and accuracy." Squire, "Biological Foundations of Accuracy and Inaccuracy in Memory," 220.
11. "Desires, goals, plans, emotions, and a sense of coherence concerning the self and its place in the world can all influence the memory consolidation process. This is where the entity comes in." Thomas J. Anastasio, Kristen Ann Ehrenberger, Patrick Watson, and Wenyi Zhang, *Individual and Collective Memory Consolidation: Analogous Processes on Different Levels* (Cambridge, MA, and London: MIT Press, 2012), 166.

17

Filling the Void

He knelt down and commenced to call upon God in great earnestness to grant him the knowledge he needed: believing fully that it would be given to him. He had but just commenced when he was seized by a power that brought with it the most dreadful apprehension of sudden destruction. He struggled to appeal for deliverance, and when he felt that he was about to be engulfed in darkness and despair, a sudden change was wrought within him, and an indescribable calm swept over his whole being.

—Don Carlos Young, 1892[1]

In the summer of 1892 the magnificent Salt Lake temple stood complete, at least the exterior. After nearly forty years of construction, the saints almost lost the building when the US government confiscated the church's valuable assets to encourage conformity. The saints relinquished polygamy to keep the temple, or at least began to do so.

Inside the temple finishers were busy preparing the sacred space for its dedication and use in April 1893. John Winder, a counselor to the church's presiding bishop, oversaw the work and Don Carlos Young worked under his direction, designing interior elements. As part of that work, a committee overseeing furnishings hired Tiffany & Company to depict Joseph Smith's first vision in stained glass.[2] Winder donated $1,500 to pay for the glass and Young sent detailed instructions for it to Tiffany in New York. "A subject has been selected for your artist to sketch out, and submit for approval," Young wrote. "The subject is the <u>first vision</u> of the Prophet Joseph Smith."[3]

Young described as graphically as he could what he called "the scene which this remarkable vision opened before the youthful 'seeker after God,'" providing in the process a particularly rich memory of the vision at the turn of the century:

This vision was received early in the spring of 1820 in Manchester, Wayne Co New York when he was in the 15th year of his age. . . . It was on the morning of a beautiful clear day that this young man retired to the woods near his father's house, to a spot of ground which he had previously selected to offer up in fervent prayer his desire that God would make known to him which of the many Christian churches was the right so that he might become a member of that church. As the distractions and confusion arising out of a revival held in the neighborhood had very much disturbed and unsettled his mind. He looked around and saw that he was alone. He knelt down and commenced to call upon God in great earnestness to grant him the knowledge he needed: believing fully that it would be given to him. He had but just commenced when he was seized by a power that brought with it the most dreadful apprehension of sudden destruction. He struggled to appeal for deliverance, and when he felt that he was about to be engulfed in darkness and despair, a sudden change was wrought within him, and an indescribable calm swept over his whole being. Simultaneously with the change of feeling he opened his eyes and saw a pillar of light exceeding the brightness of the son descending immediately over his head. This pillar of light descended so low that he became enveloped by it. And in the pillar of light he saw two heavenly personages whose brightness and glory defy all description standing above him in the air, in such close proximity as to hear one of them speak to him, calling him by name and pointing with his finger to the other personage, saying "this is my beloved Son hear him." One of the personages unfolded in this vision the benighted condition of the whole Christian world and imported to Joseph such information as to fully answer all his enquiries of the Lord in prayer.[4]

Young's description closely follows the canonized version in Joseph Smith's 1838/39 manuscript history, mirroring its arc and echoing its phrases. It represents the saints' factual memory, selected and related by Joseph Smith.

To it Young added instructions for the stained glass that represented the saints' interpretive memory. He wanted the glass scene to convey a humble, hopeful fourteen-year-old, "a healthy boy of good habits and of a thoughtfull turne of mine destined for future greatness in the world."[5] Smith himself said only that the divine beings he envisioned looked exactly alike but defied description. But Young did not leave their appearance to the artist's imagination alone. He ordered something spectacular and specified that they should appear brilliant and standing above young Joseph Smith "some distance in the air, but in such close proximity that every feature of their countenances were seen." Smith's direct accounts do not mention clothes or countenances but Young ordered them "clothed in robes of exquisite whiteness, reaching to the ankles, and the arms were covered nearly to the lower parts of the wrists. The feet were also covered with a sort of shoe apparently of the same kind of material as the garments." Joseph Smith did not describe their hair, but Young told the artist to depict it "of snowy whiteness and worne more after the early oriental style."[6]

For a moment Young felt obliged to stick to the historical record. "It is not said that the heads were covered," he wrote, "therefore they will appear uncovered," but then, given his need to describe a scene Smith left to the imagination, he returned to his interpretive mode, saying that both divine beings "were adorned with full grown Beard, also, of pure white color." To the tricky question of how to convey that the beings were identical yet one was the father of the other, Young asked that the father be shown older and pointing to his son, positioned to his right, and that both be depicted "with their heads bowed sufficiently forward to make the Boy to behold their circumstances in full." Then, underlining for emphasis, Young said he wanted them both "without wings."[7] At the bottom of the scene, Young said, the artists should include the words of James 1:5: "If any of you lack wisdom let him ask of God. Who giveth to all men liberally and upraideth not and it shall be given him." At the top, above the divine beings, he wanted "the words 'addressed by the elder personage to the young Prophet. 'This is my beloved Son: hear him.'"[8] (See figure 17.1).

Don Carlos Young's vivid description captures and conveys the saints' collective memory of the vision and reveals its increasing importance in their narrative. Kathleen Flake observed, "The First Vision contained the elements necessary to fill the historical, scriptural, and theological void left by the abandonment of plural marriage."[9] John Winder sensed that when he offered a large sum to pay for the stained glass.[10] Don Carlos Young sensed it when he pled with Tiffany for a stained-glass depiction of the vision that would "awaken reverence" in observers and cause them to sense "the presence of omnipotence . . . of infinite condescension and love." He wanted "as perfect a piece of work as can be done," and when early drawings didn't match his ideal he requested adjustments at least twice.[11] The vision in stained glass was, after all, to adorn the holiest space in the saints' holiest space.

Young described the designated setting to Tiffany & Company generically, calling it "a circular Room, a 'Chapel' in the Temple."[12] Winder

Figure 17.1 This specifically designed stained-glass depiction of Joseph Smith's first vision was chosen to adorn the saints' most sacred space in the Salt Lake temple.

Art Window in the Interior of the Salt Lake Temple. Courtesy Church History Library.

described it as the anointing room.[13] Apostle James E. Talmage, writing nearly twenty years later, described it as "The Holy of Holies: The central of three small apartments connected with the Celestial Room" and "by far the most beautiful," raised above the others, reached by a short staircase, elegantly finished and furnished, with a domed ceiling including jeweled glass windows. "On the south side of this room," Talmage wrote, "opposite the entrance doorway, and corresponding in size therewith, is a window of colored glass depicting the appearance of the Eternal Father and His Son Jesus Christ to the boy Joseph Smith. The event here delineated marked the ushering-in of the dispensation of the fullness of times."[14]

Like other late-nineteenth-century selectors and relaters, those who put a stained-glass depiction of the canonized version of Joseph Smith's vision in the Salt Lake temple tolerated inaccuracy in their shared memory better than they tolerated incoherence, but their objective differed.[15] C. C. A. Christensen painted and George Manwaring composed music and others wrote about the vision so the saints generally could sense and internalize a coherent version of it, a past that made sense in their present. Putting stained glass in the holiest temple space certainly did that too, but with the added effect of sacralizing the space and elevating the vision, endowing it with more significance, signifying its first place in the Latter-day Saint narrative both chronologically and seminally.

Notes

1. Don Carlos Young to Tiffany & Co., September 20, 1892, Joseph Don Carlos Young Letterpress Copybook, 160–71, Church History Library.

2. Don Carlos Young to Tiffany & Co., September 20, 1892, Joseph Don Carlos Young Letterpress Copybook, 160–71, Church History Library.

3. John R. Winder to Lorenzo Snow, October 8, 1900, Church History Library, Salt Lake City, Utah. Don Carlos Young to Tiffany & Co., September 20, 1892, Church History Library, Salt Lake City, Utah.

4. Don Carlos Young to Tiffany & Co., September 20, 1892, Joseph Don Carlos Young Letterpress Copybook, 160–71, Church History Library. Punctuation and capitalization standardized.

5. Don Carlos Young to Tiffany & Co., September 20, 1892, Joseph Don Carlos Young Letterpress Copybook, 160–71, Church History Library.

6. Don Carlos Young to Tiffany & Co., September 20, 1892, Joseph Don Carlos Young Letterpress Copybook, 160–71, Church History Library.

7. Don Carlos Young to Tiffany & Co., September 20, 1892, Joseph Don Carlos Young Letterpress Copybook, 160–71, Church History Library.

8. Don Carlos Young to Tiffany & Co., September 20, 1892, Joseph Don Carlos Young Letterpress Copybook, 160–71, Church History Library.

9. Kathleen Flake, *The Politics of American Religious Identity: The Seating of Senator Reed Smoot, Mormon Apostle* (Chapel Hill and London: University of North Carolina Press, 2004), 118.

10. Winder wrote to then–church president Lorenzo Snow in 1900, "I remember when we were finishing the Temple I made a vow that I would give fifteen hundred Dollars for a window to be placed in the Anointing room representing the Father and Son appearing to the Boy Prophet Joseph Smith I prize that to day as the best investment I ever made." John R. Winder to Lorenzo Snow, October 8, 1900, Church History Library. Don Carlos Young to Tiffany & Co., September 20, 1892, Joseph Don Carlos Young Letterpress Copybook, 160–71, Church History Library.

11. Young wrote to W. H. Belson at Tiffany & Company, "I write to call your attention particularly to the position of the feet of the two personages in last sketch. They appear as if mortal beings standing on terra firma. This is a wrong concept and should be corrected by the feet being in a more easy and graceful position as shown in your original sketch. Also, please do not forget that I said the two personages were too large. Please correct in your sketch." Don Carlos Young to W. H. Belson, December 1, 1892, Joseph Don Carlos Young Letterpress Copybook, 196, Church History Library.

12. Don Carlos Young to Tiffany & Co., September 20, 1892, Joseph Don Carlos Young Letterpress Copybook, 160–71, Church History Library.

13. John R. Winder to Lorenzo Snow, October 8, 1900, Church History Library. Don Carlos Young to Tiffany & Co., September 20, 1892, Joseph Don Carlos Young Letterpress Copybook, 160–71, Church History Library.

14. James E. Talmage, *The House of the Lord: A Study of Holy Sanctuaries Ancient and Modern* (Salt Lake City: The Church of Jesus Christ of Latter-day Saints, 1912 [2013 ed.]), 177–78.

15. Thomas J. Anastasio, Kristen Ann Ehrenberger, Patrick Watson, and Wenyi Zhang, *Individual and Collective Memory Consolidation: Analogous Processes on Different Levels* (Cambridge, MA, and London: MIT Press, 2012), 168.

18

The Joseph (F.) Smith Story

Is it true that God the Father and Jesus Christ the Son came to the earth in the spring of the year 1820 and revealed themselves to the Prophet Joseph Smith? Is that true? If it is you ought to know it, we ought to know it. Joseph declared that it was true. He suffered persecution all the days of his life on the earth because he declared it was true. He carried his life in his hands, so to speak, every moment of his life until he finally sacrificed in Carthage jail for the testimony that he bore.

—Joseph F. Smith, 1905[1]

In the First Vision, Joseph F. Smith had found a marker of Latter-day Saint identity whose pedigree was as great as—and would be made greater than—that of plural marriage for the twentieth-century Latter-day Saints.

—Kathleen Flake[2]

On December 23, 1894, Latter-day Saints crowded into a Salt Lake City chapel to commemorate Joseph Smith's eighty-ninth birthday. It was the largest and most formal memorial of Smith yet held. Americans were in a remembering mood at the time, an unsurpassed era of memorializing.[3]

Joseph F. Smith, nephew and namesake of Joseph Smith and now a counselor to president and prophet Wilford Woodruff, championed the event and wanted it to become an annual celebration by all Latter-day Saints. He was quickly becoming an old man and longing to remember. He typified the memorializing and meaning-making mood that motivated Americans of the era, including the Latter-day Saints among them. Joseph F. worried that his people might soon forget their founding prophet. He could find fewer than two dozen saints with first-hand memories of Joseph Smith to attend the memorial service.[4]

Fifty years had passed since Smith bounced five-year-old Joseph F. on his knee in June 1844 before leaving with his brother Hyrum, the boy's father.

They returned days later in pine boxes, their bullet-ridden, putrefying bodies making a sight and smell the boy would never forget. But even as that memory shaped Joseph F.'s life, it was not the one he wanted to share with the saints celebrating their prophet's birthday.

During the service, Joseph F. told the saints that he could pick from "many little incidents" that he remembered well, but warned them that it was often the trivial or unusual that got remembered. He illustrated with a story of playing marbles with his cousin, Joseph's son, on the sidewalk outside their home "when all of a sudden the door flew open and I looked, and there came a great big man right off the end of Joseph Smith's foot, and he lit on the sidewalk just by the gate. I saw that myself."[5]

Once Joseph F. captured the saints' attention with that memory, he made his larger point by relegating it to relative unimportance. "What I remember most," he contrasted, "and what is dearest to my memory and to my thinking, and what is greatest to my salvation," was his uncle's calling, revelations, translations, and priesthood. "For he was the only man that I have any record of, or knowledge of, or that I have ever read of in any history, that God Himself, on connection with His son Jesus Christ, deigned to visit in person and commune with in this world."[6] Joseph F. succeeded Orson Pratt as the Latter-day Saints' most important selector, relater, and repeater of his prophet-uncle's vision.

■ ■ ■

Following the death of Lorenzo Snow in 1901, Joseph F. Smith was next in the line of prophetic successors. Joseph F. became the prophet and president of The Church of Jesus Christ of Latter-day Saints in autumn. A few weeks later, on Sunday, December 22, the day before Joseph Smith's 1805 birthday, Joseph F. and his counselors in the church's presidency attended several Sabbath meetings as usual, but that day they placed unusual emphasis on helping youth remember Joseph Smith. At a Sunday school meeting Joseph F. taught "the little ones" that their Savior was Jesus Christ and that Joseph Smith was his prophet. Counselor John Winder, who had paid for the temple's stained-glass portrayal of Smith's vision, told them of seeing Joseph Smith in a dream in a beautiful place, and counselor Anthon Lund told them in his Danish accent about "Joseph's first vision and the grand work he had done."[7]

As Joseph F. visited congregations in the years that followed, he routinely "spoke to the children upon the love of Jesus and the truth of the mission of the Prophet Joseph," often making his later point by asking one of the fourteen-year-old boys to stand next to him "to give the children an object lesson of the prophet's age when he received the first vision."[8] Throughout the congregations, Joseph F. told the story of the vision over and over, acting as selector, relater, and repeater in the ongoing processes of collective memory consolidation and recursion, especially between generations.

Then, in February 1904, Joseph F. Smith received a subpoena to appear before a committee of the US Senate. Chaired by Senator Julius Caeser Burrows, a long-time antagonist to the Latter-day Saints, the committee took advantage of petitions against Reed Smoot, the apostle newly elected to the Senate, to "investigate the Mormon Church" and make its members monogamous, or "see that these men obey the law."[9] Joseph F. welcomed the investigation as "another opportunity" to declare his doctrines.[10]

For the first week of March, Joseph F. sat before the committee in the Capitol building in Washington, DC, and was grilled about whether polygamy continued among his people. The ultimate issue, however, was authority, and whether saints would obey their government or their God. So, when the committee's questions for Joseph F. Smith turned to the nature of his revelations, he had, in the words of Kathleen Flake, "to find a way to rationalize convincingly the subordination of prophecy to democracy" if he wanted to keep the Protestant establishment from crushing his church.[11]

But that task may have been the easier of his two problems, for the other seemed impossible in the face of the first. He needed "to remove his people's faith in one revelation without undermining their confidence in all revelation, as well as the revelator, namely Joseph Smith and himself as Smith's prophetic successor."[12] Joseph F. Smith succeeded in his first task—convincing the committee that he did not consider himself above the law—but that made the second one even more precarious. He returned to Utah and to the resource best suited to the task—Joseph Smith's canonized narrative of the heavenly vision in the spring of 1820—and began in earnest the work Kathleen Flake described as replacing memory.[13]

■ ■ ■

Joseph F. rose in the tabernacle on Temple Square in Salt Lake City on April 8, 1904, the final day of the saints' seventy-fourth annual conference, and, as was customary, presented his name, the names of his two counselors, and the names of the twelve apostles to the saints for their sustaining vote, which they expressed by raising their right hands on cue. "You cannot help but have noticed," Smith then said to the assembled saints, "that some of our brethren have been absent from us. I regret very much the absence of a number of the Apostles."[14] Three of the missing ones were too ill to attend, he explained, but he offered no excuse for two others—the two who had not appeared before the Senate committee to testify of their involvement in postmanifesto plural marriages, though summoned to do so. Ambiguity paralyzed the saints and they desperately needed to "know just where the Church stands on this question."[15] What they got from Joseph F. Smith was a carefully worded statement denying that the plural marriages entered since the October 1890 manifesto were "solemnized with the sanction, consent, or knowledge of the Church of Jesus Christ of Latter-day Saints."[16]

Joseph F. hoped that by prevaricating he could deflect the demands that the saints pay a price or take a punishment for their postmanifesto polygamy, but those demands increased. Either Smoot's Senate career would become a casualty, it seemed, or two other apostles would. But either of those was a small consequence compared to the faith of Latter-day Saints, especially those who were consciously trying to make the past meaningful to their present, who were working out their identity, their shared memory. Whether they thought their prophet should prevaricate for public relations (as some did) or not (as others did), these saints wanted to know the truth about their past and their present. Some wanted the polygamous past to go away. Others saw no way to accept Joseph Smith's "other revelations without accepting that also."[17]

How could Latter-day Saints put polygamy in the past once and for all without rejecting Joseph Smith as a prophet? As Joseph F. Smith stood before them that day he did not answer that question, but he clearly put polygamy in the past. He announced that anyone participating in a polygamous marriage henceforth would "be deemed in transgression against the Church" and subject to excommunication.[18]

That, Joseph F. hoped, ended the controversy, but so long as there was no action behind his words, the storm continued. He took a beating in the Salt Lake *Tribune* by Frank J. Cannon, son of George Q. Cannon and contributor to his father's biography of Joseph Smith, but no longer a Latter-day Saint and no friend of Joseph F.[19] The national press lampooned Joseph F. and assailed his church. One paper announced that "Revelations Doom

Mormonism to Extinction," and President Theodore Roosevelt, frustrated to share the same party as the controversial Smoot, told the senator apostle to abolish the saints' most sacred rituals, calling them "foolishness."[20]

Latter-day Saints were being pulled apart and smothered. Young, educated, eastward-looking saints were anxious for their faith to catch up, to be relevant in the progressive era. Many older saints, and those with fundamentalist tendencies, felt like shutting that world out, but it could not be ignored. The negative press and opinions stifled proselytizing, so much so that the church's commission to take the gospel to all, to gather Israel by making converts, and to usher in the millennial reign of Christ was jeopardized. More than at any prior time, the future depended on what the saints decided to do with their past.

Joseph F.'s response was to do what his uncle Joseph had done: bring a persecuted past to bear on the persecuted present. Acting as the primary selector, relater, and repeater with the collaboration of his fellow saints, Joseph F. raised the profile of Joseph Smith's first vision and its position as the beginning of the saints' narrative. He led the effort to replace the proximate, polygamous past with an ultimate and original, persecuted past. As he toured congregations, Joseph F. continued instructing youth by calling on a fourteen-year-old boy to stand and represent youthful Joseph Smith while he told the story of his vision and "the persecution which followed immediately."[21]

■ ■ ■

Joseph F. Smith had begun his ministry as their prophet with a declaration that "the Lord designs to change this condition of things and to make us known in the world in our true light."[22] In April 1904 he stated his resolve, "I must defend the Church," and in October 1905 he defied the forces that were suppressing the saints and declared "that 'Mormonism' is a living, moving entity; that it is not dead nor sleeping, but that it is alive and awake, growing and advancing in the land; and let the world know it."[23]

So on December 18, 1905, Joseph F. and an entourage of church leaders (excluding those still summoned to testify before the Senate committee) boarded an eastbound train and chugged up and over "the mountains behind which they had fled as children," headed for locations where they would memorialize their founding prophet.[24] For nearly a year they had planned and prepared for the celebration of Joseph Smith's hundredth

WELCOME PHOTO
DEC. 23 – 1905

Figure 18.1 Using the hundredth anniversary of Joseph Smith's birth as a fitting occasion, Joseph F. Smith led Latter-day Saints in memorializing and elevating Smith's first vision as the church relinquished polygamy in the early twentieth century. Joseph Smith Memorial Cottage and Monument, Sharon, Vermont, December 23, 1905.
Courtesy Church History Library.

birthday, having approved the purchase of the property where he was born in rural Vermont and the erection of a monument there. On the anniversary date, Saturday, December 23, a crowd gathered early, including curious locals who trickled to the site from nearby villages and farms, and more than two dozen men and women who arrived in carriages from their lodgings in nearby Royalton, Vermont.[25]

They packed the cottage built for the occasion and listened to Junius Wells tell the impressive story of constructing the monument (see figure 18.1). Others spoke, and then Joseph F. stood and offered a solemn prayer, dedicating the monument and describing it as he went—a concrete foundation on bedrock, signifying apostles and prophets; a granite base "typifying the rock of revelation"; inscriptions including "Sacred to the memory of Joseph Smith, the Prophet," "In the spring of the year of our Lord, 1820, The Father and the Son appeared to him in a glorious vision, called him by name and instructed him," and the text of James 1:5; and thirty-nine tons and nearly that many feet of polished granite shaft. Cumulatively, this was a massive monument signaling the move away from Joseph Smith's revelation

Figure 18.2 Joseph Smith Monument, Sharon, Vermont, dedicated December 23, 1905, one hundred years after Smith's birth near the site.
Courtesy Church History Library.

on plural marriage and toward his first, formative revelations (see figure 18.2).[26]

Later that day Joseph F. became emotional, overcome with joy, flooded by pleasing thoughts of standing on the same land and eating fruit from the same trees as his ancestors. These mixed with painful memories of his murdered father and uncle and being exiled with his widowed mother to refuge in Utah.[27] He felt an intense obligation to carry on the work of his

Figure 18.3 Members of the Smith family at the base of the monument. Joseph F. Smith (1838–1918) is standing on the back row, third from the right.
Courtesy Church History Library.

predecessors, to remember them well, and to pass on his memory to the next generation (see figure 18.3).

After spending Christmas morning in Boston, he and his party boarded the train again and set out to sacralize a grove. They disembarked the next day in Palmyra, New York, and hired carriages to take them a few miles to Manchester to the Smith homestead. They walked into the nearby woods and sang George Manwaring's hymn, "Joseph Smith's First Prayer." Anthon Lund picked up a stick as a memento and later wrote in his diary, "I felt as if walking on hallowed ground."[28] Two years later the saints purchased the grove (see figure 18.4).[29]

The party proceeded from the grove to the hill Joseph Smith's history described as the hiding place for the plates from which he translated the Book of Mormon, and Joseph F. was again overcome with emotion. In a trembling voice he prayed aloud a shared memory "as he remembered the Prophet and the burdens which were placed upon him and the trials."[30]

Joseph F. Smith does not seem to have masterminded this memory-making work, especially to do it deliberately in the context of contentions

Figure 18.4 Joseph F. Smith (1838–1918) in the "sacred grove" in Manchester, New York, during his December 1905 visit.
Courtesy Church History Library.

over polygamy. "There is no hint," wrote Jennifer Lund, "of a deliberate, calculated attempt to celebrate Church history on the landscape."[31] It resulted, rather, from the coincidence of the saints' dramatically decreased debt and resulting ability to spend money, the media assault against them, the Senate hearings demanding assurance that plural marriage was past, the soulful longings to remember evoked in part by centennial anniversaries, and the resolution to never let the restored gospel die.

Joseph F. used the past to ensure that the religion would not become a thing of the past. In the process he elevated his uncle's first vision in the shared story until it became "preeminently the event" of the latter days, "the most important event in the history of the world, excepting only the revelation of Godhood in the person of our Lord Jesus Christ."[32]

■ ■ ■

After a year-long recess, the Senate hearings convened again in February 1906. "It is not me that is in danger," Senator/apostle Smoot wrote to Joseph F., "but the church," and he asked for its leaders to fast and pray for a favorable outcome.[33] That April the two remaining post-1890 polygamist apostles resigned from their roles "because they found themselves out of harmony with the Presidency of the Church."[34]

Smoot held his Senate seat in the end, but the ordeal left Joseph F. resonating with his uncle's persecution-dominated narrative of his first vision. "The greatest crime that Joseph Smith was guilty of," Joseph F. declared in a sermon in London that summer, "was the crime of confessing the great fact that he had heard the voice of God and the voice of His Son Jesus Christ, speaking to him in his childhood; that he saw those Heavenly Beings standing above him in the air of the woods where he went out to pray. That is the worst crime he committed, and the world has held it against him."[35]

Joseph F. even asserted that his uncle's 1844 murder resulted from his 1820 vision.

> Is it true that God the Father and Jesus Christ the Son came to the earth in the spring of the year 1820 and revealed themselves to the Prophet Joseph Smith? Is that true? If it is you ought to know it, we ought to know it. Joseph declared that it was true. He suffered persecution all the days of his life on the earth because he declared it was true. He carried his life in his hands, so to speak, every moment of his life until he finally sacrificed in Carthage jail for the testimony that he bore. . . . He knew that the Father had spoken to him, and, pointing to the personage by His side, had declared: "This is my beloved Son, hear him." Joseph knew this.[36]

On Sunday, April 4, 1909, saints met in the tabernacle on Temple Square for their general conference. Joseph F. Smith opened the meetings with thanksgiving and a reflection on the seventy-nine years of church history.

The saints faced opposition in the beginning, just as they were in the present, he concluded.

> From the day that the Prophet Joseph Smith first declared his vision until now, the enemy of all righteousness, the enemy of truth, of virtue, of honor, uprightness, and purity of life; the enemy to the only true God, the enemy to direct revelation from God and to the inspirations that come from the heavens to man, has been arrayed against this work.[37]

In the turn-of-the-century crisis that threatened to undermine the saints, Joseph F. Smith's selection, relation, and repetition of the story of his uncle's first vision helped them navigate their way to a new narrative, one in which plural marriage could be relinquished without eroding faith in revelations received by prophets past or present.

Notes

1. *Two Sermons by President Joseph F. Smith: What It Is to Be a Latter-day Saint. Divinity of the Mission of Joseph Smith* (Chattanooga, TN: Church of Jesus Christ of Latter-day Saints, Southern States Mission, 1906), 3–6.

2. Kathleen Flake, *The Politics of American Religious Identity: The Seating of Senator Reed Smoot, Mormon Apostle* (Chapel Hill and London: University of North Carolina Press, 2004), 110, 118.

3. According to cultural historian Michael Kammen. See his *Mystic Chords of Memory: The Transformation of Tradition in American Culture* (New York: Knopf, 1991), 115. Joseph F. Smith, "Recollections of the Prophet," Discourse at the Memorial Services in honor of the Prophet Joseph Smith's Birthday, held in the Sixteenth Ward Meeting House, Sunday evening, December 23, 1894, in Brian H. Stuy, compiler and ed., *Collected Discourses*, 5 vols. (Burbank, CA: BHS Publishing, 1987–92), 5:26–30.

4. Joseph F. Smith, "Recollections of the Prophet," Discourse at the Memorial Services in honor of the Prophet Joseph Smith's Birthday, held in the Sixteenth Ward Meeting House, Sunday evening, December 23, 1894, in Brian H. Stuy, compiler and ed., *Collected Discourses*, 5 vols. (Burbank, CA: BHS Publishing, 1987–92), 5:26–30; Keith Erekson, "'Out of the Mists of Memory': Remembering Joseph Smith in Vermont," *Journal of Mormon History* 31, no. 2 (2005): 30–69.

5. Joseph F. Smith, "Recollections of the Prophet," Discourse at the Memorial Services in honor of the Prophet Joseph Smith's Birthday, held in the Sixteenth Ward Meeting House, Sunday evening, December 23, 1894, in Brian H. Stuy, compiler and ed., *Collected Discourses*, 5 vols. (Burbank, CA: BHS Publishing, 1987–92), 5:28.

6. Joseph F. Smith, "Recollections of the Prophet," Discourse at the Memorial Services in honor of the Prophet Joseph Smith's Birthday, held in the Sixteenth Ward Meeting House, Sunday evening, December 23, 1894, in Brian H. Stuy, compiler and ed., *Collected Discourses*, 5 vols. (Burbank, CA: BHS Publishing, 1987–1992), 5:29.

7. Anthon Lund, diary, Sunday, December 22, 1901, Church History Library, Salt Lake City.

8. Anthon Lund, diary, Sunday, September 21; Friday, September 26; Sunday, November 16, 1902; and Sunday, September 6; Sunday, September 13, 1903; and Sunday September 4, 1904, Church History Library, Salt Lake City.

9. Reed Smoot to C. E. Loose, January 26, 1904, Reed Smoot Collection, L. Tom Perry Special Collections, Harold B. Lee Library, Brigham Young University, Provo, Utah; Unsigned letter by Franklin S. Richards to First Presidency, January 18, 1904, Reed Smoot Collection, L. Tom Perry Special Collections, Harold B. Lee Library, Brigham Young University, Provo, Utah.

10. Joseph F. Smith to Reed Smoot, January 28, 1904, Selected Collections, 1:30; Charles W. Nibley, "Reminiscences of President Joseph F. Smith," *Improvement Era,* January 1919, 191–203.

11. Flake, *The Politics of American Religious Identity,* 77–78.

12. Flake, *The Politics of American Religious Identity,* 110, 118.

13. Flake, *The Politics of American Religious Identity,* 109–37. Also see Kathleen Flake, "Re-Placing Memory: Latter-day Saint Use of Historical Monuments and Narrative in the Early Twentieth Century," *Religion and American Culture* 13, no. 1 (2003): 69–109.

14. Elders John W. Taylor and Matthias F. Cowley. See *Seventy Fourth Annual Conference of the Church of Jesus Christ of Latter-day Saints (Deseret News,* 1904), 75, http://archive.org/stream/conferencereport1904a/conferencereport741chur#page/74/mode/2up.

15. Remarks by President Anthon H. Lund, *Seventy Fourth Annual Conference of the Church of Jesus Christ of Latter-day Saints* (Salt Lake City: *Deseret News,* 1904), 76, http://archive.org/stream/conferencereport1904a/conferencereport741chur#page/76/mode/2up.

16. "President Smith," *Seventy Fourth Annual Conference of the Church of Jesus Christ of Latter-day Saints* (Salt Lake City: *Deseret News,* 1904), 75, http://archive.org/stream/conferencereport1904a/conferencereport741chur#page/74/mode/2up.

17. Quote comes from Sarah E. Pearson, "Woman of Mormondom, Smoot Investigation," circa 1905, Church History Library, Salt Lake City. For the view that polygamy should go away, see Carl Badger to Rose Badger, January 1, 1905, in Carlos Ashby Badger Papers, L. Tom Perry Special Collections, Harold B. Lee Library, Brigham Young University, Provo, Utah: "I do not want to see polygamy reestablished, and I want to see the Church leaders tell the truth. It is absolutely impossible after the many declarations made by the leaders to tell just where we are. . . . As to the expression that I would do differently than President Smith is doing if I were in his place, and that I do not think he is doing right, what would you have me say when I believe these things." Also see Flake, "The Common Good," chap. 4 in *The Politics of American*

Religious Identity: The Seating of Senator Reed Smoot, Mormon Apostle (Chapel Hill and London: University of North Carolina Press, 2004), 82–108, for this history in greater detail.

18. "Official Statement," *Seventy Fourth Annual Conference of the Church of Jesus Christ of Latter-day Saints* (Salt Lake City: Deseret News, 1904), 75, http://archive.org/stream/conferencereport1904a/conferencereport741chur#page/74/mode/2up.

19. Kenneth L. Cannon II and Michael A. Paulos, *Selected Frank J. Cannon Salt Lake Tribune Editorials during the Reed Smoot Hearings, 1904–1907 and Snippets from Frank J. Cannon's Campaign against Mormonism during the 1910s* (Salt Lake City: DMT Publishing, 2010); Kenneth W. Godfrey, "Frank J. Cannon: Declension in the Mormon Kingdom," in *Differing Visions: Dissenters in Mormon History*, ed. Roger D. Launius and Linda Thatcher (Urbana: University of Illinois Press, 1994), 241–59.

20. Carl A. Badger, diary, February 8 and 11, 1905, Carl Ashby Badger Papers, L. Tom Perry Special Collections, Harold B. Lee Library, Brigham Young University, Provo, Utah.

21. Anthon Lund, diary, September 6, 1903, Sunday, September 13, 1903, and Sunday, September 4, 1904, in MS 2737, box 62–63, Church History Library, Salt Lake City.

22. Joseph F. Smith in *Conference Report*, November 1901, 70.

23. Joseph F. Smith, in *Conference Report*, October 1905, 97; Joseph F. Smith to Franklin S. Richards, April 16, 1904, in Joseph Fielding Smith, *Life of Joseph F. Smith: Sixth President of The Church of Jesus Christ of Latter-day Saints* (Salt Lake City: Deseret News, 1938), 376–77.

24. The quote is from Flake, *The Politics of American Religious Identity*, 111. A detailed account of the trip by one who was there is in Smith, *Life of Joseph F. Smith*, 355–56.

25. Smith, *Life of Joseph F. Smith*, 358.

26. *Proceedings at the Dedication of the Joseph Smith Memorial Monument* (Salt Lake City, privately published, 1906), 9–27. The interpretation here closely follows Flake, "Re-Placing Memory," 69–109. Also see Flake, *The Politics of American Religious Identity*, 109–37.

27. Smith, *Life of Joseph F. Smith*, 364–66.

28. Smith, *Life of Joseph F. Smith*, 370. Anthon Lund, diary entry, Edyth Romney transcript, Church History Library: "Tuesday December 26th [1905] We arrived at Palmyra in the morning. Here we hired carriages which took us to Manchester to a Mr. Chapman who lives in the house built by Joseph Smith. Sr. and was the farm on which Joseph (76) labored. . . . We went out into the grove where Joseph is said to have received the first vision. The company sang the hymn: 'Joseph's first prayer.' It was very interesting to see these places and I felt as if walking on hallowed ground I brought away a stick from there. Mr. Chapman and family were very pleasant and accomodating to us."

29. Donald L. Enders, "Sacred Grove," in *Encyclopedia of Mormonism* (New York: Macmillan, 1992), 1247.

30. Smith, *Life of Joseph F. Smith*, 370.

31. Jennifer L. Lund, "Joseph F. Smith and the Origins of the Church Historic Sites Program," in *Joseph F. Smith: Reflections on the Man and His Times*, ed. Craig K.

Manscill, Brian D. Reeves, Guy L. Dorius, and J. B. Haws (Provo, UT: Brigham Young University Religious Studies Center, 2013), 345.

32. According to a textbook written for use in Sunday Schools. John Henry Evans, *One Hundred Years of Mormonism* (Salt Lake City: *Deseret News*, 1905), 18.

33. Reed Smoot to Joseph F. Smith, January 21, 1906, Reed Smoot Collection, L. Tom Perry Special Collections, Harold B. Lee Library, Brigham Young University, Provo, Utah.

34. Francis M. Lyman, Sermon, *Conference Report,* April 1906, 93.

35. *Two Sermons by President Joseph F. Smith*, 3.

36. *Two Sermons by President Joseph F. Smith*, 3–6.

37. "Opening Address," in *The 79th Annual Conference of the Church of Jesus Christ of Latter-day Saints* (Salt Lake City: *Deseret News*, 1909), 4.

19

The Golden Age of That First
Great Revelation

There is nothing in our doctrines on Deity today but what was germinally present in that first great revelation received by the Prophet Joseph Smith.

—B. H. Roberts, 1903[1]

It was warm outside, and probably warmer still in the Assembly Hall across the square from the saints' temple in Salt Lake City, late in the evening of June 11, 1900. Members of the Young Men's Mutual Improvement Association (YMMIA) packed the pews for their annual speakers' contest. Contestants could choose their topic, and they were judged by a panel including the saints' best-known theologians and rhetoricians.[2]

After five young men spoke that night, Joseph F. Smith awarded one of them first prize for a speech claiming that "no sooner did Joseph Smith, the boy-prophet of the nineteenth century, tell of the heavenly visit which he had received, than false witnesses arose," beginning a persecuted life "from the age of fourteen until his cold body lay against the stone wall of Carthage jail."[3]

Second prize was awarded to a speech titled "Joseph Smith, His Mission and Persecution," which eloquently cast Smith as an unpretentious lad whose vision ended "darkness, delusion, and ungodliness" but evoked "bigotry." Both speakers contrasted Smith with "his avowed enemies" and ended with the "martyred hero."[4] The Latter-day Saints identified with these themes.

Joseph F. Smith's efforts to raise the profile of the vision, especially among the youth of the church, were working. The speakers had no need to introduce Joseph Smith to the audience, nor his first vision story, nor their shared persecution narrative. They needed only to evoke the vision to make several rhetorical points: that God was embodied and passionate and created humans in his image; that God and Christ were distinct, separate, yet unified; that the Christian churches and creeds were not Christ's; that God continued to reveal himself; that Joseph Smith was his revelator.[5]

These ideas were collective knowledge among Latter-day Saints in 1900. And no story captured and conveyed their shared sense of God, their relationship to him and to other Christians, as potently as the story of Smith's vision. That may help explain why the judges tended to award speakers who evoked the vision. It may also explain why the audience seemed unsatisfied with the awards; reportedly "there appeared to be a pretty general sentiment in favor of Alma Taylor" instead.[6]

Eighteen-year-old Taylor titled his talk "The First Vision." It was less rhetorical than the winning speeches but powerful, and a better story—the familiar story of spiritual darkness prior to 1820 during which "the ways of salvation became as numerous as the dispositions of men," so amid confusion, earnest Joseph Smith encountered James 1:5, and prayed humbly. Just as Joseph's "petitions ascended to God," Taylor paused and painted the same scene as George Manwaring's hymn—sunshine, birdsong, giant oaks swaying in a gentle breeze, and a plainly clothed boy kneeling, face heavenward.

Then (paraphrasing the hymn and quoting Smith's best-known line), Taylor's story climaxed: "What rapture must have filled his bosom when he saw the heavenly personages, and heard the voice of the Father say, 'Joseph, this is my Beloved Son, hear him!'"[7] Taylor's speech concluded with some didactic if poetic points, the morals to the saints' seminal story.[8] "The vision," he summed up, "was indeed the earthquake which dried up the rivers of unbelief, which started the fountains of truth, and which shook the mountain from whose side the little stone rolled forth to accomplish its destiny of filling the whole earth with the Gospel of purity."[9] Taylor and the other contestants show how young saints learned, repeated, and inevitably distorted the familiar story of the first vision, favoring coherence over accuracy.

These speeches were emblematic of a broader movement in the church during the first two decades of the twentieth century. Led by Joseph F. Smith, the saints worked more concertedly than ever at consolidating and transmitting collective memory of Joseph Smith's first vision. When antagonism waned after the Smoot hearings, no one besides Latter-day Saints showed much interest in Smith's vision.[10] But Progressive Era selectors, relaters, and tellers of the story kept the persecution narrative alive. Young Saints like

Alma Taylor inherited and repeated it. It forged group identity even without an intense, immediate threat, until saints experienced enough lessons, magazine articles, and speaking contests to share knowledge of Smith's first vision, which led to a distinctive doctrine of God and Christ and a heritage of persecution. It was the first vision's golden age.

Besides making the most of the power of the persecution narrative, tellers of the story in this era articulated increasingly coherent theology of God as corporeal, distinct from Christ, and as plural. They solidified links between history and theology, between Smith's vision and their distinctive doctrines of deity. Saints learned in Sunday school that their faith "dates its beginning from an event—the most important in its history—that occurred in the western part of New York State, in the year 1820."[11]

The saints' history and theology became increasingly inseparable. The more they related the vision to their theology of God, the more seminal the event became for them. It distinguished them from other Christians, which helped maintain difference in an era when the saints were otherwise trying desperately to fit in.

■ ■ ■

One of the judges of the YMMIA speeches that June evening in 1900 was B. H. Roberts (see figure 19.1). He must have been pleased. Though only in his early forties, he was already among the saints' leading orators and intellectuals, and the author of several theological histories. His 1893 *Outlines of Ecclesiastical History* endowed Smith's vision story with more systematic theological meaning than earlier selectors and relaters had. He listened to Alma Taylor and others repeat ideas that he selected, related, and repeated often.[12]

The present as Roberts experienced it shaped the way he related Smith's vision to theology in the early twentieth century. In 1901, Reverend Alfred Henry delivered lectures in Salt Lake City on the nature of the Mormon God. That summer a Dr. Paden, speaking to the Utah Presbytery but sending a message to progressive theologians like Roberts, argued that the saints were moving away from "heathenish" notions of a material God and of plural gods. Two days later Roberts spoke to the YMMIA annual conference.[13]

He began by restating three objections to the saints' doctrine of deity: "First . . . in a word, God is an exalted, perfected man. Second we

Figure 19.1 Brigham Henry (B. H.) Roberts (1857–1933) led Latter-day Saint efforts to maximize the theological implications of Joseph Smith's first vision. Photo courtesy Church History Library.

believe in a plurality of Gods. Third, . . . man may become like God—a God." Roberts then defended each proposition from the New Testament and the Apostles' Creed. He argued that history had seen "paganization of the Christian religion," "false philosophies," and "idle speculations of the Greeks" until the Apostles' Creed gave way to later statements that rendered God impersonal, incorporeal, passionless—"an absolute nonentity." Roberts then wielded the Bible in defense of Latter-day Saint doctrines of deity.[14]

The editors of the *Improvement Era* published the discourse late in 1901.[15] Father Cyril Van Der Donckt, a Catholic priest in Idaho, wrote a civil reply that the *Era* published in the summer of 1902, followed by Roberts's response.[16] In 1903 Roberts published a book including the debate, with this new preface:

In nothing have men so far departed from revealed truth as in their conceptions of God. Therefore, when it pleased the Lord in these last days to open again direct communication with men, by a new dispensation of the gospel, it is not surprising that the very first revelation given was one that revealed himself and his Son Jesus Christ. A revelation which not only made known the being of God, but the kind of being he is. The Prophet Joseph Smith, in his account of his first great revelation, declares that he saw "two personages," resembling each other in form and features, but whose brightness and glory defied all description. One of these personages addressed the prophet and said, as he pointed to the other—"This is my beloved Son, hear him."

Roberts argued that Joseph Smith's vision proved the Old Testament doctrine that God created man in his image and the New Testament idea that Jesus was the Son of God, separate from but like God, as well as what both Testaments taught about the plurality of Gods.

No wonder the saints' doctrine of deity was controversial, Roberts concluded,

coming so sharply in conflict with the ideas of apostate Christendom which had rejected the plain anthropomorphism of the Old and New Testament revelations of God; also the scriptural doctrine of a plurality of Gods, for a false philosophy-created God, immaterial and passionless—all this, I say, could not fail to provoke controversy; for the revelation given to Joseph Smith challenged the truth of the conception of God held by the modern world.[17]

Roberts ended his book with appendices arranged to show "that from the beginning of what the world calls 'Mormonism,' the views contended for in the body of this work, have been the doctrine of the Church."[18] The first document among them was Joseph Smith's canonized story of his vision, followed by a restatement of the theology that Roberts found in it. These were the ideas that he argued for against creedal Christians, the ideas repeated in speakers' contests and manuals and meetings.[19]

Joseph Smith told the story of his encounter with God without elaborating a theology of it, but Roberts found theological seeds in Smith's story. "There is nothing in our doctrines on Deity today," Roberts said, "but was germinally present in that first great revelation."[20]

■ ■ ■

While B. H. Roberts was defending and theologizing the first vision, it continued to modulate through other means and mediums, both visual and written. George Edward Anderson stepped off the train in Palmyra, New York, on the evening of August 12, 1907, and walked south—packing his camera, tripod, and glass plates—to a farm purchased by the church two months earlier. A second-generation Latter-day Saint in his midforties with a young family in Utah, Anderson was bound for a proselytizing mission in England but determined, while en route, to visit the sacred sites of his people and capture them in photographs.[21]

He met the caretaker of the farm and early the next morning the caretaker's twelve-year-old son led Anderson into the woods.[22]

"I wanted to show you the tree where they said Joseph Smith prayed," Anderson remembered the boy saying. "I thought you would like to make a picture of it."

"I certainly should," Anderson replied, excited and curious. "Do you know where the tree is?"

"I can take you right to it," the boy said, leading the photographer there.

Anderson studied the tree and asked the boy how he knew that it marked the site. The boy told of following a large group of visitors into the grove two years earlier and watching them gather around the tree and sing. "Then a man with a long beard prayed," the boy said.[23]

Anderson told the boy that the praying man was a prophet, and also the nephew and namesake of the murdered prophet Joseph Smith, who knelt and prayed at that site when he was fourteen.

"I am going to make a picture of the grove," Anderson told the boy, "and I would like to have you in the picture." Anderson made at least two images of the boy amid the trees, along with other photos of the grove (see figure 19.2).[24]

The church published Anderson's photos in 1909 in a book for use in Sunday schools.[25] By 1920, the centennial of Smith's vision, the photos were well known among Latter-day Saints.[26] In terms of memory consolidation, Anderson not only added elements into the memory buffer but also selected and related elements from the buffer for the saints to incorporate into their memory.

Anderson's photos were not his sole contribution, either. Through the medium of the *Improvement Era*, he told the story of the boy and another story about the caretaker, whose father's dying wish was that the grove be

Figure 19.2 George Edward Anderson's 1907 photo of site of Joseph Smith's first vision, the "sacred grove" in Manchester, New York, with local boy in the foreground.
Courtesy Church History Library.

preserved because "that is where Joseph Smith, the 'Mormon' prophet, had his first vision."[27]

No one knows the precise site.[28] Smith left no more description than "the woods," presumably somewhere near his home.[29] Joseph F. Smith's pilgrimage to *a* grove near that home site in 1905, the church's acquisition of the home site and surrounding land, the publication of Anderson's photographs of that grove, and the folk repetition of his stories all signified the sacralization of that grove, a powerful way of geographically grounding the transcendent.

That process created a specific memory of the place. A grove became *the* grove, and a certain tree marked the very spot.[30] Selectors, relaters, and repeaters favored coherence (a past with meaning in the present) over fidelity to historical records (or lack thereof). The church's goal was to transmit meaning to young saints who needed guidance in selecting the story from among alternatives, relating it to their lives, and rehearsing it repeatedly with emotional associations that would make the memory their own.

Efforts to that end were effective.[31] Families and missionaries started making pilgrimages to what they began calling "the sacred grove," to "the maple tree near the spot where Joseph offered his prayer."[32] When, in 1919, the *Improvement Era* published an article titled "The Sacred Grove," saints knew which grove was meant and why it was sacred. The author described an idealized pilgrimage to the grove and readers shared it vicariously: "As one draws near he instinctively feels the spirit of the holy spot. He treads more lightly, fearful that the snapping of a twig may break the spell. The head is bared as memory of the wonderous story fills the mind." The pilgrim and his imagined companion (the reader) enter the grove, and the companion says, "This is where little Joseph prayed," pointing to the tree that became the site in the first decade of the twentieth century, "the spot where a child's faith moved the heavens and called to earth the Father and the Son."[33]

The pilgrim continues: "O Sacred Grove, I pray thee, speak." It doesn't speak to the uninitiated, at least not the same words, but the author prayed that it would "speak to this generation" and suggested how that prayer and its answer could sound:

Are all these glories true? Breathless I waited for the answer, my heart thrilled with heavenly emotions. In a moment the answer came to my soul, soft yet vivid as the music of the leaves: . . . "I well recall the morn when Joseph came to pray. I loved the child and always in the springtime welcomed his return. Like the birds he was a carrier of gladness, strong of limb and bright of eye. This morn I shall not forget, so strange was that which fell beneath my view. He came—the boy—and looked about in youthful fear. The day was calm like this. In sympathy, I held my breath for fear of frightening the tender lad. And then, I saw him fall upon his knees, with eyes turned toward the sky. He prayed, and it seemed that all the universe stood still and hung upon a thread. Soon the sun seemed darkened. A power, black as the blackest night, seized the praying lad. I, too, did feel the wicked presence, shaking as I do before the winter gales. But still did Joseph pray. Ere long I felt a peaceful, heavenly spirit soothe the world, and lo! descending from the clouds I saw two Personages arrayed in white of purest hue. My bosom heaved with ecstasy. The birds gushed o'er with harmonies divine. The flowers changed to blooms of paradise. And a Voice, gentle and kind, yet piercing like the lightning flash, addressed the kneeling boy:

'This is my beloved Son. Hear him!'

And then One spoke in tones much like the First. And Joseph listened, his face illumined in the glorious light. In time, the Voice ceased, the light slowly faded, and then, 'twas gone. Then the youthful seer arose. I spoke to him in voice we oft had used. And Joseph, strengthened, melted into joyous tears."

However the personified grove may sound to readers today, it modulated memories then. That is, it evoked the emotion needed to contribute to consolidation.[34] The article was one of many modulators available in the early twentieth century.

Other modulators came through different genres of writing, as well as other mediums of expression. Nephi Anderson's *A Young Folks' History of the Church*, published in 1900, wasn't as popular as some of his later novels, but it told an accessible, fast-paced story in which the problem of Christian apostasy is resolved when God and Christ visit a compelling protagonist, young Joseph Smith.[35] Anderson was a good modulator, not only as a writer of history but also as the author of novels whose characters speak of Smith's vision or sing George Manwaring's hymn about it.

One of the earliest novels to evoke the vision was Ben Rich's *Mr. Durant of Salt Lake City: That Mormon* in 1893. Set in the New South, the novel introduces readers to the restored gospel via a missionary, Charles Durant, whom Mr. and Mrs. Marshall welcome into their mansion in Westminster, Tennessee, for candid visits. The Marshalls and their guests hang on Durant's every word. In their final meeting one guest confesses that "like most good people of this nation, we have been in possession

Figure 19.3 Relief Society theology class in Salt Lake Seventeenth Ward with stained glass of Joseph Smith's first vision in the background, 1942.
Courtesy Church History Library.

of only one side of the question regarding your people," and asks Durant for Joseph Smith's own claims "in regard to his being a prophet." Pleased, Durant offers Smith's "own statement"—the canonized account of his vision.[36]

In 1907, the same year the church acquired the grove and Anderson photographed it, saints in Salt Lake City's seventeenth ward installed stained glass in their new chapel that depicted Joseph Smith kneeling before two divine beings (see figure 19.3). Similar windows soon graced other chapels (see figure 19.4).[37] About 1910 the church began publishing Smith's canonized account of his vision in a pamphlet.[38] In 1912 the novel-like biography *From Plowboy to Prophet* told the story for young readers, illustrated with a painting of Joseph Praying in the Grove.[39]

The church even made a silent movie, *One Hundred Years of Mormonism*, in 1913. It has not been seen since its initial run at the Salt Lake Theater,

Figure 19.4 Stained glass of Joseph Smith's first vision, Adams Ward, Los Angeles. See figure 21.1.
Courtesy Church History Library.

and no one knows if or how it depicted Smith's first vision.[40] But it bore the same title as the saints' 1905 Sunday school manual, which emphasized the vision as the seminal event of the faith.[41]

Even the high priests—often the older men in the church—studied the story in their curriculum. And, though the format was not nearly as conducive as other media to stirring emotions that could modulate enduring memory, most of them could already recite the story in their sleep.[42]

        ■ ■ ■

On April 6, 1902, church leaders appointed B. H. Roberts an assistant church historian and tasked him with turning Smith's history, originally serialized in 1842 in the *Times and Seasons*, into published volumes.[43] No one was better positioned to mine the story for its theological potential. B. H. Roberts had edited the *Millennial Star*, the saints' British periodical, in the late 1880s.

While in that role, he had gathered the serialized "History of Joseph Smith" from back issues and bound it into three volumes that he kept and annotated.[44] Roberts worked fast. Within a year he published Smith's history through mid-May 1834, working not from manuscripts but from his copy of the *Millennial Star*.

Roberts experienced dissonance when he came to Smith's account of what happened when he saw the divine beings. In the 1838/39 manuscript history (as published in 1842), Smith said he "asked the personages who stood above me in the light, which of all the sects was right, (for at this time it had never entered into my heart that all were wrong,) and which I should join." Earlier in the same account, however, Smith said that prior to his vision he had "often said to myself, what is to be done? Who of all these parties are right? Or are they all wrong together?"[45]

The two lines seemed a contradiction to Roberts. He knew that Smith's 1842 letter to John Wentworth said that at about age fourteen he began to notice "a great clash" between churches and considered "that all could not be right, and that God could not be the author of so much confusion."[46] So Roberts silently elided the line "for at this time it had never entered into my heart that all were wrong."[47]

Roberts's interaction with the first vision text shows how memories consolidate in layers that blend but also compete with each other—like the 1838 history, lost but rewritten in 1839, published in 1842 and again in 1852, and edited by Roberts in the first volume of his *History of the Church of Jesus Christ of Latter-day Saints* in 1902. Distortions occur all along the way as selectors and relaters like B. H. Roberts suit the past to the present.

Roberts inherited a complex amalgamation of material that has only been untangled recently. He knew that Joseph Smith was not solely responsible for the contents of his history and felt licensed to edit as his predecessors in the Church Historian's Office did—redacting with no hint to readers that the end result was anything other than Smith's voice, or, as the title page said, "History of Joseph Smith, the Prophet, by Himself."[48]

The editorial practices of B. H. Roberts made no difference to Latter-day Saints in the early decades of the twentieth century. The source material available for shaping their shared memory was the canonized account, and now they had Roberts's *History*—together with a common hymn, stained glass, lessons, and popular histories and novels that selected, related, and repeated it. During this golden era for Smith's vision, no one was attacking the vision. Roberts was the closest thing to a source critic, and his *History* elided dissonance between versions of Smith's story.

Then, just when things seemed about as good as they could be for the saints, *American Historical Magazine* published a series of articles in 1906–7 attacking the story of the divinely revealed, miraculously translated Book of Mormon. B. H. Roberts asked the publisher for room to respond in the *American Historical Magazine*. The society welcomed the debate, doubled the number of issues, renamed their periodical *The Americana*, and invited Roberts to serialize a "History of the Mormon Church," all of which indicated a receptive national audience.[49] Even as they kept the persecution complex from fading, church leaders had worked hard to brand the saints as mainstream, and it seemed to be working.

The third installment of Roberts's history appeared in September 1909, illustrated by George Anderson's photograph over the caption: "The Sacred Grove." Roberts wrote well and augmented the usual story with sources besides Smith's canonized account, acknowledging in a footnote that he purposely blended Smith's two narratives—the only two known at the time, from 1838/39 and 1842. "Not that there are any irreconcilable differences in the two," he added quickly. "One is given in greater detail than the other, and in each there are some details not mentioned in the other, hence the blending of the narratives," Roberts explained.[50]

Roberts's narrative was the most comprehensive vision story yet. He followed it with ten pages of analysis, justifying God's denunciation of Christian creeds in Smith's vision. It was characteristic of Roberts to situate the vision as the solution to the problem of Christian apostasy. He began his histories with long, academic descriptions of primitive Christianity's fall, followed by the story of Smith's vision—the antidote to Christian apostasy. Roberts had long since developed the practice of harvesting the saints' distinctive theology from Smith's vision narratives, as he did when he spoke to the YMMIA in 1901.

Other relaters followed the same line of thought, teaching "the first thing the Prophet Joseph Smith did was to restore to the world the lost knowledge of the true God."[51] The vision was likewise evoked as defense against insiders and outsiders who argued for any God but the separate, embodied, passionate father and son that B. H. Roberts and others found in Smith's first vision.[52] Likewise, Smith's vision had become a resource for defending peripheral "doctrines," similar to how George Q. Cannon had used the first vision to argue against Darwinism in the late nineteenth century. In the early twentieth century, B. H. Roberts and others found in the vision the seeds of a theology in which humans evolve into gods.[53]

The first vision had become an uncontested instrument for explaining what it meant to be a Latter-day Saint. Throughout the vision's golden age among the general church membership, however, an undercurrent of scholarship was calling the event into question.

Notes

1. B. H. Roberts, *The Mormon Doctrine of Deity: The Roberts-Van Der Donckt Discussion* (Salt Lake City, 1903), preface, http://www.gutenberg.org/files/45464/45464-h/45464-h.htm#.

2. The setting for the Speakers' Contest is described in Stan Larson, ed., *A Ministry of Meetings: The Apostolic Diaries of Rudger Clawson* (Salt Lake City: Signature, 1993), 175–77. For details of the meeting, also see "The Speaker's Contest," *Improvement Era* 3, no. 9 (July 1900): 666–78.

3. Walter J. Sloan, "Thou Shalt Not," *Improvement Era* 3, no. 9 (July 1900): 666–68.

4. Mark C. Brown, "Joseph Smith—His Mission and Persecution," *Improvement Era* 3, no. 9 (July 1900): 673–78.

5. B. H. Roberts, *Outlines of Ecclesiastical History* (Salt Lake City: George Q. Cannon and Sons, 1893), 305–8.

6. "The judges rendered their decision giving to W. J. Sloane the first prize and to Mark C. Brown the 2nd prize. It was truly a most interesting and instructive contest, though the audience did not seem to be altogether satisfied with the decision. There appeared to be a pretty general sentiment in favor of Alma Taylor." Stan Larson, ed., *A Ministry of Meetings*, 175–77.

7. Alma O. Taylor, "The First Vision," *Improvement Era* 3, no. 9 (July 1900): 682–86.

8. Latter-day Saint young men were being taught that Smith's vision began the final and full dispensation of God's blessings to mankind. See General Board of the Young Men's Mutual Improvement Associations, *Dispensation of the Fullness of Times* (Salt Lake City: Deseret News, 1899), 23.

9. Taylor, "The First Vision," 682–86.

10. The 1883 *Encyclopedia Britannica* article "Mormons," for example, referred to Smith's "alleged visions" but began describing them with the 1823 visit of an angel who "told him that the Bible of the Western Continent, the supplement to the New Testament, was buried in a certain spot" nearby. *Encyclopedia Britannica*, 1883, s.v. "Mormons," 825–27. William Linn's 1902 *Story of the Mormons*, based on Mormon sources, said nothing of the vision, perhaps because, as Linn claimed, he could not access the *Times and Seasons*, nor did he list among his sources the *Pearl of Great Price*, and so, in terms of consolidating a memory, the vision was not available or meaningful to the world beyond Mormondom. "Joseph Smith, Jr., is known, where known at all, only in the most general way as the founder of the sect," Linn deduced. William Alexander Linn, *The Story of the Mormons: From the Date of Their Origin to the Year 1901* (New York: Macmillan, 1902), v–vii.

11. John Henry Evans, *One Hundred Years of Mormonism: A History of the Church of Jesus Christ of Latter-day Saints from 1805–1905* (Salt Lake City: Deseret Sunday School Union, 1909), 1.

12. Roberts, *Outlines of Ecclesiastical History*, 305–8.
13. B. H. Roberts, *The Mormon Doctrine of Deity* (Salt Lake City, 1903), 3–4, 10 in Project Gutenberg Ebook.
14. Roberts, *The Mormon Doctrine of Deity*, 3 in Project Gutenberg Ebook.
15. B. H. Roberts, "Characteristics of Deity," *Improvement Era* 5 (November, December 1901): 29, 119.
16. B. H. Roberts, "Jesus Christ: The Revelation of God," *Improvement Era* 5 (August, September, October 1902): 787–98, 886–89, 969–79, respectively.
17. Roberts, *The Mormon Doctrine of Deity*, 3–4, 10 in Project Gutenberg Ebook.
18. Roberts, *The Mormon Doctrine of Deity*, 144 in Project Gutenberg Ebook.
19. Roberts, *Outlines of Ecclesiastical History*, 305–8.
20. Roberts, *The Mormon Doctrine of Deity*, 5 in Project Gutenberg Ebook.
21. Nelson Wadsorth, "A Village Photographer's Dream," *Ensign*, September 1973), https://www.lds.org/ensign/1973/09/a-village-photographers-dream?lang=eng. Richard Nietzel Holzapfel, T. Jeffrey Cottle, and Ted D. Stoddard, eds., *Church History in Black and White: George Edward Anderson's Photographic Mission to Latter-day Saints Historical Sites* (Provo, UT: Brigham Young University Religious Studies Center, 1995), 164. For church acquisition of the farm, see footnote 446.
22. Holzapfel, Cottle, and Stoddard, eds., *Church History in Black and White*, 164.
23. George Ed. Anderson, "Boy in the Picture of the Sacred Grove," *Improvement Era* 23, no. 7 (May 1920): 638–40, https://archive.org/stream/improvementera2307unse#page/636/mode/2up.
24. Holzapfel, Cottle, and Stoddard, eds., *Church History in Black and White*, 6, 164, 180, 182–83. Anderson, "Boy in the Picture of the Sacred Grove," 638–40, https://archive.org/stream/improvementera2307unse#page/636/mode/2up.
25. See *Birth of Mormonism in Picture: Scenes and Incidents in Early Church History* (Salt Lake City: Deseret Sunday School Union, 1909).
26. According to the editors of the *Improvement Era*. See Anderson, "Boy in the Picture of the Sacred Grove," 638–40, https://archive.org/stream/improvementera2307unse#page/636/mode/2up.
27. Anderson, "Boy in the Picture of the Sacred Grove," 638–40, https://archive.org/stream/improvementera2307unse#page/636/mode/2up. For a 1934 variation on the caretaker story; see John Wells to Joseph Fielding Smith, July 17, 1934, MS 19247, Church History Library, Salt Lake City.
28. T. Edgar Lyon, "How Authentic Are Mormon Historic Sites in Vermont and New York?," *BYU Studies* 9, no. 3 (Spring 1969): 343–45.
29. "The wilderness" in 1832: "History, circa Summer 1832," p. 3, *The Joseph Smith Papers*, accessed October 24, 2018, http://www.josephsmithpapers.org/paper-summary/history-circa-summer-1832/3. "The silent grove" in 1835: "Journal, 1835–1836," p. 23, *The Joseph Smith Papers*, accessed October 24, 2018, http://www.josephsmithpapers.org/paper-summary/journal-1835-1836/24. "The woods," in 1838/39: "History, circa June 1839–circa 1841 [Draft 2]," p. 3, *The Joseph Smith Papers*, accessed October 24, 2018, http://www.josephsmithpapers.org/paper-summary/history-circa-june-1839-circa-1841-draft-2/3. "A secret place in a grove,"

in 1842: "'Church History,' 1 March 1842," p. 706, *The Joseph Smith Papers*, accessed October 24, 2018, http://www.josephsmithpapers.org/paper-summary/church-history-1-march-1842/1.

30. In a pioneering study of collective memory, Maurice Halbwachs analyzed how a similar process created what he called "the legendary topography of the gospels in the Holy Land." See his *On Collective Memory* (Chicago: University of Chicago, 1992), esp. part 2.

31. These efforts are summarized by James B. Allen in "Emergence of a Fundamental: The Expanding Role of Joseph Smith's First Vision in Mormon Religious Thought," in *Exploring the First Vision,* ed. Samuel Alonzo Dodge and Steven C. Harper (Provo, UT: Brigham Young University Religious Studies Center, 2012), 244–45.

32. Frederick A. Herman to Frank Mitchell, Logan, Utah, November 9, 1909, p. 4. Also see Newell J. Crookston, Journal Extracts, August 18, 1915, pp. 474–76, Church History Library, Salt Lake City.

33. Charles F. Steele, "The Sacred Grove," *Improvement Era* 23, no. 8 (June 1920): 720–21, https://archive.org/stream/improvementera238unse#page/720/mode/2up.

34. Benno Roozendaal and James L. McGaugh, "Memory Modulation," *Behavioral Neuroscience* 125, no. 6 (December 2011): 797–824.

35. Nephi Anderson, *A Young Folks' History of the Church of Jesus Christ of Latter-day Saints* (Salt Lake City: George Q. Cannon and Sons, 1900), accessed through Google Books.

36. Ben E. Rich, *Mr. Durant of Salt Lake City: That Mormon* (Salt Lake City: George Q. Cannon & Sons, 1893), 13–15, 111–31.

37. Joyce Athay Janetski, "The First Vision and Mormon Stained Glass," *Stained Glass* 75 (1980): 47–50.

38. According to James B. Allen in "Emergence of a Fundamental," 245. It was included in Ben E. Rich's circa 1910 publication of "Religious Tracts." See Rich, *Scrapbook of Mormon Literature* 1: 11, http://babel.hathitrust.org/cgi/pt?id=njp.32101068997913; view=1up;seq=23.

39. William A. Morton, *From Plowboy to Prophet: Being a Short History of Joseph Smith, for Children* (Salt Lake City: Deseret Book, 1943), 1–12.

40. Randy Astle, "One Hundred Years of Mormonism," accessed October 9, 2015, http://mormonarts.lib.byu.edu/works/one-hundred-years-of-mormonism.

41. Evans, *One Hundred Years of Mormonism*, 1.

42. *Course of Study for the Quorums of the Priesthood: High Priests, Second Year, History of the Gospel* (Salt Lake City: Church of Jesus Christ of Latter-day Saints, 1910), lessons 27 and 28, pp. 87–89.

43. Truman G. Madsen, *Defender of the Faith: The B.H. Roberts Story* (Salt Lake City: Bookcraft, 1980), 162–64, 289–90.

44. *History of Joseph Smith*, 3 vols., in B. H. Roberts collection, MS 1278, Church History Library, Salt Lake City.

45. Joseph Smith, History, circa June 1839–1841, handwriting of James Mulholland and Robert B. Thompson, in Joseph Smith, History, 1838–1856, vol. A-1, Church History

Library, Salt Lake City. Compare to "History of Joseph Smith," *Times and Seasons* 3, no. 11 (April 1, 1842): 748.

46. Joseph Smith, "Church History," *Times and Seasons* 3, no. 9 (March 1, 1842): 706.

47. On p. 3 of his "History of Joseph Smith from the Millennial Star," Roberts wrote the following in pencil: "contradiction with statement in Wentworth letter [one illegible word] see preceding." *History of Joseph Smith*, 3 vols., in B. H. Roberts collection, MS 1278, Church History Library, Salt Lake City.

48. Truman Madsen analyzes Robert's editorial hand in *Defender of the Faith: The B.H. Roberts Story* (Salt Lake City: Bookcraft, 1980), 289–94.

49. B. H. Roberts, *A Comprehensive History of the Church of Jesus Christ of Latter-day Saints*, 6 vols. (Salt Lake City: Deseret News Press, 1930), 1:v–vi. "Announcements," *Americana* 4, no. 4 (July 1909): 466–67.

50. B. H. Roberts, "History of the Mormon Church: Chapter 5, The Early Visions of Joseph Smith," *Americana* 4, no. 6 (September 1909): 610–27. Roberts relied also on William Smith's memories and Joseph Smith's 1842 account for John Wentworth.

51. George F. Richards to S. C. Brown, March 28, 1911, in George F. Richards journal entry of that date, MS 1307, box 2, folder 5, Church History Library, Salt Lake City; Orson F. Whitney, Discourse, Ogden, Utah Weber North Stake Quarterly Conference, General Minutes, June 25, 1916, LR 9969/11, Church History Library, Salt Lake City. Whitney reportedly said of Smith's vision: "Joseph Smith did not give us anything new; he brought back the old; old things are best. The eternal truth of God must be old, it cannot be new for it never had a beginning, it will never have an end. That is the first thing that Joseph Smith did for the world: To restore this precious knowledge of the true God. And, it is a little singular and yet it is very beautiful to me, that when Joseph went into the woods to ask in his simple manner which of all the Christian churches was the true Church, God gave him a greater answer than he was looking for. Joseph wanted to know which of all the churches was the true church. It had never dawned upon this boy's mind but that one of them was right, and he was told that none of them was right, that they had all gone out of the way; that they were teaching for doctrine the commandments of man, and that God was about to restore the gospel to the earth again and that he had a mission in connection therewith. But that was not the greatest part of that wonderful revelation. The greatest part is the part that He did not speak. The boy saw two beings before him – two glorious beings in the form of man and, before a word had been uttered that great truth had been restored that God is indeed what Moses said, in the form and image of man, and one of these glorious Beings said of the other: 'this is my beloved son, hear Him.' The inference is therefore that the one who spoke first was our Father in heaven who had come down to open this new dispensation for the love of His children, and had brought with Him the Savior who had died that His children might live. We can approach with confidence such a God, who notes the sparrow's fall, and knows that there is no man, no woman, no human soul so little, so insignificant but God has a care over them and desires to bless them and save them."

52. George F. Richards to S. C. Brown, March 28, 1911, in George F. Richards journal entry of that date, MS 1307, box 2, folder 5, Church History Library, Salt Lake City; Orson F. Whitney, Discourse, Ogden, Utah Weber North Stake Quarterly Conference, General Minutes, June 25, 1916, LR 9969/11, Church History Library, Salt Lake City.

53. On this point, see Kurt Widmer, *Mormonism and the Nature of God: A Theological Evolution, 1830–1915* (Jefferson, NC: McFarland, 2000), 91–106.

20

The Objective Reality of the First Vision
Is Questioned

I myself have gone through the critical period when science and religion seemed to rise up against one another; and can sympathize keenly with every young person who is in the same condition.
—John A. Widtsoe, 1898[1]

Benjamin Cluff was thirty-five and the assistant principal of Brigham Young Academy in Provo, Utah, when he finished his master's degree at the University of Michigan in 1893. Before returning to the academy, he visited several universities. At a Harvard reception he met William James, who invited him to dinner the following evening.[2]

By then the Harvard professor was in his early fifties, renowned as the father of American psychology, and characteristically curious to comprehend his visitor.[3] After dinner, James asked Cluff "to give in brief an account of the vision of Joseph Smith." Cluff did so and then one of James's students "asked the Doctor how he would explain the vision scientifically."

"On the theory of hallucination," James replied. "Joseph Smith had a hallucination." Cluff explained that Joseph Smith saw an angel and translated the Book of Mormon from writing on metal plates. James said it would make a difference "if others had seen the angel or the plates," and Cluff assured him "that others, three witnesses had seen the angel and the plates and eight had seen the plates."[4]

"That changes it then," James said, and he asked how he could get what Cluff called "a set of our books from which he could read up on this subject." Cluff wrote to the First Presidency and they sent James "a full set of works."[5]

To Benjamin Cluff it may have felt like a triumph for someone of James's reputation to take his religion seriously. Though James was open to Joseph Smith's gold plates as evidence of their reality, however, Smith's first vision remained in the subjective realm. Such things happened, James granted, as "inner religious phenomena," but even if he read every book church leaders sent him in March 1894, he found nothing to overturn his subjective explanation of divine beings appearing to Joseph Smith.[6]

Late nineteenth- and early twentieth-century academic interest in Joseph Smith added an alternative to overt hostility or total disregard. It also added a new risk that believers in the historical appearance of divine, embodied beings could find more dangerous than persecution. Pluralism and pragmatism—as William James articulated them—could undermine the exceptionalism saints found in Smith's first vision.[7]

■ ■ ■

The year following Cluff's Harvard visit, a Yale graduate student named Woodbridge Riley visited Salt Lake City to research Joseph Smith's psychology.[8] Nearly a decade later, Riley published *The Founder of Mormonism: A Psychological Study of Joseph Smith, Jr.* Riley situated Smith's first vision at the intersection of genetic inheritance and evangelical revivalism. By turns sardonic and scientific in tenor, Riley showed that "the erratic tendencies in Joseph's mind appear constitutional." The conversion narrative of Smith's maternal grandfather, Riley noted, "fulfills three out of the five general causes of hallucination." It was obvious to Riley that Smith inherited "neural instability."[9]

After analyzing Smith's 1838/39 and 1842 accounts, along with Orson Pratt's 1841 account, in the context of "analogous experiences," Riley concluded by "applying the principles of the modern psychology of religion, as derived from cold blooded statistics," that Smith's visions evidenced more than conversion in the wake of evangelical angst. The visions "put him in the rarer third of youth who have dreams and hallucinations."[10]

Riley interpreted Smith's hallucinations in what he called "psychophysical terms, for the apparent objective manifestations were actually subjective symptoms." Riley explained, "the theophanic portions of his visions are precisely what occur in a certain form of visual disturbance akin to vertigo." Riley's diagnosis: ophthalmic migraine compounded by melancholic depression and epilepsy.[11]

An earlier critic of Smith dismissed him as "either crazy or a very shallow imposter," but not Riley. "There is no call for so harsh a judgment," he noted. "There is a truer and, at the same time, more charitable explanation," Riley concluded.[12]

A reviewer for the *Dial* noted that Riley's "point of view makes it easier to be dispassionate, although to the devout Mormon the very point of view itself must seem hostile. Mr. Riley shows, and without much difficulty, that Joseph Smith, Jr. was pronouncedly neurotic." The reviewer concluded that there were still many inherently gullible people whose right to proselytize should be restricted.[13]

Riley's interpretation of Joseph Smith reveals academically oriented undercurrents of doubt running through the first vision's golden age in the first decade of the twentieth century. Just as Joseph F. Smith was leading Latter-day Saints to make his prophet-uncle's first vision foundational to their faith, and B. H. Roberts was showing them the theological potential of Smith's vision, academics began offering sophisticated reasons to young scholars like Benjamin Cluff why they could not make Smith's vision the basis for a rational faith. Those ideas soon migrated, making their way from the minds of a few peripheral intellectuals to the heart of Mormondom.

＊ ＊ ＊

In 1903, Benjamin Cluff became the first president of Brigham Young University, the rechristened Brigham Young Academy. His tenure was short-lived and naming the school a university did not make it one, but it was a start. In April 1906 the church's general board of education—including the First Presidency and several of the apostles—chose Horace Cummings to be their general superintendent. Cummings had been a teacher at the University of Utah for over a decade. He was a workhorse but he protested that he lacked the advanced education needed for the job. That didn't matter much to the members of the board, who knew that Cummings shared their first priority, "to teach and train the students in the principles of the gospel."[14] He set to work outlining religion curriculum to be implemented in the fall.

Joseph Peterson, a psychology professor, came the following year as the first PhD on the faculty. He was followed by a few other scholars who added academic credibility to the campus. Soon Peterson and other psychologists, philosophers, and scientists were teaching theology, as well as their disciplines.[15] Many students appreciated how they squared the restored gospel with biblical source criticism and Darwin's theory of evolution, and the Jamesian idea that visions like Joseph Smith's were better understood as subjective experience than as historical events.

Not all the students liked the new ideas. "Complaints soon began to come to me against these teachings," Cummings noted. He visited the campus, explained what he'd heard to the faculty and students, pled with them for orthodoxy, and reminded them that the "school was established to teach the gospel of Christ and not its opposite, to destroy faith."[16]

The only change, however, was that more faculty accepted the "new thought," more students embraced the teaching, the ideas began spreading to other church schools, and more complaints reached headquarters.[17] In January 1911, the board sent Cummings to investigate. "I spent about nine days," he wrote, "visiting classes, talking with teachers and students, and in the evenings I visited some of the parents to see what they thought of the situation."

On January 21, Cummings submitted his written report to the board "concerning the nature and effect of certain theological instructions given, mostly by the College professors." The report included ten unorthodox teachings Cummings observed, including the idea that "visions and revelations are mental suggestions. The objective reality of the presence of the Father and the Son, in Joseph Smith's first vision, is questioned."[18] When Cummings pressed this point, he found that some of the faculty "strenuously denied" a historical, corporeal visit of God and Christ to Joseph Smith.[19]

Cummings also discovered that for every student or parent who objected to the unorthodox instruction, others felt inspired by it. He spoke with many who described a painful reorientation process. He noted that the theology classes had never been so popular, and he felt caught between the demands of orthodox patrons and students and faculty who accused him of destroying "academic liberty" and killing their school.[20]

In February 1911 the board listened to Cummings and appointed a subcommittee to hear Joseph Petersen and two other professors answer for their teaching. They "admitted teaching everything I had charged in my report," Cummings noted. "It was decided that, since they would not promise to refrain from such objectionable teachings in the future, that their services be dispensed with."[21] Most of the student body protested and signed a petition "endorsing the teaching of the professors, and praying for their retention by the Board."[22] Their prayers were not answered. The three professors were fired and like-minded faculty members resigned or their contracts were not renewed.

When Benjamin Cluff visited Harvard in 1893, John Widtsoe was one of James's students there (see figure 20.1). Born in Norway in 1872, Widtsoe migrated with his mother to Utah and became a Latter-day Saint. He was among the first saints to seek higher education, graduating from Harvard in 1894 with highest honors after three years. Besides studying psychology with James, Widtsoe took philosophy from Josiah Royce, and he majored in chemistry under the tutelage of renowned professors he admired.[23] He questioned his faith as he drank in the materialist paradigm many of his professors shared.[24] "Was Mormonism what it pretended to be? Did Joseph Smith tell the truth?" he wondered.[25]

Widtsoe's most significant mentor at Harvard turned out not to be William James or Josiah Royce, but Josiah Cooke, Erving professor of

Figure 20.1 John A. Widtsoe (1872–1952) reconciled robust faith in Joseph Smith's first vision with advanced academic training and intellectual distinction. His example, teachings, and writings helped other Latter-day Saints reach similar conclusions.
Photo courtesy Church History Library.

chemistry and mineralogy. He had delivered lectures at Union Theological Seminary in 1888 and published them as *The Credentials of Science, the Warrant of Faith* (1888). A second edition came out while Widtsoe was his Harvard student in 1893, worried whether his faith was valid, and engaged in what he called "a real search for truth," reading much and listening to various perspectives.[26] It seemed that materialism "permeated every classroom," Widtsoe recalled, except Cooke's.[27]

The chemistry professor preached a peculiar epistemology, arguing that "knowledge of God has come to man through nature precisely in the same way as the generalizations of science, and is subject to the same limitations."[28] Both God and science, Cooke claimed, could be known only in part, by what he alternately called induction or inspiration.[29]

Inspiration was the beginning of knowing either God or gravity. From there one could deduce more by observation and experiment, to be sure. "I have the greatest respect for the love of truth and accuracy which the positive philosophy so strongly inculcates," Cooke wrote, "but, as it seems to me, this doctrine finds its chief disciples among scholars who have been so engrossed in deductive methods as to overlook the mental visions by which the broader relations of truth have been discovered."[30]

Professor Cooke was attentive to his student, and during visits to Cooke's library, Widtsoe admired the ease with which he spoke and cherished his advice about the best way to choose from "contending doctrines." When Widtsoe left Harvard in 1894, he took with him "certain knowledge that the restored gospel is true and that Joseph Smith was indeed a Prophet." He wrote in his autobiography, "In finding my way to spiritual truth, Dr. Cooke's steady certainty of the pre-eminence of religion was a great help."[31]

In 1894 Benjamin Cluff recruited Widtsoe to join the BYU faculty.[32] The best of the several offers he received, however, led him to Logan to work as a chemist at the Utah State Agricultural College.[33] He went from there to Germany, earning a PhD in 1899, before becoming the director of the Agricultural Experiment Station at the Agricultural College. In 1907, at about the same time Joseph Peterson became the first PhD on the BYU faculty, Widtsoe became president of Utah Agricultural College in Logan.

During much of this time, Widtsoe was a regular contributor to the church's new periodical, the *Improvement Era*, begun in 1897 with Joseph F. Smith as editor. During his graduate studies in Germany, Widtsoe acknowledged in an article, "I myself have gone through the critical period when science and religion seemed to rise up against one another; and can sympathize keenly with every young person who is in the same condition."[34] In a subsequent article, Widtsoe echoed Josiah Cooke, positing that scientists walked by faith in what they could not see just as believers did. Both kinds of truth seeking, Widtsoe argued, began with faith in the unseen and proceeded toward verification based on experience and observation.

If he took little from William James, Widtsoe at least shared his view that religions should integrate science if they hoped to endure.[35] With encouragement from Joseph F. Smith, Widtsoe wrote a series of articles for the *Era*, published in 1903–4 and in 1908 as *Joseph Smith as Scientist*.[36] Featuring Joseph Smith's idea on the eternal nature of matter and some of its implications, Widtsoe worked toward a version of Josiah Royce's ideal: "discovery of the unity of apparently diverse lines of investigation."[37]

Joseph F. Smith and the *Era*'s readers alike praised John Widtsoe's orthodox negotiation of modern thought and the restored gospel.[38] As he gained academic prominence for his science, Widtsoe grew in favor with intellectual young saints and their leaders, who in 1921 would call him to be an apostle and put him in charge of the church's schools.

Widtsoe lent intellectual credibility to miracles in the modern era. "I cannot satisfy myself with the theory that the vision of Joseph Smith was merely subjective," he wrote in 1930, careful with every word. "I can conceive it more than possible that another man standing by the side of Joseph, not touched with the same powers, would be unable to see what Joseph saw. That, however, does not in any degree destroy the reality of Joseph's vision."[39]

Notes

1. John A. Widtsoe, "A Voice From the Soil," *Improvement Era* 2 (December 1898): 109.
2. Benjamin Cluff, Diary, MS 1667 (US 620), box 1, folder 2, pp. 138–40, L. Tom Perry Special Collections, Harold B. Lee Library, Brigham Young University, Provo, Utah.
3. Linda Simon, *Genuine Reality: A Life of William James* (New York: Harcourt Brace, 1998), xxii.
4. Benjamin Cluff, Diary, MS 1667 (US 620), box 1, folder 2, pp. 138–40, L. Tom Perry Special Collections, Harold B. Lee Library, Brigham Young University, Provo, Utah.
5. Benjamin Cluff, Diary, MS 1667 (US 620), box 1, folder 2, pp. 138–40, L. Tom Perry Special Collections, Harold B. Lee Library, Brigham Young University, Provo, Utah; George Reynolds to William James, March 13, 1894. William James to George

Reynolds, March 28, 1894. George Reynolds to William James, April 11, 1894, Church History Library, Salt Lake City.

6. A list of the books church leaders sent to James is in William James to George Reynolds, March 28, 1894, Church History Library, Salt Lake City. On James's thought, see William James, *The Varieties of Religious Experience: A Study in Human Nature* (New York: Penguin, 1982), 482–84; Robert D. Richardson, *William James: In the Maelstrom of American Modernism* (New York: Houghton Mifflin, 2006). I'm indebted to Jed Woodworth for sharpening my thought on William James regarding Joseph Smith.

7. Linda Simon provided these succinct definitions: "Pragmatism is a method of problem solving that looks to the consequences of ideas to define the truth of those ideas. Pluralism urges our openness to multiple perspectives because, James wrote, 'there is no possible point of view from which the world can appear an absolutely single fact.'" Simon, *Genuine Reality*, xix.

8. I. Woodbridge Riley, *The Founder of Mormonism: A Psychological Study of Joseph Smith Jr.* (New York: Dodd, Mead and Company, 1903), ix.

9. Riley, *The Founder of Mormonism*, 19, 33, 64.

10. Riley, *The Founder of Mormonism*, 58–62.

11. Riley, *The Founder of Mormonism*, 67–70.

12. Riley, *The Founder of Mormonism*, 69–70.

13. W. H. Carruth, "Mormonism and Its Founder," *The Dial* 34, no. 397 (Chicago, January 1, 1903): 16–18.

14. Horace Cummings, Autobiography, chap. XXXVI, L. Tom Perry Special Collections, Harold B. Lee Library, Brigham Young University, Provo, Utah.

15. Gary James Bergera, "The 1911 Evolution Controversy at Brigham Young University," in *The Search for Harmony: Essays on Science and Mormonism,* ed. Gene A. Sessions and Craig J. Oberg (Salt Lake City: Signature Books, 1993), 23–41.

16. Horace Cummings, Autobiography, 41–42, L. Tom Perry Special Collections, Harold B. Lee Library, Brigham Young University, Provo, Utah.

17. Board Minutes, February 3, 1911, 180–86. Quote on p. 182. Also Cummings, Autobiography, 3, 41–42, L. Tom Perry Special Collections, Harold B. Lee Library, Brigham Young University, Provo, Utah.

18. Board Minutes, February 3, 1911, 183.

19. Cummings, Autobiography, 41–44.

20. Cummings, Autobiography, 41–45.

21. Cummings, Autobiography, 41–45.

22. Deseret News, March 11, 1911; Salt Lake Tribune, March 12, 1911, Chamberlain Oral History, 8. Cited in *Brigham Young University: A House of Faith*, 143n23, 426.

23. John A. Widtsoe, *In a Sunlit Land* (Salt Lake City: Deseret News Press, 1952), 34–35.

24. Alan K. Parrish, *John A. Widtsoe: A Biography* (Salt Lake City: Deseret, 2003), 57–78. Quote on p. 63.

25. Widtsoe, *In a Sunlit Land*, 37. Emphasis added.

26. For analysis of the various arguments by and between Widtsoe's Harvard professors, see Clyde D. Ford, "Materialism and Mormonism: The Early Twentieth Century

Philosophy of Dr. John A. Widtsoe," *Journal of Mormon History* 36, no. 3 (Summer 2010): 1–26.

27. Widtsoe, *In a Sunlit Land*, 37.

28. Josiah Parsons Cooke, *The Credentials of Science, the Warrant of Faith* (New York: D. Appleton and Company, 1893), 3.

29. Cooke, *The Credentials of Science*, 3–4, 211.

30. Cooke, *The Credentials of Science*, 211–12.

31. Widtsoe, *In a Sunlit Land*, 37. "I have also traveled a devious road to attain my present convictions in which I find a great and continuous satisfaction. As a child, three days old, I was baptized into the Lutheran Church, and until I was nearly twelve years of age, was taught in and out of school the doctrines of that Church. In fact I was destined for the priesthood of that Church. My mother then brought me to Utah, and soon afterwards I requested baptism into the Mormon Church. Some six years later I entered upon my College course at Harvard, and soon came under the influence of men who had no religion beyond their daily scientific work. I passed through a struggle which cut to the bone. God was denied: then again humbly affirmed. Several of the leading denominations were studied earnestly and compared with Mormonism. When the struggle was over, and supreme peace had come to me, I found myself with the conviction that the eternal scheme of salvation was held by the Church of Jesus Christ of Latter-day Saints. Since that day I have given much time to the study of the Gospel, and my testimony of the truth of Mormonism has remained unshaken." Quoted by Ardis E. Parshall, accessed August 25, 2018, http://www.keepapitchinin.org/widtsoe-on-facebook/. Original source not cited.

32. Benjamin Cluff, Jr. to John A. Widtsoe, March 29, 1894, Church History Library, Salt Lake City.

33. John A. Widtsoe to J. H. Paul, July 11, 1894, Church History Library, Salt Lake City.

34. John A. Widtsoe, "A Voice from the Soil," *Improvement Era* 2 (December 1898): 108–9.

35. Clyde D. Ford, "Materialism and Mormonism: The Early Twentieth Century Philosophy of Dr. John A. Widtsoe," *Journal of Mormon History* 36, no. 3 (Summer 2010): 7. Also see footnote 23.

36. John A. Widtsoe, *Joseph Smith as Scientist: A Contribution to Mormon Philosophy* (Salt Lake City: General Board, Young Men's Mutual Improvement Associations, 1908).

37. Josiah Royce, *The Spirit of Modern Philosophy* (Boston and New York: Houghton Mifflin Company, 1892), 297.

38. Edward H. Anderson to John A. Widtsoe, August 13, 1900, and February 20, 1901, Church History Library, Salt Lake City; Joseph F. Smith to John A. Widtsoe, September 24, 1903, Church History Library, Salt Lake City.

39. John A. Widtsoe to Susa Young Gates, March 19, 1930, Church History Library, Salt Lake City.

21

One Hundred Years of Mormonism

Through the vision of that unlearned boy, who knelt in humble prayer before his Maker, I bear testimony that I am what I am. The glory of God has been engraved in my heart, and belief in the truths of His Gospel has caused me to rejoice, and to go ever onward and upward to a higher and nobler plane. I have learned to have faith in a living God who loves all men and is never known to desert them when in need. I have learned that it is better to walk with Him in the dark, that to attempt to find my way alone in the light.

—Mildred Boyer, 1920[1]

Commemoration, when successful, unites the past and the present.

—Amy Corning and Howard Schuman, *Generations and Collective Memory*, 2015[2]

Joseph F. Smith died in November 1918. He was one of the few remaining saints who walked westward across the American plains and over the Rocky Mountains in the 1840s, seeking a place where they could worship as they pleased. He was also one of the few who had known Joseph Smith personally. He had become his generation's foremost selector, relater, and repeater of his prophet-uncle's first vision, turning saints from polygamy toward the vision and changing "the arena of confrontation over differences," as Kathleen Flake put it, "from social action to theological belief." He adapted "the Latter-day Saints' necessary sense of otherness to fit safely within the politics of American religion."[3] He led them in creating a new narrative, consolidating a new memory. But it was as subject to change as life itself.

The nature of the saints' memory had to change as Joseph Smith's vision sank deeper into the past and its foremost selectors, relaters, and repeaters passed away. Jan Assman's terms *communicative* and *cultural* memory characterize the change. Communicative memory is temporary. It can last one generation, maybe two, depending on how long contemporaries of the event live and how well they transfer memory.[4] "To make sure that this memory does not die with them," Assman wrote, "it has to be transmuted into tradition, into the symbolic forms of cultural memory."[5]

Cultural memory concerns the more distant past. It remembers extraordinary events formally and ceremonially. Intentional commemoration typifies cultural memory, and often memorial events multiply as time passes. Cultural memory that is not memorialized will weaken.

There is no guarantee that a group will develop or perpetuate cultural memory of a specific event. It was almost certain, however, that Latter-day Saints would try to consolidate cultural memory of Joseph Smith's first vision. Early in 1920, Heber J. Grant, Joseph F. Smith's successor as church president and prophet, received a letter from John Widtsoe expressing delight at the news he had just read of the plan to commemorate the one hundredth anniversary of Smith's vision. "The First Vision was a marvelous event which thrills to the core every latter-day Saint," Widtsoe wrote. He sent Grant his own writings on the vision and suggested the publication of "a memorial volume."[6] Grant shared Widtsoe's views, "read every word with pleasure," and heartily approved the book idea.[7]

Grant told Edward Anderson, long-time editor of the *Improvement Era*, that he had "read a very splendid article by Dr. Widtsoe on the subject of the First Vision." Grant solicited Widtsoe's essay for a special spring issue devoted "exclusively to the vision and its world-wide significance and far-reaching results." Anderson wanted Grant to write an article as well, but the president balked. There were more talented writers, he said, Widtsoe among them. Anderson replied that he had solicited essays from them but couldn't go to press without a statement on Smith's first vision from his successor as the prophet.[8] Grant thought about it for a couple of weeks, but as the press deadline loomed he told Anderson he had decided not to write on the first vision for the special issue of the *Improvement Era*.[9]

Meanwhile he read the proofs, including Anderson's poem "The Divine Answer," based on the canonized account of Smith's vision, and Orson F. Whitney's ode "The Messenger of Morn." Grant read essays by his counselors in the First Presidency, Anthon Lund and Charles Penrose, who made a case that the nineteenth century was more impressive than any previous, and Smith's vision was its most important event.[10]

Lund wrote of his 1905 trip to the grove with Joseph F. Smith and declared three truths derived from the vision but "contrary to the belief of the

Christian world." First, God is embodied and passable. Second, Christianity was apostate at the time of Smith's vision. To his third point, namely, that Christians were wrong to deny that God and Christ revealed themselves to Joseph Smith, Lund told a story of his Danish boyhood and Lutheran education. "We learned much that was very good," he admitted, "but also some doctrines that I could not accept." He paraphrased his catechism, "if any one should say he had received new, divine revelation, we must not put any faith in such a declaration; for God has nowhere promised to give any more revelation." Not so, Lund argued.[11]

Grant continued reading, a dozen essays in all, each selecting Joseph Smith's vision for saints to remember, relating it to other information in ways both old and new, applying the past to the present and vice versa, and repeating it over and over.

Susa Gates's essay was the least long-winded and the most original. She asked the novel question: "Can you conceive, then, what the Vision meant to women?" She interpreted God's intervention in history (via the vision) as the catalyst of equal suffrage. She was completely conscious as she wrote that the constitutional amendment long sought by Mormon women and others, the amendment to forbid voting discrimination based on gender, had gained Utah's support the previous fall and now needed just one more state to ratify it.

"The Vision held the bright promise of equality and freedom for women," Gates asserted, linking those two elements of the past for the first time in a present where both mattered. For her, Smith's revelation evoked the doctrines of Latter-day Saint feminism. "It meant woman's free agency," she wrote, "the liberation of her long-chained will and purpose." And it meant both a Mother and a Father in heaven, who revealed their will personally, individually, without respect to gender.[12]

Grant read every page of the proofs. "I thoroughly enjoyed every article from start to finish," he wrote to Anderson. "I think it is the finest number that has ever been issued by the *Era*. It is a wonderful missionary. I want ten thousand extra copies printed."[13] Ultimately, he couldn't resist including his own contribution, a three-page article celebrating "the most wonderful vision ever bestowed upon mortal man."[14]

The special issue of the *Improvement Era*, published in April 1920, is a memory capsule. It included a photo of "The Sacred Grove in Summer," captioned as "showing the Sacred Tree said to be nearest the space where the Father and Son appeared to the boy Joseph,"[15] and "a sacred historical cantata" by Evan Stephens, "written and composed especially for the centennial."[16] It contained elements long since selected for inclusion in the saints' collective memory buffer. It introduced new elements into that buffer. It represented the saints' robust and relentless will to remember Smith's vision. But alone it was an insufficient memory modulator.

The saints' cultural memory depended on what they decided to do with the available information. It was one thing for the *Era* to publish a special commemorative edition (or the *Young Woman's Journal* to publish "The First Vision of Joseph Smith the Prophet," by John A. Widtsoe). It was another for young women or old men to understand or remember ideas communicated via the professor's prose and advanced reasoning.[17] No matter how many periodical pages or memorial books were printed, cultural memory depended on whether Latter-day Saints internalized the words on the pages. That depended on whether they could effectively ritualize the ideas and repeatedly rehearse them.

■ ■ ■

On the second day of the saints' general conference in April 1920, Joseph Fielding Smith, son and namesake of the recently deceased prophet, stood at the tabernacle pulpit in Salt Lake City. "One theme has stood out very prominently, and properly so," he said, "in the remarks of the speakers who have addressed this conference. That has been the subject of the great vision given to the Prophet Joseph Smith."

He had just listened to the scientist James Talmage, a fellow apostle and sometimes theological rival. "You know the story, I know," Talmage had said, "but it is well sometimes to be reminded of what we know." He rehearsed Smith's canonized vision narrative again and asserted that because of it The Church of Jesus Christ of Latter-day Saints "stands aloof and alone."[18] Joseph Fielding Smith agreed heartily with all Talmage had said.[19]

That evening Latter-day Saints packed the tabernacle again, filling every seat and standing in the aisles. In his midsixties, Evan Stephens, Welsh-born director of the Mormon Tabernacle Choir until 1916, returned to the rostrum after four years of feeling he had "been upon the shelf as a worn out vessel." Now he was back in the conductor's spot that had been his for a quarter century, leading the choir in his cantata, *The Vision*.[20]

Heber J. Grant thought the performance was a "regular triumph."[21] So did Samuel Mitton. He had first attended general conference in his teens in October 1880, when Joseph Smith's first vision was canonized. He had loved the tabernacle organ and choir and listening to Orson Pratt rehearse and relate the vision.[22] Now in his midfifties, an admirer and friend of Evan Stephens, and director of the saints' choir in Cache Valley to the north, Mitton noted in his journal each part that was sung, the speech on "the vision of the Father and Son," and the singer who played Joseph Smith. He summed up the experience as "the greatest music I ever heard."[23]

■　■　■

The April 1920 general conference, together with that month's issues of the *Improvement Era* and *Young Woman's Journal*, were just the beginning. The Mutual Improvement Association commemorated Smith's vision church-wide on May 1.[24] There are few records of this celebration, but they show that at least some of the celebrations were impressive. Young saints in the California mission performed music and gave commemorative speeches (see figure 21.1).[25]

Figure 21.1 Los Angeles Stake M Men's and Gleaner Girls' Chorus, March 20, 1927, set to perform "The Vision," by Evan Stephens. Adams Ward, Los Angeles. Note the stained glass of Joseph Smith's first vision in the background. See figure 19.4.
Photo courtesy Church History Library.

In Provo, Utah, students and faculty from the sixth grade through college shared testimonials. "Joseph Smith's first prayer proves to me that there must be a Mother in Heaven," said seventh grader Inez Taylor, perhaps taking her cue from Susa Young Gates's recently published essay, "for if there is a Father and Son, there must be a Mother."[26]

These precocious, commemorative statements are revealing samples of cultural memory. For the first time in the historical record, young saints—some very young—described how Smith's vision resonated with them. Printed beside their professors' comparatively didactic statements, the students told "what the first vision has done for me," "what the first vision means to me," and "how the prophet's vision has affected my life."[27]

Several students linked their identity, their very selves, to the vision, and none more cogently than Mildred Boyer, a student at Brigham Young University, who said the vision began the movement that led her future mother to migrate from Europe to America, where she married a man

> whose parents pulled a handcart across the plains of America because of that same wonderful revelation. . . . Through the vision of that unlearned boy, who knelt in humble prayer before his Maker, I bear testimony that I am what I am. The glory of God has been engraved in my heart, and belief in the truths of His Gospel has caused me to rejoice, and to go ever onward and upward to a higher and nobler plane. I have learned to have faith in a living God who loves all men and is never known to desert them when in need. I have learned that it is better to walk with Him in the dark, that to attempt to find my way alone in the light.[28]

The youth in Provo internalized Joseph Smith's first vision and made it their own as they commemorated with *The Return of Truth Triumphant: A Pageant of the Restored Gospel*, in which one of them acting as "the boy prophet" took center stage, while many others formed the chorus and supporting cast.[29]

In Logan, after five weeks of intensive rehearsal, Samuel Mitton's choir of 160 singers performed *The Vision*. "Oh how grateful I feel," he noted afterward in his journal, "to have the privilege of singing this great composition of so great an event—and on the 100th anniversary of the time when the Vision was given to Joseph the prophet."[30]

■ ■ ■

As similar commemorations occurred throughout Mormondom, a French sociology professor in his early forties, Maurice Halbwachs, was still a few years away from publishing his seminal study *Social Frameworks of Memory*.[31] If he had witnessed the concerts and pageants, they may have informed his book. They may have made him recall the words of his recently deceased mentor, Émile Durkheim (1858–1917): "So we have here a whole group of ceremonies whose sole purpose is to awaken certain ideas and sentiments, to attach the present to the past, or the individual to the group."[32]

Halbwachs would have concluded that the students, however sincere, were "but an echo" of the saints' society. "Often we deem ourselves the originators of thoughts and ideas, feelings and passions actually inspired by some group," he would later write, going so far as to argue that individual memories were incoherent outside of a society, because "every memory, however personal, is linked with an entire set of notions that many others possess . . . with the entire material and moral life of the societies in which we participate."[33]

If the French historian Marc Bloch (1886–1944), a contemporary critic and admirer of Halbwachs, could have observed the Mormon commemorations with him, they would have agreed that "remembering is always an active process," but Bloch would have thought his colleague was so focused on shared memory that he missed the phenomenon of sharing, of "memory transmission," of watching "the oldest memories of the group transmit these representations to the youngest." Use the term *collective memory* all you want, Bloch would say, "but we must remember that at least a part of what we are referring to is simply everyday communication between individuals."[34]

If the French psychiatrist Charles Blondel (1876–1939) had witnessed the commemorations, he would not dispute "that we reconstruct our past in large part through the use of materials which are collective," but he would maintain that each individual's memory came from "something more than commonly shared materials." Halbwachs would have been most interested in groupthink, Bloch in transmitting memory from one generation to another, and Blondel in the individual testimonies or "sensory intuitions."[35]

Memory researchers Amy Corning and Howard Schuman were born after the 1920 centennial commemoration of Joseph Smith's first vision. If they could interview the young saints who participated, however, they would find evidence for their conclusions about how commemoration affects collective memory. Based on Corning and Schuman's findings, we can conclude that commemorating Joseph Smith's vision created greater awareness and knowledge of it. But commemoration also enhanced subjective judgments about the vision's significance. Those effects were especially pronounced for Latter-day Saints who were coming of age in 1920, youth and young adults. Commemoration solidified their memory of the vision, making it less vulnerable to erosion over time.[36]

■ ■ ■

Ten years later, in 1930, Latter-day Saints commemorated the centennial of their church. Probably few, if any, of them had even heard of Halbwachs's work on collective memory. Unconscious of the nascent theorizing, still they longed to plant and awaken shared sentiments, "to attach the present to the past, or the individual to the group."[37] So, beginning April 6, the saints convened a centennial conference in Salt Lake City, broadcasting on radio to tens of thousands who could not attend.[38]

Saints too far away to hear the radio broadcast were instructed to gather and commemorate locally and invited to include in their celebration a letter from Heber J. Grant and his counselors. It said:

> In humility, and with full consciousness of the responsibility involved, we bear witness to the people of the world that with the appearance of the Father and the Son to the Prophet Joseph Smith, in the early spring of 1820, the greatest gospel dispensation of all time was ushered in, a dispensation of light, radiating from the presence of God.[39]

A talented committee was called to produce a pageant for the centennial, "Message of the Ages," on a scale that dwarfed prior Mormon commemorations.[40] The message was that God ordained a plan of salvation in premortal councils and revealed it to people anciently. Christ preached it and, by his suffering, death, and resurrection, fulfilled it. But then the full terms of the plan were lost to mankind until Joseph Smith prayed and experienced his first vision, and God restored knowledge of the plan through him. In this telling, Smith's vision catalyzed the climactic act not only of the pageant but also of human history.[41]

Figure 21.2 "The First Vision," published in *The Message of the Ages.*

Fifteen hundred saints of all ages gave repeat performances of "Message of the Ages" for a month on a massive, tiered stage in the Salt Lake tabernacle. The combined audience totaled two hundred thousand, and the performances still couldn't satisfy the demand (see figures 21.2 and 21.3).

❚ ❚ ❚

Two years after the centennial commemoration, British psychologist Frederic Bartlett published *Remembering: A Study in Experimental and Social Psychology*. He granted Maurice Halbwachs's main claim that individuals remembered in groups, in social frameworks, but Bartlett asked a different question: "Does the group remember?" Try as he might, he could find no way to arrive at an answer. "Whether the social group has a mental life over and above that of its individual members is a matter of speculation and belief," he concluded. "That the organized group functions in a unique and unitary manner in determining and directing the mental lives of its individual members is a matter of certainty and fact."[42]

Figure 21.3 Filming the Centennial Pageant on the steps of the Utah state capitol. Orchestra and choir in the foreground. Tableau of Joseph Smith's first vision in the background.
Courtesy Church History Library.

As scholars racked their brains to discern the nature of collective memory between 1920 and 1930 and the last saints to know Joseph Smith passed away, those who remained commemorated Joseph Smith's first vision and that vision's role in initiating their church. They turned communicated memories "into tradition, into the symbolic forms of cultural memory."[43]

Young saints who came of age in that decade were the most likely to acquire enduring cultural memory of Smith's vision as a result.[44] The Church of Jesus Christ of Latter-day Saints matured as it turned one hundred. It was no longer a marginalized sect. It had a usable past that situated it safely within host cultures. It had a robust rising generation that could generally identify with Smith's first vision while accommodating modern challenges to it. It had cultural memory. It had a story, a message for the ages.

Notes

1. Mildred Boyer, "The Vision," in Sketches Commemorating the Centenary of the Prophet Joseph Smith's First Vision, *Brigham Young University Quarterly* 14, no. 4 (May 1, 1920).

2. Amy Corning and Howard Schuman, *Generations and Collective Memory* (Chicago: University of Chicago Press, 2015), 209.

3. Kathleen Flake, *The Politics of American Religious Identity: The Seating of Senator Reed Smoot, Mormon Apostle* (Chapel Hill and London: University of North Carolina Press, 2004), 120–21.

4. Anne Whitehead, *Memory: The New Critical Idiom* (London and New York: Routledge, 2009), 132.

5. Jan Assman, "Introduction: What Is Cultural Memory," in *Religion and Cultural Memory: Ten Studies*, trans. Rodney Livingstone (Stanford, CA: Stanford University Press, 2006), 17.

6. John A. Widtsoe to Heber J. Grant, January 17, 1920, Church History Library, Salt Lake City.

7. Heber J. Grant to John A. Widtsoe, January 22, 1920, Church History Library, Salt Lake City.

8. This correspondence is at the Church History Library, Salt Lake City. See Edward H. Anderson to Heber J. Grant, January 7, 1920; Heber J. Grant, Santa Monica, to Edward H. Anderson, January 24, 1920; Edward H. Anderson to Heber J. Grant, January 28, 1920; Anderson to Heber J. Grant, February 4, 1920; Heber J. Grant to Anderson, February 10, 1920.

9. Heber J. Grant to Edward H. Anderson, February 19, 1920, Church History Library, Salt Lake City, "I dislike very much to disappoint you but I have finally concluded not to try to write a piece for the April Era on the First Vision. I may say something on it at the Tabernacle meeting on the 29th inst, but that will be too late."

10. Charles W. Penrose, "The Edict of a Century," *Improvement Era* 23, no. 6 (April 1920): 484–87.

11. Anthon H. Lund, "Joseph Smith's First Vision and Scripture Promises," *Improvement Era* 23, no. 6 (April 1920): 476–83.

12. Susa Young Gates, "The Vision Beautiful," *Improvement Era* 23, no. 6 (April 1920): 542–43, https://archive.org/details/improvementera2306unse.

13. Heber J. Grant to Edward H. Anderson, March 31, 1920, Church History Library, Salt Lake City.

14. Heber J. Grant, "A Marvelous Work and a Wonder," *Improvement Era* 23, no. 6 (April 192): 472–74.

15. "The Sacred Grove in Summer," frontispiece, *Improvement Era* 23, no. 6 (April 1920), https://archive.org/details/improvementera2306unse.

16. Evan Stephens, "The Vision," *Improvement Era* 23, no. 6 (April 1920): 532–38; Evan Stephens, *The Vision: A Sacred Historical Cantata* (Salt Lake City: Church of Jesus Christ of Latter-day Saints, 1920).

17. John A. Widtsoe, "The First Vision of Joseph Smith the Prophet," *Young Woman's Journal* 31, no. 4 (April 1920): 179–91.

18. Conference Report, April 1920, 100–104, https://archive.org/stream/conferencereport1920a/conferencereport901chur#page/132/mode/2up.

19. Conference Report, April 1920, 105.

20. Evan Stephens to Heber J. Grant, April 13, 1920, Church History Library, Salt Lake City.

21. Evan Stephens, *The Vision: A Sacred Historical Cantata* (Salt Lake City: Church of Jesus Christ of Latter-day Saints, 1920); Heber J. Grant to Frances Grant, April 15, 1920, and Evan Stephens to Heber J. Grant, March 30, 1920, Church History Library, Salt Lake City.

22. Victor L. Lindblad, *Biography of Samuel Bailey Mitton* (Salt Lake City: by the author, 1965), 5–6.

23. Samuel B. Mitton, Journal, April 6, 1920, 70–72, Church History Library, Salt Lake City.

24. Edward H. Anderson to Heber J. Grant, March 25, 1920, Church History Library, Salt Lake City.

25. California Mission MIA, Program of Exercises in Commemoration of Joseph Smith's First Vision, Church History Library, Salt Lake City.

26. Inez Taylor, "What the Vision Means to Me," in Sketches Commemorating the Centenary of the Prophet Joseph Smith's First Vision, *Brigham Young University Quarterly* 14, no. 4 (May 1, 1920). Newell Bown, also in seventh grade, made a similar assertion. See his "What the First Vision Means to Me" in the source noted previously.

27. All in Sketches Commemorating the Centenary of the Prophet Joseph Smith's First Vision, *Brigham Young University Quarterly* 14, no. 4 (May 1, 1920).

28. Mildred Boyer, "The Vision," in Sketches Commemorating the Centenary of the Prophet Joseph Smith's First Vision, *Brigham Young University Quarterly* 14, no. 4 (May 1, 1920).

29. "The Return of Truth Triumphant," in Sketches Commemorating the Centenary of the Prophet Joseph Smith's First Vision, *Brigham Young University Quarterly* 14, no. 4 (May 1, 1920).

30. Victor L. Lindblad, *Biography of Samuel Bailey Mitton* (Salt Lake City: by the author, 1965), 82. Samuel B. Mitton, Journal, May 27, 1920, 73–76, Church History Library, Salt Lake City.

31. Maurice Halbwachs, *On Collective Memory* (Chicago: University of Chicago Press, 1992). Translated from *Les cadres sociaux de la mémoire* (Paris: Presses Universitaires de France, 1952), originally published in *Les Travaux de L'Année Sociologique* (Paris, F. Alcan, 1925). Edited, translated, and introduction by Lewis A. Coser, includes a translation of the conclusion of *La Topographie légendaire des évangiles en terre sainte: étude de mémoire collective* (Paris, Presses Universitaires de France, 1941).

32. Jeffrey K. Olick, Vered Vinitzky-Seroussi, and Daniel Levy, *The Collective Memory Reader* (New York: Oxford University Press, 2011), 136.

33. Olick et al., *The Collective Memory Reader*, 139–49, 151; quotes on 139–40.

34. Olick et al., *The Collective Memory Reader*, 153.

35. Olick et al., *The Collective Memory Reader*, 156.

36. Corning and Schuman, *Generations and Collective Memory*, 82, 177–81, 198–99, 207. For the May 1, 1920, MIA commemoration, see Edward H. Anderson to Heber J. Grant, March 25, 1920, Church History Library, Salt Lake City.

37. Olick et al., *The Collective Memory Reader*, 136; Corning and Schuman, *Generations and Collective Memory*, 209.

38. *One Hundred Years 1830–1930: Centennial Celebration of the Organization of The Church of Jesus Christ of Latter-day Saints Beginning April 6, 1930*, 27, 42, 45, 50–51.

39. *One Hundred Years 1830–1930: Centennial Celebration of the Organization of The Church of Jesus Christ of Latter-day Saints Beginning April 6, 1930*, 27–29.

40. *One Hundred Years 1830–1930: Centennial Celebration of the Organization of The Church of Jesus Christ of Latter-day Saints Beginning April 6, 1930*, 45.

41. Pageant Committee, *The Message of the Ages: A Sacred Pageant Commemorating the One Hundredth Anniversary of the Organization of the Church of Jesus Christ of Latter-day Saints* (Salt Lake City: Corporation of the President of the Church of Jesus Christ of Latter-day Saints, 1930).

42. Frederick C. Bartlett, *Remembering: A Study in Experimental and Social Psychology* (Cambridge: Cambridge University Press, 1932, repr. 1954), 296–300.

43. Jan Assman, "Introduction: What Is Cultural Memory," 17.

44. Based on the findings of Corning and Schuman, *Generations and Collective Memory*, 82, 177–81, 198–99, 207.

PART III
CONTESTED MEMORY

22

Fundamentalism

The second of the two things to which we must all give full faith
is that the Father and the Son actually and in truth and very deed
appeared to the Prophet Joseph in a vision in the woods.

—J. Reuben Clark Jr., 1938[1]

We just repeat words, don't do any thinking, don't do any
questioning, don't do any studying, don't question anything. We
don't think we have any right to.

—Isaac E. Brockbank, 1946[2]

At a mountain retreat on a summer day in Utah in 1938, there was a meeting
of the 142 faculty employed by The Church of Jesus Christ of Latter-day
Saints to teach the faith to its youth. They had been camped with their families for six weeks of instruction and some relaxation in the spectacular setting. Then on a rainy morning, J. Reuben Clark—formerly a Washington,
DC, lawyer, then a diplomat, and at the time a counselor to church president Heber J. Grant—addressed the teachers about a topic he and other
church leaders had worried about for several years.[3]

The next day the *Deseret News* carried excerpts and characterized
Clark's talk as "an official pronouncement of the First Presidency of the
Church," giving "direct counsel" to its religious educators.[4] Within a week
the *Deseret News* printed the entire talk and within a month the church's
Improvement Era published it again, but before the sun set on the day that
Clark spoke, those who heard him segregated themselves over it.[5] "There
was considerable discussion about it around our campfires," one of them
remembered. "We divided ourselves up pretty quickly into liberal and conservative camps." One of them even rose from an impassioned discussion
and announced that he was going to resign.[6]

What had Clark said to catalyze such feelings pro and con, to galvanize
such action? He drew a line around orthodoxy, around "two prime things
that may not be overlooked, forgotten, shaded, or discarded." First, Jesus

Christ is the Son of God, the crucified and risen Christ. "The second of the two things to which we must all give full faith is that the Father and the Son actually and in truth and very deed appeared to the Prophet Joseph in a vision in the woods," Clark said.[7] With the first, he declared that everyone who taught the restored gospel must be a Christian. With the second, he declared that they must be fundamentally Latter-day Saints.

The litmus test of belief in the literal, historical appearing of God and Christ to teenage Joseph Smith in 1820 could have disqualified the earliest saints. Not long ago the best scholarship said that few if any knew of the vision in the 1830s, and not many more even after it was published in the 1840s, and that it only became a collective memory with shared meaning for most saints post-1880, when it was canonized in the *Pearl of Great Price*.

More recently discovered evidence reveals that Joseph Smith told of the vision regularly beginning by the mid-1830s and that several such tellings were recorded, that Orson Pratt's 1840 tract of it circled the globe, that Pratt coined the term *first vision* (at least in print) by the late 1840s, and that he and others made it the collective memory of the Latter-day Saints by 1880 by selecting the story for inclusion in the narrative they related meaningfully to the present, rehearsing it repeatedly. That's how collective memories form or consolidate—someone selects them, relates them meaningfully to the group's identity and shared story, and tells that story again and again until it becomes common knowledge, so common that everyone in the community knows it while few if any know or question its source or veracity.[8]

Joseph Smith created four accounts of his vision that persist in the historical record, but when J. Reuben Clark told the religion faculty that they must give full faith to the idea "that the Father and the Son actually and in truth and very deed appeared to the Prophet Joseph in a vision in the woods," he and those hearing him shared knowledge only of the canonized story in the *Pearl of Great Price*.[9] While additional accounts were known to some scholars, including B. H. Roberts and Woodbridge Riley, the laity and even most members of the seminary faculty were familiar with only the canonized 1838/39 version.

Saints for more than a generation had shared faith in Smith's canonized narrative as their founding story with no interference from other versions, and with little if any opposition to it from the wider world. Clark and his audience shared a narrative, a genesis story for their faith, a *fundamental*, as Clark consciously called it. But the tranquil alpine setting in which he spoke belied tension beneath the surface. J. Reuben Clark knew, as his hearers knew, that there was a war going on, and the polarized reactions to his talk evidenced that they were now in it.

Every major Protestant denomination in the country was torn by the same conflict. The Bible was a battleground. Was it inerrant? Was its Pentateuch the work of Moses's pen? Were its sacred history and its miracles reconcilable with modern science? The most educated members of Clark's audience were trained by university faculties who answered these questions liberally, and some of the educators leaned that way with their mentors. Others responded to the controversy moderately, while still others responded as the most conservative Christians had, by laying down fundamentals of the faith.[10]

Mormon scriptures expanded far beyond the Bible and gave the saints a comparatively moderate hermeneutic that resisted erosion from historical or source criticism.[11] The Bible, therefore, was not the primary battlefield. For saints, Clark declared, the line was drawn at Joseph Smith's first vision, and it remains a battleground over which people fight, negotiating their identities and relationships relative to the restored gospel as they join or leave, fight for or against the faith.

■ ■ ■

Two days after J. Reuben Clark made belief in the canonized version of Joseph Smith's first vision a test of orthodoxy, Dale L. Morgan, just graduated from the University of Utah, began work as a historian as part of the New Deal (see figure 22.1).[12] Raised as a Latter-day Saint and already a gifted writer, Morgan was haunted by meningitis-induced deafness that struck just as he was coming of age. Then, in college, he traded faith-based explanations for psychological ones and began to view his society through a sociological lens. He was "undergoing a wholesale revision of all my beliefs," he said, just as he went to work surveying records and compiling county histories.[13]

The work convinced Morgan that "practically nothing worthwhile" had been written on church history but that the rich source material awaited only "some gifted writer to produce the first extensive, penetrating work on the whole amazing phenomena of Utah, the West, and the Mormon relation to itself and both."[14]

Morgan began research for a history magnum opus. He dug into the canonized part of Smith's 1839 history and compared it closely with Oliver

Figure 22.1 Dale L. Morgan (1914–71) pioneered source criticism of Joseph Smith's first vision and advised Fawn Brodie.

March 1964 photo by George P. Hammond. Courtesy Bancroft Library, University of California, Berkeley.

Cowdery's historical 1834-1835 letters, becoming the first serious source critic of the saints' genesis story, the first to ask when and why the sources were created and how they compared to each other, the first to ask questions about the historical memory of Joseph Smith and his followers.

Still without any idea that an 1832 Joseph Smith autobiography and an 1835 journal entry reposed in the church's archive, Morgan felt sure "that no man in his church, not even Joseph himself, suspected in 1835 that he had been visited in his youth by the Father and the Son."[15] The later discovery of those sources and others would prove Morgan wrong on that point; once discovered, they added complexity to the historical record being read and interpreted along the critical lines Morgan pioneered.

Morgan knew that the laity accepted the canonized story at face value, while outsiders simply dismissed Smith's story as either ridiculous or evidence of psychosis. Morgan thought metaphorically of the source texts as a mural whose visible layer obscured "underpaint."[16] He was the first to painstakingly peel back the layers insofar as the available sources allowed, and behind only Orson Pratt and B. H. Roberts to find dissonance between and in these sources.

He concluded "that the idea of a visitation from the Father and the Son was a late improvisation" by Joseph Smith, "no part at all of his original design."[17] Morgan's source criticism led to his conclusion that Joseph Smith enlarged his story over time, that there was no 1820 vision, only Smith's later "conception investing him with an ineffable dignity, for in all recorded history, to what other men have the Father and the Son appeared?"[18]

Morgan proved to be not only a skeptical source critic but also a researcher. He used a 1947 Guggenheim Foundation grant to discover evidence that led him to conclude (further to his developing point that Smith invented the story of an 1820 theophany) that Smith's memory of evangelical revivalism catalyzing his vision and, specifically, Oliver Cowdery's 1835 claim that the preaching of Reverend George Lane triggered it were anachronistic.[19]

Morgan's claims were potentially devastating to the canonized account of Joseph Smith's first vision, but only potentially. They made little difference so long as they remained in Morgan's mind, unarticulated by a man who had much to say but who could not hear and rarely spoke and had thus far not written his arguments except possibly in early drafts. Then Fawn McKay Brodie, a friend and protégé of Morgan's and a niece of apostle David O. McKay, unleashed the potential (see figure 22.2).

In 1945 Knopf published her biography of Joseph Smith, *No Man Knows My History*. Brodie had persuaded Knopf of her "attitude of complete objectivity," but she had confided to Morgan about her psychological need to understand Smith's life and escape his influence. She reflected later that writing the biography enabled her to assert her independence, providing the resolution to what she called her "compulsion to liberate myself wholly from Mormonism."[20]

Brodie followed but simplified Morgan's interpretation, completely rejecting the orthodox position Clark stated in 1938 "that the Father and the Son actually and in truth and very deed appeared to the Prophet Joseph in a vision in the woods."[21] Instead, Brodie argued in lucid prose that Smith had no theophany in 1820 but simply combined his past (a half-remembered dream induced by the anxieties of revival culture) with his late 1830s present (the need for the credibility inherent in divine authority).[22]

She set forth the ideas so boldly that Morgan was "struck," as he told her, "with the assumption your MS makes that Joseph was a self-conscious

Figure 22.2 Fawn M. Brodie (1915–81) published *No Man Knows My History* (1945), a biography of Joseph Smith that did not take his descriptions of his first vision at face value.

Photo courtesy of Special Collections, J. Willard Marriott Library, University of Utah.

imposter." She was not a careful historian, and he worried about what he called her "bold judgments on the basis of assumptions," a critique shared by later reviewers.[23] But Brodie wrote for the public, not for source critics. In abridging the argument she made it accessible and interesting, giving a wider audience than ever a plausible alternative to orthodox belief. The war of words was on. The sacred narrative of a people was at stake.

■ ■ ■

Before Fawn Brodie's biography of Joseph Smith even reached mass audiences, an advance copy circulated among some Latter-day Saints. They met one Sunday evening to discuss it. Could it be true, they wondered, as Brodie asserted, that no known scrap of evidence existed from the spring of 1820 to show that Joseph Smith claimed to see God and Christ in the woods near his home? "I was somewhat startled to find that statement," Isaac Brockbank confessed, "probably a little more startled to find that it is probably true."[24]

A lawyer in his late fifties, Brockbank prided himself on his extensive library of Latter-day Saint history and doctrine. He embarked on a lecture circuit, deconstructing Brodie's biography for audiences including the Brigham Young University faculty. On April 26, 1946, saints gathered to hear him in a Salt Lake City chapel. They sang George Manwaring's hymn, the one that shaped their shared memory of Smith's first vision and the meaning they found in it.[25]

Then Brockbank began his remarks with an indictment—not of Fawn Brodie but of Mormon culture. "We think we know without doing any studying," he said, adding that he was glad at least that the book forced him to re-examine the saints' history, to ask questions and seek answers. Brockbank pointed unknowingly to the paradox between his actual audience and the saints' ideal, the archetypical truth seeker. "We just repeat words," Brockbank lamented. "Don't do any thinking, don't do any questioning, don't do any studying, don't question anything. We don't think we have any right to."[26]

Brockbank eventually turned to Brodie's book and took it apart page by page, highlighting errors of fact and emphasizing speculative conclusions. But he had no apologetic for Brodie's critique of the vision. "That is her opinion" is all he could muster when it came to her appraisal of the founding event of his faith.[27]

▪ ▪ ▪

By the time Fawn Brodie published *No Man Knows My History* in 1945, John A. Widtsoe's Harvard days were a half century behind him and he had been a apostle for more than two decades, with a distinguished academic career in between. Shaped by his own "religious battles," Widtsoe thought of himself as a "firm believer in religious education for youth."[28] Latter-day Saints young and old looked to him as an authority who could provide "evidences and reconciliations" for any argument, someone who could clarify ambiguity, who could "set straight" ideas that were at odds.[29]

Widtsoe responded to private inquirers about Brodie's book by dismissing it as the devil's work and assuring them of the ultimate triumph of truth. But he worried about the book's power to undermine faith, and as an editor of the *Improvement Era*, he used his "evidences and reconciliations" column to answer the question, "When did Joseph Smith have the First Vision?"[30]

Widtsoe began with a cool summary of the orthodox position based on the canonized account. Then, without naming Brodie, he stated the problem—because the earliest known account of Smith's vision dated many years after 1820, "some enemies to the Church have cast doubt upon the authenticity of the date claimed for the vision. They have suggested that the vision was invented by the Prophet in 1838." Then Widtsoe attacked what he called the "preposterous claim," countering Brodie's argument point by point with supposition similar to hers. Brodie argued that Smith could not have envisioned God and Christ in the woods in 1820 without the neighbors hearing all about it.[31] Widtsoe argued that "the people in Joseph's neighborhood would pay little attention to the claim of a fourteen-year-old boy that he had a visitation from God."[32]

His argument could not have been weaker. Brodie took her interpretive cue from the canonized account itself, where Smith reflects on how strange it was that telling his vision "excited a great deal of prejudice" and of how he, "a boy of no consequence," became the focus of the local clergy, whose only ecumenical activity was "to persecute me."[33] Weak as it was, Widtsoe's authoritative article gave Latter-day Saints the impression that the research was done and all evidence, whether produced by Joseph Smith or his enemies, proved beyond doubt that his first vision occurred in 1820. Widtsoe won praise from admiring saints, among whom his arguments were unquestioned. Seminary teachers used the article to arm their pupils against the new attack.[34]

Widtsoe knew a good argument, a valid proof. He knew that his protested too much and made a circular case, and that a source critic like Dale Morgan could have demolished it. Widtsoe began to build a better case for Smith's first vision, a quest that would lead to correspondence between him and Morgan.[35]

In December 1946 Widtsoe returned to Logan, Utah, where he had been president of Utah Agricultural College, and delivered the third annual Joseph Smith Memorial Sermon at the LDS Institute of Religion near campus. He titled his sermon "The Significance of the First Vision." Inspired by his Harvard days and the Morgan/Brodie argument against the vision, Widtsoe addressed the students and their religion teachers. Widely circulating books, he said—meaning Brodie's biography—threw doubt on Joseph Smith's first vision, claiming that he invented the idea in 1838. He dismissed the argument again.

This time, however, Widtsoe made no attempt to dig into the historical record, to get into the fine points of when the vision occurred, and who knew, and when. Instead, he presented the vision as archetype, Joseph Smith as the ultimate truth seeker, the truth he found as the ultimate goal, and untruth as the great obstacle. "The first vision was not only the Prophet's first great religious experience and, therefore, of great consequence, but it seems to me to be an epitome of the approach to all truth," Widtsoe said, giving the young saints and their teachers an inspiring epic, a compelling character who typified their own quests, overcoming every obstacle in the process. He advised the students to read the canonized account, to memorize it.[36]

That day in Logan, as John Widtsoe upheld the vision as a historical reality, he passed Clark's orthodoxy test. He did not stop there, however. Clark had told educators what they could believe about Smith's vision. Widtsoe invited his audience to enact Smith's epistemology, as he had successfully done at Harvard. Thinking and believing like a Latter-day Saint, Widtsoe reminded them, meant they could seek and receive their own revelations. "We must all find truth," Widtsoe taught, "and find it as the Prophet Joseph Smith found it in his first vision."[37]

Faced with a new attack on Smith's canonized account, prophets and apostles stood with the story, trusting it as history and upholding it as a model for young, increasingly educated Latter-day Saints to follow. It remained to be seen whether rising generations would follow them, and whether saints could possibly live up to the rule of accepting Smith's first vision as a historical reality in the face of new evidence and interpretations.

Notes

1. J. Reuben Clark Jr. "The Charted Course of the Church in Education," Address to seminary and institute of religion leaders at the Brigham Young University summer school in Aspen Grove, Utah, on August 8, 1938 (Salt Lake City: Church of Jesus Christ of Latter-day Saints, 1992), www.lds.org/bc/content/ldsorg/manual/seminary/32709_000.pdf.

2. Isaac E. Brockbank, "Address Regarding Fawn Brodie's *No Man Knows My History*," 5–7, Church History Library, Salt Lake City.

3. Scott C. Esplin, "Chartering the Course: President Clark's Charge to Religious Educators," *Religious Educator* 7, no. 1 (2006): 103–19; Joseph Fielding Smith to J. Reuben Clark Jr., August 15, 1938, and J. Reuben Clark Jr. to Joseph Fielding Smith, August 15, 1938, J. Reuben Clark Jr. Papers, L. Tom Perry Special Collections, Harold

B. Lee Library, Brigham Young University, Provo, Utah (hereafter LTPSC, BYU). Just one week after the Aspen Grove address, Joseph Fielding Smith, acting as church historian, wrote to Elder Clark and informed him that he had "been hoping and praying for a long time for something of this kind to happen." Smith continued, furthermore, to support the First Presidency's decision to deliver the address, claiming that he had personally spoken to many teachers and the church's commissioner of education, he "realizing thoroughly the need of such counsel and wisdom." In a response to Smith dated that same day, Elder Clark wrote that the First Presidency had "felt for some time—as you say you have felt—that something of this sort should be said"; J. Reuben Clark Jr. to Merrill Y. Van Wagoner, September 3, 1938, J. Reuben Clark Jr. Papers, LTPSC, BYU. In a written reply to BYU student Merrill Y. Van Wagoner, who had responded to Elder Clark's address with a letter voicing his perceived failure of BYU in teaching doctrine, Elder Clark affirmed to Van Wagoner that his was "not the only statement of this sort that comes to us" and that it would be valuable to the First Presidency in its attempt to remediate the current "difficult situation" within the church's educational system; Jesse W. Richins to J. Reuben Clark Jr., September 5, 1938, J. Reuben Clark Jr. Papers, LTPSC, BYU. Jesse W. Richins of the Twin Falls Idaho Stake Presidency wrote to Elder Clark on September 5, following Clark's address, expressing his surety that the message had been "not only very timely but very much needed"; William T. Tew to J. Reuben Clark Jr., September 8, 1938, J. Reuben Clark Jr. Papers, LTPSC, BYU. Writing from the Louisville office of the Central States mission, mission president William T. Tew responded to Clark's address (which he had obtained via the *Improvement Era*) with sentiments similar to Smith and Bischoff: "many of us who have been in this system for years," wrote Tew, "have long since recognized the need of such a barometer in our teachings." Jacob H. Trayner to J. Reuben Clark Jr., September 14, 1938, and J. Reuben Clark Jr. to Jacob H. Trayner, September 22, 1938, J. Reuben Clark Jr. Papers, LTPSC, BYU. Jacob P. Trayner, Superintendent of the LDS Hospital at Idaho Falls, wrote to Elder Clark on September 14, inquiring whether the First Presidency might consider issuing the Aspen Grove address in pamphlet form.

4. "Pres. Clark Sets Forth Church Seminary Policies," *Deseret News*, August 9, 1938. Clipping included in J. Reuben Clark Jr. Papers, MS 303, box 215, folder 8, LTPSC, BYU.

5. "First Presidency Sets Standards for Church Educators," *Deseret News*, August 13, 1938.

6. Sterling M. McMurrin and L. Jackson Newell, *Matters of Conscience: Conversations with Sterling M. McMurrin on Philosophy, Education, and Religion* (Salt Lake City: Signature, 1996), 115. Also see N. L. Nelson to J. Reuben Clark, September 2, 1938, J. Reuben Clark Jr. Papers, LTPSC, BYU.

7. J. Reuben Clark Jr., "The Charted Course of the Church in Education," Address to seminary and institute of religion leaders at the Brigham Young University summer school in Aspen Grove, Utah, on August 8, 1938 (Salt Lake City: Church of Jesus Christ of Latter-day Saints, 1992), www.lds.org/bc/content/ldsorg/manual/seminary/32709_000.pdf.

8. Thomas J. Anastasio, Kristen Ann Ehrenberger, Patrick Watson, and Wenyi Zhang, *Individual and Collective Memory Consolidation: Analogous Processes on Different Levels* (Cambridge and London: MIT Press, 2012).

9. J. Reuben Clark Jr., "The Charted Course of the Church in Education," Address to seminary and institute of religion leaders at the Brigham Young University summer school in Aspen Grove, Utah, on August 8, 1938 (Salt Lake City: Church of Jesus Christ of Latter-day Saints, 1992), www.lds.org/bc/content/ldsorg/manual/seminary/32709_000.pdf.

10. A good survey of the Protestant controversy is George M. Marsden, *Understanding Fundamentalism and Evangelicalism* (Grand Rapids, MI: William B. Eerdmans, 1991), esp. see 56–61.

11. Philip L. Barlow, *Mormons and the Bible: The Place of the Latter-day Saints in American Religion* (New York: Oxford University Press, 1991).

12. Richard Saunders, "'The Strange Mixture of Emotion and Intellect': A Social History of Dale L. Morgan, 1933–1942," *Dialogue* 28, no. 4 (Winter 1995): 48.

13. Saunders, "The Strange Mixture of Emotion and Intellect," 49, cites Morgan to Jerry Bleak, May 22, 1938, Bleak Letters, in footnote 30, but on the page says it was May 1939.

14. Morgan to Jerry Bleak, November [Dec.] 31, 1938, Bleak Letters, quoted in Saunders, "The Strange Mixture of Emotion and Intellect," 50n33.

15. John Philip Walker, ed., *Dale Morgan on Early Mormonism: Correspondence and a New History* (Salt Lake City: Signature Books, 1986), 249.

16. Morgan uses this metaphor throughout his draft chapter. See Walker, ed., *Dale Morgan on Early Mormonism*, 245–61

17. Walker, ed., *Dale Morgan on Early Mormonism*, 247. See p. 255 for Morgan's awareness that he was the first to make such observations.

18. Walker, ed., *Dale Morgan on Early Mormonism*, 253.

19. Dale L. Morgan to Wesley P. Walters, Berkeley, California, November 27, 1967, in Walker, ed., *Dale Morgan on Early Mormonism*, 209–10, and Morgan's draft history of Mormonism, chap. 3, in the same volume pp. 245–61.

20. Newell G. Bringhurst, *Fawn McKay Brodie: A Biographer's Life* (Norman: University of Oklahoma Press, 1999), 80, 87, 95, 105, 115.

21. J. Reuben Clark Jr., "The Charted Course of the Church in Education," Address to seminary and institute of religion leaders at the Brigham Young University summer school in Aspen Grove, Utah, on August 8, 1938 (Salt Lake City: Church of Jesus Christ of Latter-day Saints, 1992), www.lds.org/bc/content/ldsorg/manual/seminary/32709_000.pdf.

22. Fawn M. Brodie, *No Man Knows My History: The Life of Joseph Smith the Mormon Prophet* (New York: Alfred A. Knopf, 1945), 25; Fawn M. Brodie, *No Man Knows My History: The Life of Joseph Smith the Mormon Prophet,* 2nd ed. (New York: Vintage, 1995), 25.

23. Bringhurst, *Fawn McKay Brodie: A Biographer's Life*, 80, 87, 95, 105, 115.

24. Isaac E. Brockbank, "Address Regarding Fawn Brodie's *No Man Knows My History*," 2, MS 545, Church History Library, Salt Lake City. For biographical information on

Isaac E. Brockbank, see *An Historical and Genealogical Record of Isaac Brockbank Sr.* (n.p.: n.p., circa 1959), 194, available at the Church History Library, Salt Lake City.

25. Isaac E. Brockbank, "Address Regarding Fawn Brodie's *No Man Knows My History*," MS 545, Church History Library, Salt Lake City. For Brockbank's address to BYU faculty see p. 37; for his occupation see p. 52. For biographical information on Isaac E. Brockbank, see *An Historical and Genealogical Record of Isaac Brockbank Sr.* (n.p.: n.p., circa 1959), 194.

26. Isaac E. Brockbank, "Address Regarding Fawn Brodie's *No Man Knows My History*," 5–7, Church History Library, Salt Lake City; John A. Widtsoe, "Joseph Smith: The Significance of the First Vision," in *The Annual Joseph Smith Memorial Sermons*, vol. 1, sermons 1–10 (Logan, UT: Institute of Religion, 1966), 28.

27. Isaac E. Brockbank, "Address Regarding Fawn Brodie's *No Man Knows My History*," see p. 47, Church History Library, Salt Lake City.

28. John A. Widtsoe, *In a Sunlit Land* (Salt Lake City: Deseret News Press, 1952), 25.

29. Grover C. Cochran Junior to John A. Widtsoe, November 24, 1945, Church History Library, Salt Lake City. Also see Ariel N. Benson to John A. Widtsoe, June 10, 1951, Church History Library, Salt Lake City. Thanks to Ardis E. Parshall for bringing these documents to my attention.

30. John A. Widtsoe to Grover C. Cochran Junior, November 26, 1945, Church History Library, Salt Lake City. Thanks to Ardis E. Parshall for bringing this correspondence to my attention. John A. Widtsoe, "Evidences and Reconciliations: When Did Joseph Smith Have the First Vision?," *Improvement Era* 49, no. 7 (July 1946): 449, 478–79. For evidence of Widtsoe's concern about Brodie's book, see John A. Widtsoe to Carter E. Grant, July 23, 1946, in John A. Widtsoe Papers, CR 712/2, box 70, folder 16, Church History Library, Salt Lake City. Thanks to Chad Foulger for bringing this document to my attention.

31. Fawn M. Brodie, *No Man Knows My History: The Life of Joseph Smith*, 2nd ed., rev. & enl. (New York: Vintage, 1995), 25.

32. Widtsoe, "Evidences and Reconciliations," 449.

33. "History, circa June 1839–circa 1841 [Draft 2]," 4, *The Joseph Smith Papers*, accessed October 26, 2018, https://www.josephsmithpapers.org/paper-summary/history-circa-june-1839-circa-1841-draft-2/4.

34. Carter E. Grant to John A. Widtsoe, July 24, 1946, John A. Widtsoe Papers, CR 712/2, box 70, folder 16, Church History Library, Salt Lake City.

35. Widtsoe's more mature argument is in his biography, *Joseph Smith: Seeker after Truth, Prophet of God* (Salt Lake City: Deseret News, 1951), esp. chap. 1. I am grateful to Richard Saunders for making me aware of the correspondence between Dale L. Morgan and John A. Widtsoe.

36. Widtsoe, "Joseph Smith: The Significance of the First Vision," 28–30.

37. Widtsoe, "Joseph Smith: The Significance of the First Vision," 28–30.

23

Censoring Joseph Smith's Story

The story of the First Vision need only be studied from original sources to assure the seeker not only of its truth, but also of the time of its occurrence.

—John A. Widtsoe, 1951[1]

Memory was simple for S. Dilworth Young. He could not remember *not* knowing the standard story of Joseph Smith's first vision. Born in 1897 to parents whose parents were early Latter-day Saints, he came of age during the decade of commemoration. Young became a general authority, one of the seven members of the Council of Seventy, the third ranking body in LDS Church, just as Fawn Brodie published *No Man Knows My History* in 1945.

He was not unsettled by the biography, but in 1957 he was shocked to learn the rumors spreading through the ranks that Joseph Smith

evolved his doctrine from what might have been a vision, in which he is supposed to have said that he saw an angel, instead of the Father and the Son. According to this theory, by the time he was inspired to write the occurrence in 1838, he had come to the conclusion that there were two beings.[2]

Speaking at the general conference in April 1957, Young rejected any version of the vision but the canonized account of two divine personages, Father and Son. He said:

I can see no reason why the Prophet, with his brilliant mind, would have failed to remember in sharp relief every detail of that eventful day. I can remember quite vividly that in 1915 I had a mere dream, but I can remember every detail of it as sharply and clearly as though it had happened yesterday. How then could any man conceive that the Prophet, receiving such a vision as he received, would not remember it and would fail to write it clearly, distinctly, and accurately?[3]

Young's uncle and leader in the Council of Seventy, Levi Edgar Young, sat behind him in the tabernacle as he spoke. Levi shared his nephew's conviction

> that Joseph Smith walked into a grove in 1920, inspired of the Lord to do so, knelt down, as he said, among the silent trees, offered up a prayer, and there he was given a vision in which he saw God the Eternal Father, who in his turn introduced to Joseph his beloved Son.[4]

However, Levi did not share his nephew's simple sense of memory.

He knew that memories could be complex and historical documents full of ambivalence. He had studied at Harvard, earned an MA from Columbia, and been a history professor at the University of Utah. He also knew that the church possessed another account of Joseph Smith's first vision. Earlier, he had gotten permission from Heber J. Grant to see documents B. H. Roberts used to compile the *Comprehensive History of the Church*. As a result, Joseph Fielding Smith, church historian and apostle, pulled an old record book from his office safe and handed it to Levi, who studied it long enough to know that its contents varied from the standard story.[5]

It did not explicitly say two personages appeared to Joseph. Levi was fascinated by the discovery but not shocked to learn of varying explanations or interpretations of Joseph Smith's first vision. He regarded the historical record as ambivalent, while S. Dilworth assumed it was clear, accurate, and obvious.

■ ■ ■

So did most Latter-day Saints. LaMar Petersen, for example, was a classically trained organist in his midforties when he decided to dig into church history. When his suburban Salt Lake bishop could not answer his questions, they visited the Church Historian's Office together. The bishop came away edified, Petersen dissatisfied. He was referred to Levi Edgar Young and they met several times. Young was candid and open, with deep faith in the saints' story. Petersen left feeling validated but skeptical, lacking Young's equanimity in the face of ambivalence. "The thing that interested me most,"

Petersen recalled, "was his reference to what he called a strange account of Joseph's first vision."[6]

Georgia McGee, in Southern California, was another example. She was traumatized by her reading of Fawn Brodie's *No Man Knows My History*. A great-granddaughter of Brigham Young, Georgia married a man who had also grown up in a devout family. They moved to California with their children in the early 1940s, where Georgia's husband continued to believe in the restored gospel but stopped attending church. Georgia attended but started questioning until she was unwelcome in Sunday school and embarrassing her children.[7]

Her daughter Sandra tried to help. Sometimes Sandra came home from high school to find her mother sitting with several books and photocopies strewn across the front room floor, searching for answers. "I don't know the answers," she would tell her mom. "I just know the Church is true." When a friend questioned what temples were all about, Sandra asked her seminary teacher, who encouraged her to "start with the first vision."[8] By the time she was a senior in high school and attending LDS Institute classes near UCLA, Sandra was questioning too.[9] Then in early 1959 she visited Salt Lake City to see her grandmother, who invited Sandra to a meeting she thought would be a typical "Mormon fireside."[10]

Instead, a reserved man in his early twenties, Jerald Tanner, played a recording of Pauline Hancock, founder of the Church of Christ in Independence, Missouri, an offshoot sect that rejected Joseph Smith's first vision and most of his revelations after 1830. Jerald had grown up in Utah in a nominal Mormon family but felt unsatisfied. When he learned of Hancock's teachings, he visited her church in Independence in 1957 and again in 1958, when Hancock baptized him.[11]

Sandra was attracted to Jerald and his faith. She asked him to teach her more. Soon they became engaged, then married in June 1959 (see figure 23.1).[12] In 1960, at nineteen, Sandra declared, "after much prayer and study, I am withdrawing from the Church of Jesus Christ of Latter-day Saints." She listed several reasons. The most extensive read:

> Today the church teaches that the personages in the First Vision were God and Christ, but, in studying I have found that until after the death of Brigham Young the church proclaimed that *angels* appeared in the First Vision. There is no testimony in existence dated within the 50 year period, "1820 to 1870," claiming the personages in the Vision of 1820 were

Figure 23.1 Sandra McGee Tanner (b. 1941) and Jerald Tanner (1938–2006) on their wedding day, June 14, 1959. Sandra and Jerald publicized criticism of Joseph Smith's first vision.

Photo accessed November 27, 2018, at http://www.utlm.org/images/newsletters/108/108jeraldsandrawedding.jpg.

God the Father, and His Son, Jesus Christ. . . . For 50 years no testimony or sermon by Joseph Smith, Brigham Young, the Twelve Apostles, church historians, wittnesses [*sic*] to the Book of Mormon, Joseph Smith's own family, friends, relatives or acquaintances, Mormon or Anti-Mormon literature proclaims a visitation of God and Christ to Joseph Smith in 1820.[13]

Sandra's sweeping claim was naïve, as she soon began to realize.[14] Saints knew Joseph Smith's canonized account said that two personages appeared to him, one unmistakably identifying the other as his "beloved Son."[15] Orson Pratt wrote in 1849:

> In the first vision which Joseph Smith received in the spring of the year 1820, he being between fourteen and fifteen years of age, both the Father and the Son, while he was praying, appeared unto him. He said, "When the light rested upon me, I saw two personages, whose brightness and glory defy all description, standing above me in the air. One of them spake unto me, calling me by name, and said—(*pointing to the other*)—This is my beloved, Son, hear him." Thus we find that the visions both of the ancient and modern prophets agree, and clearly demonstrate the existence of two distinct persons—the Father and Son.[16]

Sandra wrongly assumed that if she did not know about a source, it did not exist. She was right, however, that church leaders between 1850 and 1880 had said that an angel or angels appeared to Joseph in his first vision. No one had yet shown that until 1880 Latter-day Saints were still selecting and relating elements of the story and deciding how much to emphasize it and to what uses they might put it.

■ ■ ■

It jarred midcentury saints, including S. Dilworth Young, LaMar Petersen, Georgia McGee, her daughter Sandra, and Jerald Tanner, to learn that there were other pieces of the past than the ones that had been selected and related and repeated until they consolidated as the collective memory. Many saints, it turns out, assumed that if they did not know about a source, it did not exist.

There were a range of responses when they heard there was more to know. S. Dilworth approached the canonized account of the first vision dogmatically. LaMar Petersen thought in similarly inflexible ways. He felt nonplussed when he talked to scholars who knew the issues he was discovering but who had not assumed, as Petersen had, "a clear choice between black and white" but rather "many possible choices for each of us which from our finite perspective are mostly from the grays."[17]

Several other Latter-day Saints visited or wrote to Joseph Fielding Smith or his associates in the Church Historian's Office, asking for access to historical records. The records remained closed.[18] Suspecting "that the church had an account of the First Vision in Joseph Smith's own handwriting," Sandra asked Joseph Fielding Smith for a copy. "I was refused," she wrote in the summer of 1960, explaining her reasons for leaving the church. "There would be no reason to keep this from me if it read the same as the account the church releases today."[19]

Instead of opening the records for inquirers to research, Joseph Fielding Smith addressed frequently asked questions in the *Improvement Era*. In the February 1960 issue he tackled the question "What evidences have we to substantiate the first vision of Joseph Smith to prove the truth of his story and that he was not deceived or a deceiver?" The details of the canonized account proved it true, he explained, reasoning that Joseph would not have imagined two divine personages in his creedal context, nor been so fool-hardy as to make up such a controversial story. Besides, Joseph Fielding Smith explained, "Joseph Smith's story harmonizes with divine truth."[20] If that answer satisfied saints who shared Smith's views, it seemed like obfuscation to the growing group of disaffected saints who wanted to evaluate the records themselves.[21]

■   ■   ■

To further address the issue, church leaders enlisted Hugh Nibley, an ancient history professor at BYU who had published a satirical review of Fawn Brodie's *No Man Knows My History* in 1946.[22] In July 1961, the *Improvement Era* published the first of Nibley's four-part essay "Censoring the Joseph Smith Story," beginning with this statement of the problem:

> Joseph Smith's official account of his first vision and the visits of the angel Moroni was written in 1838 and first published in the *Times and Seasons* in 1842. Since the writing took place from eleven to eighteen years after the events described, anti-Mormon writers were quick to exploit the time-lag as a welcome chink in the Mormon armor. "Why," they asked, "did Smith wait so long to make his official statement?" And they insisted that the only possible answer was that the stories of the first vision and the golden plates were invented in retrospect—they were pure fabrications.[23]

Nibley situated Brodie's biography in a genre of hearsay-based pseudo-history, evoking antagonistic writers since 1842 who charged Joseph Smith with making up his story late and then changing it.

What Sandra Tanner and others noticed, however, was an aside from Nibley's argument. He said his great-grandfather wrote a journal entry about hearing Joseph Smith tell his vision. "Because it was a sacred and privileged communication," Nibley said, "it was never published to the world and never should be."[24]

Sandra wrote to Nibley, asking for access to the entry. "The day my great-grandfather heard that remarkable account of the First Vision from Joseph Smith," Nibley replied,

> he wrote it down in his journal: and for 40 years after he never mentioned it to a soul. Therefore, when I came across the story unexpectedly I handed the book over to Joseph Fielding Smith and it is now where it belongs—in a safe. The prophet did not like to talk about the First Vision and those to whom he told the story kept it to themselves. It was only when inevitable leaks led to all sorts of irresponsible reports that he was "induced" to publish an official version.[25]

Sandra wrote to Joseph Fielding Smith, asking for access. He replied, "private journals are filed in this office with the understanding that they will be available to members of the family, but not to the general public."[26] Nibley wrote to Sandra again, revealing the name of his ancestor, saying,

> the reason that Alexander Neibaur told no one of his experience for forty years is that it was strictly confidential and should remain so. I think we should respect his confidence. Actually, the last time I asked permission to see the Journal, I was refused. Any attempt to reproduce it at this time is out of the question.[27]

Joseph Fielding Smith answered another woman's question about the Neibaur journal entry, saying, "it was written following a conversation Bro. Neibaur had with the Prophet. The account is somewhat similar to that given by Joseph Smith, with the wording being given as 'this is my Beloved Son harken ye him.'" He invited her to visit his office if she had further questions.[28]

Meanwhile, Jerald Tanner's mother, Helen, wrote repeatedly to church president David O. McKay demanding to see the Neibaur journal. She got no response. Finally she sent an ultimatum. Either she would be shown the journal, she said, or she would publicize her letter and leave the church. "I do not wish to be a member of a church which does not love the truth and that hides its history," she wrote.[29]

■ ■ ■

James B. Allen earned a PhD in history from the University of Southern California in 1963 and joined the history department faculty at BYU in 1964 (see figure 23.2). Soon thereafter a graduate student named Paul Cheesman approached him excitedly and said he wanted to write his thesis on the first vision. "I think I can prove that it really happened," he said.[30]

"What makes you think that?" Allen asked, believing in the vision but not that it could be proved by the historical method.[31]

"I have found another version of Joseph Smith's first vision," Cheesman answered. Curious, Allen listened to his student describe the document.[32] It was an undated manuscript in the voice of Joseph Smith, written apparently by a scribe in the early 1830s on the first six pages of a ledger book, before being cut out. Cheesman had been shown the document in the Church Historian's Office.[33] Allen went there promptly and asked to see it too. "You

Figure 23.2 James B. Allen (b. 1927) became a leading scholar of Joseph Smith's first vision in the 1960s.

Photo courtesy Church History Library.

can't see the book," he was told, "but we can give you a microfilm copy of it."
He laced the film through the spools on the microfilm machine, sat down,
and started reading the lines of what he later called "a handwritten story
that didn't have very good grammar and maybe two sentences in the whole
thing."[34]

As he read, Allen was moved by Joseph Smith's struggle to represent his
youthful experience. "This young man is telling the truth," Allen thought,
and he began formulating a new research agenda.[35] "When did Joseph
Smith begin to tell this story?" he wondered. "When did he stop telling it, or
did he stop telling it?" He wanted to know when saints began to know the
story of Joseph Smith's first vision.[36]

He started his research in diaries from the 1830s and autobiographies
that reflected on that decade, discovering that none of them mentioned
it. Neither did the saints' periodicals. "Why not?" he wondered. He knew
Smith wrote accounts of the vision at least twice in the 1830s. He surmised,
based on what Nibley had written about his ancestor's experience, that
Joseph Smith may have told the vision "privately to a few people once in
a while, but the story wasn't being spread privately and it certainly wasn't
being published."

■ ■ ■

Paul Cheesman finished his MA thesis in 1965. It included Joseph Smith's
1832 vision account in an appendix, the first time the document had ever
been printed. "This thesis is not an effort to prove beyond all doubt that
Joseph Smith was telling the truth," a wiser Cheesman began, "for this
cannot be done by empirical methods." He wrote candidly about "the various sources" that had emerged, raising questions. He argued that Joseph
Smith told a generally consistent story over time and offered plausible
reasons why Smith apparently did not write or tell about the vision for years
after it occurred.[37]

Very soon afterward, Jerald and Sandra Tanner printed their pamphlet,
Joseph Smith's Strange Account of the First Vision. They copied Cheesman's
transcription of the new source document—claiming it had been
"suppressed for 130 years"—but otherwise disagreed with Cheesman's every
argument. He had sought to minimize dissonance in the historical record.
They tried to maximize it and to prove that Joseph Smith "did not see the
father and the son in 1820."[38]

James Allen, meanwhile, tried to understand the historical record. He presented his research in Logan, Utah, to a group of scholars who were thinking of forming a Mormon history association. Allen showed them that Smith's first vision was not a factor in the conversions of early saints, nor was it common knowledge among them or their critics. Smith was telling it, however, earlier than Fawn Brodie had claimed, as some late reminiscences suggested and the new document seemed to confirm.

Allen posited that Smith's rejection by the Methodist minister kept him from telling his story publicly earlier than he did. At the small gathering of historians, Allen proved himself the best analyst of the available evidence, and giddy to have an account of what he later called "Joseph Smith pure and simple, giving his feelings as best he could remember them and writing them out by himself."[39]

For James Allen and his peers, Joseph Smith's multiple memories, and the memories of his followers, were complex. They were fascinated by the historical record, not fearful of it. They expected it to be ambivalent and open to various interpretations. And in that small way, their expectations were met.

Notes

1. John A. Widtsoe, *Joseph Smith: Seeker after Truth, Prophet of God* (Salt Lake City: Deseret News Press, 1951), 26.

2. S. Dilworth Young, "The First Vision," *Improvement Era* 60, no. 6 (June 1957): 436–38.

3. Young, "The First Vision," 436–38.

4. Young, "The First Vision," 436–38. See pp. 409 and 479 for Levi E. Young being in attendance and speaking.

5. LaMar Petersen memoir, J. Willard Marriott Library Special Collections Division, University of Utah, Salt Lake City, 20–22 (hereafter cited as UUSC); S. Dilworth Young, "A Scholar, a Gentle Man, President Levi Edgar Young," *Improvement Era* 67, no. 1 (January 1964): 16–20, 39–40.

6. LaMar Petersen memoir, UUSC, 20–22.

7. Scott Faulring interview of Sandra Tanner, January 24, 1981, MS 1580, box 1, folder 2, pp. 6–7, L. Tom Perry Special Collections, Harold B. Lee Library, Brigham Young University, Provo, Utah (hereafter LTPSC, BYU).

8. Scott Faulring interview of Sandra Tanner, January 24, 1981, MS 1580, box 1, folder 2, p. 5, LTPSC, BYU. Georgia McGee had apparently written to church headquarters about Reverend George Lane's role in Joseph Smith's first vision. Church librarian Earl. E. Olson wrote back to her on the subject on April 21, 1958. See Earl L. Olsen to

Mrs. Georgia McGee, April 21, 1958, LaMar Petersen Papers, MS 524, box 8, folder 11, UU Special Collections, Marriott Library.

9. Scott Faulring interview of Sandra Tanner, January 24, 1981, MS 1580, box 1, folder 2, pp. 5–6, LTPSC, BYU.

10. Scott Faulring interview of Sandra Tanner, January 24, 1981, MS 1580, box 1, folder 2, pp. 10–13, LTPSC, BYU.

11. Scott Faulring interview of Sandra Tanner, January 24, 1981, MS 1580, box 1, folder 2, pp. 10–18, LTPSC, BYU. Jerald Tanner described a similar meeting in which Pauline Hancock spoke. See Jerald Tanner to Charles Bytheway, July 1958, Church History Library. Jerald Tanner, *Jerald Tanner's Testimony* (Salt Lake City: Utah Lighthouse Ministry, 1987), 9–10.

12. Scott Faulring interview of Sandra Tanner, January 24, 1981, MS 1580, box 1, folder 2, pp. 19–21, LTPSC, BYU. Tanner, *Jerald Tanner's Testimony*, 9–10.

13. Sandra McGee to Dear Friend [Roger Flick], [June or July 1960], in Scott Harry Faulring, "An Oral History of the Modern Microfilm Company," 1983, MS 1580, LTPSC, BYU.

14. Sandra soon realized that she had claimed too much. She subsequently wrote, "Some time ago I wrote a letter stating my reasons for withdrawing from the church. In it I stated that there was no Mormon or anti-Mormon literature published before 1870 which identified the personages in the first vision as God the Father and His Son, Jesus Christ. I would like to apologize, for I have found that an anti-Mormon writer named John Hyde, in his book 'Mormonism,' published in 1857, states that Joseph Smith saw God and Christ in 1820." She then noted several reasons that her general claim remained sound. Sandra Tanner to Dear Friend, [July or August 1960], in Scott Harry Faulring, "An Oral History of the Modern Microfilm Company," 1983, MS 1580, box 3, folder 3, LTPSC, BYU.

15. "History, circa June 1839–circa 1841 [Draft 2]," 3, *The Joseph Smith Papers*, accessed December 21, 2017, http://www.josephsmithpapers.org/paper-summary/history-circa-june-1839-circa-1841-draft-2/3.

16. Orson Pratt, "Are the Father and the Son Two Distinct Persons," *The Latter-Day Saints' Millennial Star* 11, no. 20 (October 15, 1849): 310.

17. Anthony I. Bentley to LaMar Petersen, March 16, 1957, in LaMar Petersen Papers, memoir, 23–26, UUSC.

18. See Jerald Tanner to Charles Bytheway, August 18, 1960, and Helen Tanner to David O. McKay, April 23, 1961, MS 3793, Church History Library, Salt Lake City. Also see the following, all in the LaMar Petersen Papers, MS 524, box 8, folder 3, UUSC: LaMar Petersen to Joseph Fielding Smith, October 16, 1953, and Joseph Fielding Smith to LaMar Petersen, October 21, 1953; Earl E. Olson to Jerald Tanner, April 24, 1961; Ralph W. Hansen to Jerald Tanner, December 7, 1961; A. W. Lund to Sandra Tanner, April 17, 1961; Frances Cardall to Sandra Tanner, April 10, 1861; Lauritz Petersen to Jerald Tanner, April 19, 1961; Pauline Hancock, *The Godhead: Is There More Than One God* (Independence, MO: Church of Christ, n.d.), 12–13.

19. Sandra McGee to Dear Friend [Roger Flick], [June or July 1960], in Scott Harry Faulring, "An Oral History of the Modern Microfilm Company," 1983, MS 1580,

LTPSC, BYU. Also see Jerald and Sandra Tanner, *Mormonism* (n.d. [1963 according to *Jerald Tanner's Testimony*]), 12, 69–70.

20. Joseph Fielding Smith, "Evidences of the First Vision," *Improvement Era* 63, no. 2 (February 1960): 80–81.

21. In Hancock, *The Godhead*, 12–14.

22. On Nibley being enlisted, see David J. Whittaker's introduction to his anthology of Nibley essays, *Tinkling Cymbals and Sounding Brass* (Salt Lake City: Deseret, 1991), where he claims twice that Nibley was asked by leaders.

23. High W. Nibley, "Censoring Joseph Smith's Story: Part I," *Improvement Era* 64, no. 7 (July 1961): 490–92.

24. Nibley, "Censoring Joseph Smith's Story: Part I," 522.

25. Hugh Nibley to Sandra Tanner, March 8, 1961, in Hancock, *The Godhead*, 12–13.

26. Joseph Fielding Smith to Sandra Tanner, March 13, 1961, in Hancock, *The Godhead*, 13.

27. High Nibley to Sandra Tanner, March 21, 1961, in Hancock, *The Godhead*, 13–14.

28. Joseph Fielding Smith to Christine Sweet, August 29, 1961, in Lamar Petersen Papers, MS 524, box 8, folder 11, UUSC.

29. Helen Tanner to David O. McKay, April 23, 1961, Church History Library, Salt Lake City.

30. James B. Allen, interview by Samuel A. Dodge and Steven C. Harper, 2009.

31. James B. Allen, interview by Samuel A. Dodge and Steven C. Harper, 2009.

32. James B. Allen, interview by Samuel A. Dodge and Steven C. Harper, 2009.

33. Paul R. Cheesman, "An Analysis of Accounts Relating Joseph Smith's Early Visions" (MA thesis, Brigham Young University, 1965), 126; Dean C. Jessee, "The Early Accounts of Joseph Smith's First Vision," *BYU Studies* 9 (Spring 1969): 275–94; Karen Lynn Davidson, David J. Whittaker, Mark Ashurst-McGee, and Richard L. Jensen, eds., *Joseph Smith Histories, 1832–1844*, vol. 1 of the Histories series of *The Joseph Smith Papers*, ed. Dean C. Jessee, Ronald K. Esplin, and Richard Lyman Bushman (Salt Lake City: Church Historian's Press, 2012), 2–23

34. James B. Allen, interview by Samuel A. Dodge and Steven C. Harper, 2009.

35. James B. Allen, interview by Samuel A. Dodge and Steven C. Harper, 2009.

36. James B. Allen, interview by Samuel A. Dodge and Steven C. Harper, 2009.

37. Paul R. Cheesman, "An Analysis of Accounts Relating Joseph Smith's Early Visions" (MA thesis, Brigham Young University, 1965), 1–2, 126.

38. Jerald Tanner and Sandra Tanner, *Joseph Smith's Strange Account of the First Vision* (n.p.: n.d. [1965]).

39. James B. Allen, interview by Samuel A. Dodge and Steven C. Harper, 2009. Also see James B. Allen, "Significance of Joseph Smith's 'First Vision' in Mormon Thought," *Dialogue* 1 (1966): 29–45.

24

New Light

All students of Mormon history will be forced to reconsider the reliability of Joseph's first vision story.

        —Wesley P. Walters, 1967[1]

On a Sunday morning in April 1954, David O. McKay, prophet to the world's 1.3 million Latter-day Saints, commissioned them repeatedly to teach all nations "Ours is the responsibility, greater than ever before, to proclaim that the Church is divinely established by the appearance of God the Father and his Son Jesus Christ to the Prophet Joseph Smith."[2]

In the 1950s United States, Christianity had begun to decline as the Protestant establishment lost hegemony over the diversifying population.[3] Saints, meanwhile, multiplied around the world. Big families answered McKay's call, sending unprecedented numbers of their sons and daughters to more missions than ever.[4] These missionaries shared (in multiple senses) what they called "the Joseph Smith story."[5] In 1960 in the northern British mission, a missionary noted that an interested family "knew the Joseph Smith story" and that another man "said the Joseph Smith story gave him goose pimples."[6]

Paul Thiruthuvadoss was in his native India, deeply frustrated by the behavior of Christian clergymen he closely observed. He was about to give up on all of them and return to the Hinduism of his ancestors when he went into a used bookstore. He located the book he was looking for, opened it, and found in it a tract that told how Joseph Smith's frustration with Christian clergy was resolved by a heavenly vision. "I read it two or three times and found it to be a revelation to me," Thiruthuvadoss later said, "the things for which I had been searching for over twenty-five years."[7]

Nigerian Reverend Honesty John Ekong felt similarly when he read a tract telling the same story in 1959. He detached the request for more information and sent it to Salt Lake City.[8]

When missionaries called at the home of Jack Baker, an Australian veteran of World War II, he welcomed them out of gratitude to American soldiers with whom he had served, but he was candid about the mission-aries' chances. "Listen mates," he said, "you will have to bring Jesus Christ to the front door and let me see the holes in his hands and feet before I could believe anything about this Joseph Smith."[9]

The missionaries couldn't arrange that, so Baker remained friendly but outside the fold. Then, his sixteen-year-old son Philip read the Joseph Smith story and felt an overwhelming spiritual awakening. Shortly there-after Philip and his mother and siblings were baptized as Latter-day Saints. Jack followed two years later.

In England in 1962 missionaries gave a woman a tract of "The Joseph Smith Story." She sent it to a preacher in Ghana named R. A. F. Mensah. It converted him and he began converting others with it, including Joseph William Billy Johnson, though it would be nearly two decades before they could be baptized as Latter-day Saints.[10] Meanwhile, in the summer of 1974 a twenty-one-year-old Ghanian man, Tony K. Moses, was walking along the street when a stranger handed him a pamphlet titled "The Prophet Joseph Smith's Testimony." He read it, wrote to church headquarters in Salt Lake City "I have been totally moved and inspired," and asked for more information.[11]

In 1962 Patricia Bean and her husband were some of the Americans in Vietnam fighting the Cold War on that front. While teaching English, Patricia introduced interested students to Joseph Smith's first vision. Two young women converted as a result. One of them, Duong Thuy Van, soon began translating "The Joseph Smith Story" into Vietnamese.[12]

Across the South China Sea in Taiwan, Janice Bair drilled her new mis-sionary companion, Mary Ellen Edmunds, on the story. "You're ready," Janice finally said one day. "I'm not," Mary Ellen protested, but before long a woman named Lin invited them in and Mary Ellen tried to make her mouth speak Mandarin. "I did the best I could do to say my little noises, moving my head, and the Holy Ghost took those noises, my very best effort," she said, "and by the time they got to Sister Lin, a boy went into a grove of trees and knelt and prayed."[13] These were just a few of the 1.6 million people around the world who converted between McKay's 1954 commission and 1970, more than doubling the number of saints, who were increasingly spread out across the globe.[14]

Joseph Smith's story was a powerful determinant in many of these converts' decision to join The Church of Jesus Christ of Latter-day Saints. Missionaries gave the story in tract form to a British literature professor,

Arthur Henry King, early in 1966. He was struck by Smith's candor and sincerity. "I am in this church because of the Joseph Smith story," he later wrote. "My fundamental act of faith was to accept this as a remarkable document."[15]

■ ■ ■

Missionaries in the mid-twentieth century narrowly missed some converts, thanks in part to a Baltimore teen named Wesley Walters. A friend warned Walters that two peers were planning to meet with missionaries and were dangerously close to converting. "There are two of them and only one of me," Wes's friend said, speaking of the missionaries. "Would you come along?" Wes agreed. "They dug into the Book of Mormon, and were able to refute the Elders," and got their friends "out of Mormonism and into the Kingdom of God."[16]

Wesley Walters had only recently become a Christian himself. Earlier he had been resigned to eternal damnation, having an evangelical upbringing but no personal conversion. Then some peers invited him to listen to the preaching of Reverend Donald Barnhouse, an impressive minister visiting from Philadelphia's Tenth Presbyterian Church.[17]

Wedged between concerned friends in a pew in the balcony of the tightly packed church, Walters received the good news that he was not damned. With his arresting appearance and a commanding voice, Barnhouse evoked a metaphor Walters never forgot. He proposed that "when you look through a piece of red glass, everything looks red, and when you look through a piece of blue glass, everything looks blue, so when God looks at you through his perfect and sinless son Jesus, he sees you as without sin," despite your sinful nature.

To Walters, who had given up in despair trying to counter his sinful acts with godly ones, the reverend's antidote seemed too easy to be true, but it stuck. As his wife later described, Walters "was captivated by the marvelous love of God who would provide such a great salvation, and the love of the Lord Jesus, who would die for such a miserable sinner."[18]

Unbeknownst to him at the time, Wesley Walters's conversion to evangelical Christianity and his rescue of friends from Latter-day Saint missionaries started a cascade of events that would profoundly shape memories, meanings, and representations of Joseph Smith's first vision in the late twentieth and early twenty-first centuries. Walters committed fully to conservative evangelicalism, becoming a member of the United Presbyterian Church and pursuing a seminary education and ordination. By the time David O. McKay recommissioned Latter-day Saints to teach all nations, Walters was pastor of a small church near Pittsburgh, which enabled him to take a course from John Gerstner at what was soon to become Pittsburgh Theological Seminary. Perhaps spurred by what he had experienced refuting the missionaries, Walters chose "Inspiration in Mormonism" as the topic for his term paper.

By 1960 Walters and his wife, Helen, were parents of four children and he was pastor of a United Presbyterian congregation in Marissa, Illinois. Then out of the blue came an invitation for him to publish an essay in *Christianity Today*, the popular new conservative evangelical periodical.[19] Editor Carl Henry recruited heavyweights to write about the standard constellation of cults—Jehovah's Witnesses, Adventists, Christian Scientists—but could think of no one to write the essay on Latter-day Saints until Gerstner recommended Walters based on his earlier paper.

Walters balked, feeling inadequate. He spoke to one of the elders of his church, a fatherly figure named Harry Hamilton. "I think it's a great compliment that you were asked," Hamilton told him, and then asked, "what would you need to do to learn enough?"[20] Walters thought that at the very least he would need to spend a week in Salt Lake City to talk to both saints and evangelicals. Hamilton offered to pay for the trip and Walters accepted the challenge.

Church leaders in Salt Lake City received him cordially, and he learned much from "other Christians who were knowledgeable about Mormonism." He originally wrote much more than the 1,800 words that Henry finally allowed for the essay when it was published in 1960. The published essay began by painting readers a picture of missionaries like the ones Walters and his companion had met and bested in their teens:

> Almost anywhere in America today one may see two alert, conservatively-dressed young men, knocking on doors and approaching their prospect pleasantly with, "We are from the Church of Jesus Christ of Latter-day Saints." By means of the best modern sales techniques, these somewhat mysterious and intriguing figures of the "Mormon" Church then offer a religion that claims to be the only authentic church of God, restored in these latter days by God and Christ in person.[21]

Then the essay distilled Joseph Smith's first vision to its offensive essence—
"Smith's first 'vision' (allegedly received in 1820 but not published until
20 years later and now somewhat altered) informed him that all churches
are wrong and all their creeds an abomination."[22]

For Walters, defending his faith and giving it to others became relentless
motivations. The missionaries and the growth of the church generally, and
the first vision particularly, posed a threat to Walters's own conversion and
to the conservative evangelical Christianity to which he had devoted his life.
Eternal life was at stake for him. If Joseph Smith's vision story was true, then
Presbyterianism was not. He understood the implications personally and
keenly felt the threat pastorally. Any convert was a casualty. But after the
publication of his essay in *Christianity Today* he did not intend to continue
studying the saints.[23]

Then the editor forwarded him "an indignant letter" submitted by
Louis Midgley, a political science professor at Brigham Young University,
protesting Walters's assertion of alterations in the published account of the
first vision.[24]

With characteristic tenacity, Walters determined to find out how, not
whether, Joseph Smith was wrong. Like Smith himself, Walters had been
undeniably and irreversibly converted, only to an opposing truth. In
Smith's memory a divine revelation proved a Methodist minister wrong,
Presbyterianism false, and the creeds of Christendom abominable to God.
Since Walters could not accommodate the possibility of such a revelation,
the flaw, he knew, had to be in Smith's memory of the experience.[25]

Walters turned to a form of source criticism to prove his conclusion.
When he began his quest, the widely known sources were limited to Smith's
canonized account and Oliver Cowdery's 1834-1835 letters to the editor of
the *Messenger and Advocate*. Smith had confidently placed the vision in the
spring of 1820. After a false start that suggested that same dating, Cowdery's
next letter offered a correction, claiming that the religious excitement in
"Palmyra and vicinity" occurred in Smith's seventeenth year, not fifteenth—
in 1823, not 1820.[26]

"Which date was right?" Walters asked, strategizing that he could not dis-
prove a vision but he could verify the facts Smith had set forth as context for
it. Looking for evidence of unusual religious excitement—or lack thereof—
in 1820 among the Protestants Smith specified, Walters discovered that the
Methodists were not yet organized well enough to have kept local records.

Relevant Presbyterian records had been lost. Baptist records did not extend back far enough.[27]

Walters reasoned that Smith's description of unusual religious excitement in his region or district matched a full-blown revival, and "a revival of this magnitude would certainly have been written up." He began taking a detour when returning home from visits to hospitalized parishioners, stopping at McKendree College to search back issues of *Methodist Magazine*. He worked his way through 1819 issues, finding plenty on revivals but nothing in Palmyra. He found nothing for 1820, nor 1821, and so on. "I'll go through 1825," Walters thought. "That'll be an easy round number to remember."

January yielded nothing, nor February, but in the March 1825 issue he discovered Reverend George Lane's account of a Palmyra revival that started the preceding summer, 1824, when a young woman found salvation in Christ, married, and then died of typhus within weeks, praising God and urging her unredeemed peers to come to Christ.[28]

The discovery elated Walters.[29] It stimulated and focused further research. For the next few years, each August for his annual vacation he and Helen loaded their children in their car and camped along the way from Illinois to Baltimore. There she and the children visited relatives while he read microfilmed records at Johns Hopkins, accumulating evidence of the 1824 Palmyra revival until Helen wondered whether it was overkill.[30]

■ ■ ■

While Wesley Walters was scouring archives in the Midwest and East, Dean Jessee (see figure 24.1) was hired to help catalog manuscripts piled in boxes behind a screen of wire mesh in the basement of the LDS Church Administration Building in downtown Salt Lake City. Jessee loved it in "the cage" as he called it, screened off from the world, surrounded by Joseph Smith's papers. As an MA student, he had tried to get access to some of these records and could not. Now he was immersed in them. Soon he was the only source critic with full access to the sources. He traced Joseph Smith's Manuscript History—compiled mainly by Willard Richards and others in the 1840s and 1850s—to the sources behind it. He discovered the 1835 journal entry in which a scribe recorded Smith's telling of his vision to a visitor. Richards had left it out of the Manuscript History.[31]

A rising generation of educated saints, interested in the intersections between their faith and their cultures, began publishing a new periodical

Figure 24.1 Dean C. Jessee (b. 1929) became a leading scholar of Joseph Smith's first vision in the 1960s.

Photo courtesy Church History Library.

in 1966: *Dialogue: A Journal of Mormon Thought*. The third issue featured James Allen's research on Smith's first vision, including a discussion of the accounts recently discovered by Cheesman and Jessee.[32]

Meanwhile, by 1967 the Evangelical Theological Society had been defending the idea of an inerrant Bible for nearly two decades. That fall, behind a trio of articles written by doctors of sacred theology and philosophy, the society's periodical published an unheralded essay, but it was probably the most historically significant article to appear in the *Bulletin's* pages. Titled "New Light on Mormon Origins from Palmyra (N.Y.) Revival," it was the fruit of several years of determined research, a paper delivered the previous December at a society meeting, authored by Wesley P. Walters, Bachelor of Divinity.[33]

The essay made a cool, historical argument. Granting that he could not prove whether Smith envisioned divine beings in the woods of western New York, Walters asserted that he could use historical records to check Smith's verifiable facts, especially his 1839 claim that unusual religious excitement in his region led him to seeking and ultimately to the spring 1820 vision. Having scoured the records, Walters made the case that historical evidence disproved any sizeable revival in Smith's vicinity in 1820, and therefore that Smith made up his story later, situating it in the context of a well-documented 1824 revival.

"The statement of Joseph Smith, Jr. *can not be true* when he claims that he was stirred up by an 1820 revival to make his inquiry in the grove near his home," Walters concluded.[34] There was no shortage of pages aimed at undermining the saints when Walters wrote, but his thesis and his method were altogether novel. He rightly concluded that as a result of his work "all students of Mormon history will be forced to reconsider the reliability of Joseph's first vision story."[35]

To that end, Walters had also submitted his essay to *Dialogue*. The editors postponed publication until they could muster a response, so Walters published first in the *Bulletin* and also as a stand-alone pamphlet published by the Utah Christian Tract Society, headquartered in California.[36]

Notes

1. Wesley P. Walters, "New Light on Mormon Origins from Palmyra (N.Y.) Revival," *Bulletin of the Evangelical Theological Society* 10, no. 4 (Fall 1967): 241.
2. David O. McKay, "Present Responsibility of the Church in Missionary Work," *Conference Report*, April 1954, 22–26.
3. J. Tobin Grant, "Measuring Aggregate Religiosity in the United States, 1952–2005," *Sociological Spectrum* 28, no. 5 (2008): 460–76.
4. The Annual Report of the Church, *Ensign*, July 1972.
5. Lon Bailey, Northern British Mission Journal, February 1, 1960, Church History Library, Salt Lake City. Also see James B. Allen, "The Significance of Joseph Smith's 'First Vision' in Mormon Thought," *Dialogue* 1 (1966): 39.
6. Lon Bailey, Northern British Mission Journal, February 1, 1960, Church History Library, Salt Lake City.
7. Paul Thiruthuvadoss, "First Indian Convert's Testimony," *Dialogue* 13, no. 1 (Spring 1980): 96–99. Thiruthuvadoss contacted church headquarters and asked for more information. He received scriptures and other materials. He later said, "For three years I read the Book of Mormon and other church literature—asked many questions concerning the church and cleared my doubts. After fully convinced of the Truth of the Church Faith, I accepted the Church as the only True church in this universe after the ascension of Jesus Christ." He and his family joined The Church of Jesus Christ of Latter-day Saints in 1965. See Paul Thiruthuvadoss story, Southern Far East Mission, Church History Library; also Paul Thiruthuvadoss, "A Report about the LDS Church in Coimabatore Area," December 1979, Church History Library, Salt Lake City; also Richard L. Evans, Report of World Tour, Church History Library, Salt Lake City.

8. James B. Allen, "Would-Be Saints: West Africa before the 1978 Priesthood Revelation," *Journal of Mormon History* 17, no. 1 (1991): 212–13.

9. Oceania: Australia, Phillip Baker, 1960s, p. 420, Church History Library, Salt Lake City.

10. Allen, "Would-Be Saints," 239–40.

11. Tony K. Moses to Dear Sir, June 2, 1972, Africa and India Correspondence, Church History Library, Salt Lake City.

12. Quarterly Historical Report for the Southern Vietnam Zone, Southern Far East Mission, 2, Church History Library, Salt Lake City.

13. Mary Ellen Edmunds Oral History, interviewed by Brian D. Reeves, pp. 20–21. The James Moyle Oral History Program, Archives, Historical Department of The Church of Jesus Christ of Latter-day Saints, Salt Lake City.

14. The Annual Report of the Church, *Ensign*, July 1972. From 1950 until 1960, membership grew from 1,111,314 to 1,693,180. By 1970, it was 2,930,810. Also see *Deseret News 2012 Church Almanac* (Salt Lake City: Deseret Book Co., 2012), 204–5; Tim B. Heaton, "Vital Statistics," *Encyclopedia of Mormonism*, http://eom.byu.edu/index.php/Vital_Statistics.

15. Arthur Henry King, *The Abundance of the Heart* (Salt Lake City: Bookcraft, 1986), 25–26. Also see Arthur Henry King, *Arm the Children: Faith's Response to a Violent World* (Provo, UT: BYU Studies, 1998), 42–43.

16. Helen Walters, "Wesley Walters, Sleuth for the Truth," 2, unpublished manuscript in Presbyterian Church of America Historical Archives, St. Louis, Missouri.

17. Walters, "Wesley Walters, Sleuth for the Truth," 1.

18. Walters, "Wesley Walters, Sleuth for the Truth," 2. On Barnhouse's appearance and voice, see Margaret N. Barnhouse, *That Man Barnhouse* (Wheaton, IL: Tyndale House, 1983).

19. Carl F. H. Henry, *Confessions of a Theologian: An Autobiography* (Waco, TX: Word, 1986).

20. Walters, "Wesley Walters, Sleuth for the Truth," 4.

21. Wesley P. Walters, "Mormonism," *Christianity Today* 5, no. 6 (December 19, 1960): 8.

22. Walters, "Mormonism," 8.

23. Walters, "Wesley Walters, Sleuth for the Truth," 4.

24. Walters, "Wesley Walters, Sleuth for the Truth," 4.

25. Walters, "Mormonism," 8.

26. "History, 1834–1836," 61, *The Joseph Smith Papers*, accessed August 26, 2018, http://www.josephsmithpapers.org/paper-summary/history-1834-1836/65.

27. Walters, "Wesley Walters, Sleuth for the Truth," 5.

28. Walters, "Wesley Walters, Sleuth for the Truth," 5.

29. Walters, "New Light on Mormon Origins from Palmyra (N.Y.) Revival," 231.

30. Walters, "Wesley Walters, Sleuth for the Truth," 6.

31. Dean C. Jessee, "The Early Accounts of Joseph Smith's First Vision," *BYU Studies* 9, no. 3 (Spring 1969): 275–96. Samuel A. Dodge interview of Dean C. Jessee, copy in author's possession.

32. James B. Allen, "The Significance of Joseph Smith's 'First Vision' in Mormon Thought," *Dialogue* 1, no. 3 (Autumn 1966): 29–45.

33. *Bulletin of the Evangelical Theological Society* 10, no. 4 (Fall 1967). See Wesley P. Walters to James B. Allen, November 3, 1967, Wesley Walters Papers, Presbyterian Church of America Historical Archives, St. Louis, Missouri.
34. Walters, "New Light on Mormon Origins from Palmyra (N.Y.) Revival," 227–44.
35. Walters, "New Light on Mormon Origins from Palmyra (N.Y.) Revival," 241.
36. "The Question of the Palmyra Revival," *Dialogue: A Journal of Mormon Thought* 4 (Spring 1969): 59–100.

25

Under Attack

The first vision has come under severe historical attack.
—Truman Madsen, 1968[1]

By submitting his essay to *Dialogue* in 1967, Walters awakened a faithful intelligentsia, among whom it caused "consternation."[2] That fall, five intellectuals met in Salt Lake City to strategize. Truman Madsen, who, like Walters, was in his early forties, was a Harvard-educated philosophy professor and director of the Institute of Mormon Studies at Brigham Young University. Having recently returned after three years' service as president of the New England mission, headquartered in Cambridge, Massachusetts, he was devoted to proclaiming and defending Joseph Smith's story.

When he learned of the article and assessed its potency, Madsen gathered a "steering committee or advisory council" that dubbed itself "Mormon Origins in New York." The senior member of the committee, at age sixty-four, was T. Edgar Lyon, a beloved educator and soon-to-be president of the nascent Mormon History Association. Forty-year-old James Allen was the leading scholar of Smith's first vision, having recently published his study of its significance in *Dialogue*.[3] The other two members of the committee were also members of *Dialogue*'s editorial board: fifty-year-old historian and economist Leonard Arrington, professor at Utah State University, and thirty-six-year-old Richard Bushman, whose newly published dissertation *From Puritan to Yankee* was about to win the Bancroft Prize.[4]

This committee recruited a talented, committed cadre of young historians, sending them to New York and elsewhere to study the historical record. Madsen envisioned something more than a reply to Walters. He wanted a concerted, cooperative study done by dozens of talented researchers. He wanted every piece of evidence that bore on Smith's first vision published together as an overwhelming defense.[5]

By spring 1968 a network of around three dozen scholars, women and men spread from California to New York, were on a shared quest to "uncover the context, background, and original documents" needed to counter

Reverend Walters.[6] To Ruth Shinsel, whom Madsen described as "a fantasti-
cally well-informed historian of the early life of Joseph Smith," he wrote, "we
need an answer to Walters and we need it soon."[7] This group tenaciously determined to find out how, not whether, Joseph Smith was right. They flirted
with granting that Smith may have misdated his theophany, though none of
this group questioned the event's historicity.[8]

"The first vision has come under severe historical attack," Truman
Madsen reported in April 1968 to David O. McKay and his counselors
in the church's First Presidency. He updated them on the coordinated effort "of some forty scholars throughout the Church to recover and collage
basic documentary material on the New York period of Church history,"
predicting that the effort would "dissolve this case," meaning the Walters
critique. He assured the presidency that his team was making headway
but they had a problem—depleted research funding at Brigham Young
University and desperate need to send scholars to New York for the summer
to research. So he asked for seven thousand dollars, or permission to raise it
from private donors.[9]

The funding came, the historians were sent, and while they were at
work Madsen's committee continued to strategize responses based on the
reports they received, gaining confidence as evidence mounted that could
be interpreted to mean that "the available sources confirm the chronology"
of Joseph Smith's manuscript history.[10] Along with the dialogue to be
published in the aptly named *Dialogue*, they planned a series of monologues
for the spring 1969 issue of *BYU Studies* and an accessible summary for the
Improvement Era, and tried to coordinate a nearly simultaneous release.[11]

Madsen guest-edited the *BYU Studies* issue, leading off with a prologue
that championed cooperative research and called for more of it. Obliquely
responding to Walters, Madsen raised philosophical objections to the reverend without mentioning his name or his work. Madsen preferred the
"indirect" strategy for *BYU Studies* to avoid the appearance of answering
Walters at all.[12]

In the article following Madsen's prologue, James Allen and Leonard
Arrington presented a historiographical study of the saints' origins in
New York. They credited Walters by name for casting doubt on the idea that
Methodist minister George Lane could have influenced Smith's 1820 theophany and for challenging the idea of unusual religious excitement in the
vicinity of Palmyra that year. But, contextualized as these two paragraphs
were amid thirty-plus pages of similar analysis, they put Walters in his

historical place even as they understated the power he had wielded in catalyzing their essay and others.[13]

Dean Jessee's edition of Smith's 1832, 1835, and 1838/39 vision accounts
followed next in the spring 1969 issue of *BYU Studies*. Madsen had looked
to Jessee as the scholar who could best reveal the sources behind Joseph
Smith's Manuscript History and "gather together the basic standard accounts of the First Vision—all of them." Given Jessee's access to the archives,
Madsen hoped he could "do this in a quiet way and perhaps get them all
together for comparative purposes without a lot of red-tape clearance with
the powers that be."[14] Jessee did not disappoint. He gave everyone access to
the 1835 account for the first time, and to critical, contextual editions of the
1832 and 1838/39 accounts.

Next came historian Milton Backman's essay, which did not mention
Walters but replied directly to the reverend's argument that there was no
unusual religious excitement "in the vicinity of Palmyra, New York" in
1820.[15] Walters had previously titled his essay in the *Bulletin* "New Light on
Mormon Origins from the Palmyra Revival"; Backman replied with "New
Light on the Historical Setting of the First Vision." He showed there was
more evidence for religious excitement in Palmyra than Walters acknowledged, but mainly argued that Walters too narrowly confined Joseph Smith
in time and space.

Noting that Smith had said religious excitement occurred in his region
and district (not solely the neighboring village of Palmyra) and that it began
well before his vision in spring 1820, Backman presented lots of circumstantial evidence supporting Smith's description. In the same *BYU Studies*
issue, Richard Anderson relied on reminiscences of people who knew
Joseph Smith in spring 1820 to argue "that Joseph Smith is more accurate
on his early history than any of his current critics."[16]

Meanwhile, Truman Madsen and Wesley Walters coincidentally crossed
paths. "Wesley Walters!" Madsen said, eyeing the reverend's nametag at a
symposium at Southern Illinois University hosted in 1968 to draw attention to its new collection of documents relating to the saints' history in the
state. "So you're the one who dropped the bomb on BYU!" The two struck
up a conversation and Madsen thanked Walters for stimulating a flow of
research funds. "They're giving us all the money we want to try to find
answers to you."[17]

The next spring, *Dialogue* lived up to its name when it featured a three-part exchange between Walters and Richard Bushman. An editor's preface explained why the journal had postponed publication of the Walters essay, and why it was taking the unusual step of republishing it now.[18]After the Walters essay came Bushman's, "The First Vision Story Revived," and then Walters offered "A Reply to Dr. Bushman."

The Walters argument seemed overwhelming, the evidence apparently airtight. But Bushman was well suited to meet Walters on his own terms. He began by unmasking the essay as "another piece of anti-Mormonism," though neither wrote with a polemical tone.

Bushman had been nominated to respond because he seemed to Madsen and others the least likely to be too defensive.[19] Bushman's cool, reasoned response matched Walters in tone and acknowledged the reverend's success at avoiding tired issues and genuinely puzzling the saints' historians. Even so, Bushman casually predicted a positive result for his side since the essay had galvanized research. "Without wholly intending it," Bushman understated, "Mr. Walters may have done as much to advance the cause of Mormon history within the Church as anyone in recent years."[20]

Bushman challenged Walters's argument by showing inconsistencies in its evidence and offering alternative interpretations of the facts. Walters did the same in his reply, by the end of which readers could easily have felt bewildered. But when all was said the historical facts meant deceptively little. The debate turned on perceptions of how Smith remembered, not what. Smith's memory, according to Walters, "becomes somewhat suspect," or "hazy," or "extremely confused," not merely regarding the date of the event but "the very fabric of the story itself."[21]

As Bushman noted, Walters arrived at this conclusion largely by trusting Oliver Cowdery's memory while impugning Smith's, or, rather, asserting that Smith did not misremember the experience but manufactured it later using elements of an 1824 revival (that Cowdery remembered accurately) but projecting them back to 1820. Bushman responded that it was more Cowdery than Smith who "scrambled the two events, putting together parts of two stories to make one," and faulted Walters for trusting Cowdery's memory as "virtually Joseph's own personal narrative."[22]

Walters conceived of Smith's memory hypothetically (as it should have been if it were reliable) as a static picture of a simple, objective past. Bushman conceived of memory as fluid, adaptable, a mix of past and present. These positions were predictable results of each writer's orientation, training, and thus philosophical perspective. Walters came at Christianity conservatively, with some fundamentalist tendencies. His commitment to an objective biblical truth responded to childhood concerns about relativism and subjectivity. He saw the past "as a timeless mirror to be looked at for accurate reflections of historical events."[23] He thought he could recover an external world with fixed properties that exist independently of observers.

Bushman came at Joseph Smith as a believer, willing to embrace Smith's version of the supernatural, but also inclined to and trained in a skeptical historical method, making him apt to be skeptical of skepticism itself, and convinced that only subjective pasts could be recovered. He regarded the past as "variable, contested and subject to varieties of interpretation."[24] And he came to the project fresh from an interdisciplinary fellowship at Brown University in which he learned to apply psychology to history.[25]

As Walters argued, then, that the evidence for revivalism was too little and too far from Joseph Smith in 1820 to meet the standard, Bushman repeatedly reminded him that there was no objective standard; there was only Joseph Smith's subjective description. Walters had oversimplified objectivity, Bushman contended, making himself the subjective judge of "how near is near and how big is big" when it came to Smith's subjective experience of unusual religious excitement in his region.

Bushman argued, as an alternative, for seeing the subjectivity and resulting complexity in Smith's recorded memories. "Behind the simplest event are complex motives and many factual threads conjoining that will receive varying emphasis in different retellings," he reasoned, adding, "the reasons for reshaping the story usually have to do with changes in immediate circumstances." Thinking this way about memory, Bushman offered a brief rehearsal of some of the concerns Smith had as he remembered his experience. Then, having interpreted the historical facts from the perspective of Smith's subjective memory, Bushman dubbed it "folly to try to explain every change as the result of Joseph's calculated efforts to fabricate a convincing account."[26]

As with the essay by Reverend Walters, Bushman's article is a landmark, evidence of what has become axiomatic in his work—the inescapable subjectivity inherent in historical subjects, including Joseph Smith. But in the late 1960s and probably still, many more Latter-day Saints shared Walters's view of static memory and objective history. Walters had begun his essay by citing the saints' own prophets and apostles affirming the vision's significance as second only to Christ's resurrection and ministry. "The Church of Jesus Christ of Latter-day Saints and the story of Joseph Smith must stand or fall on the authenticity of the First Vision," Walters noted, quoting apostle Bruce R. McConkie's *Mormon Doctrine* (1958).

Latter-day Saints in the 1960s generally read their redacted, canonized slice of Joseph Smith's history the way Reverend Walters read his Bible, unaware of how memories consolidate either in individuals or in groups. They knew little if anything of the transmission, composition, redaction, and canonization that had catalyzed their collective memory. And, like Walters, if Latter-day Saints knew about these potential threats to their memory, they rejected them. Understanding that, Walters ironically aimed a similar critique at Smith's story as a source critics had long since used to examine the Bible.

"Wes," Helen once complained, "you are beating a dead horse. You have proved when the revival was, you've shown that Joseph Smith's account of his vision can't be factual. Why do you keep looking for more evidence?" He paused, then soberly explained his rationale. "When liberals come up with what they claim are contradictions in the Bible, we don't give up on our faith right away. We look for any possible explanation or way out. And even if we can't explain one contradiction, or two, we don't give up on our faith in God's word. . . . Mormons are the same way."[27]

■ ■ ■

When David O. McKay told the world's 1.3 million saints in 1954 "to proclaim that the Church is divinely established by the appearance of God the Father and his Son Jesus Christ to the Prophet Joseph Smith," they shared a single, scriptural memory of their origin story.[28] By 1970 there were 1.6 million more saints and two new collective memories available for selecting and relating. One was the critical memory of Dale Morgan, Fawn Brodie, Sandra and Jerald Tanner, and Wesley Walters among others, namely: Joseph Smith did not see God in 1820. He made the story up much later.

The second collective memory was offered by historians. Informed by the two rediscovered accounts (1832, 1835) and lots of contextual research, they forged a faithful, complex understanding of Smith's vision that accounted for the incongruity critics saw in the historical record.

James Allen published this new memory for the laity in the April 1970 issue of the *Improvement Era* as "Eight Contemporary Accounts of Joseph

Smith's First Vision: What Do We Learn from Them?"[29] It was a sophisticated yet accessible synthesis of the historical record and recent scholarship. Milton Backman followed with a monograph in 1971, *Joseph Smith's First Vision*, including all the evidence for religions excitement in western New York State through 1820 and the texts of nine accounts of the vision—four from Smith or his scribes and five from contemporaries, including the Alexander Neibaur journal entry.[30] The historians added items to the saints' collective memory buffer. They selected and related these new items to old ones. They showed how these elements could be integrated recursively with the long-established story. The laity hardly noticed, however.

The two new alternative memories formed with stunning speed compared to the original memory. Both of them carried potential to disrupt, maybe even displace, the deeply embedded Joseph Smith story. In the meantime, however, the standard story continued to contribute to the conversion of more than a million new saints.

In the late 1960s, Chris Crowe, a Catholic from Mesa, Arizona, committed to play football at BYU and fell in love with a Latter-day Saint woman. She explained that she loved him too, so they'd have to break up because she was only going to marry for eternity in a temple. She cleared out her books from their shared locker, gave him a copy of the Book of Mormon, and walked away.[31]

He threw the book into the locker and slammed it. Weeks later he took the book home and stuffed it in a drawer. Weeks more later, on a Saturday morning, he dug it out and opened it. The tone and style seemed too serious. He started skimming for something interesting. He focused on some words in the front matter: "So it was with me. I had actually seen a light, and in the midst of that light I saw two Personages, and they did in reality speak to me." He felt captivated and wanted to know the speaker and their story.

And though I was hated and persecuted for saying that I had seen a vision, yet it was true; and while they were persecuting me, reviling me, and speaking all manner of evil against me falsely for so saying, I was led to say in my heart: Why persecute me for telling the truth? I have actually seen a vision; and who am I that I can withstand God, or why does the world think to make me deny what I have actually seen? For I had seen a vision; I knew it, and I knew that God knew it, and I could not deny it, neither dared I do it; at least I knew that by so doing I would offend God, and come under condemnation.[32]

Crowe sensed that whoever the writer was, the experience was real. He understood the implications. Trembling, he called his former girlfriend and she explained that the words were Joseph Smith's, describing his first vision. She said he should talk to missionaries. Crowe knew he couldn't, and that he had to. But he finally did, infuriating his father. He was baptized as a Latter-day Saint in summer 1972.[33]

As the number of converts like Chris Crowe pushed toward two million, Wesley Walters was not able to keep them from becoming Latter-day Saints. But he forced all serious scholars of Mormon history to reconsider the reliability of Joseph Smith's first vision story.[34] He also accurately predicted their response. Scholars, however, were nearly powerless to alter the saints' collective memory or make it more resilient to critics. The disruptive potential of the newly discovered records and ways of interpreting them remained latent, waiting for an information age to unleash it.

Notes

1. Truman G. Madsen to First Presidency, April 17, 1968. Truman G. Madsen to John Wilde, January 4, 1967. Truman G. Madsen Papers, Wheatley Institution, Brigham Young University, Provo, Utah. Hereafter cited as TGM Papers.
2. Bushman, "The First Vision Story Revived," reports consternation on p. 83. James B. Allen had been aware of Walters and his research since at least 1966. See James B. Allen to Rev. Wesley P. Walters, December 6, 1966, and Rev. Wesley P. Walters to Dr. James B. Allen, October 23, 1967, and Allen to Walters, October 30, 1967, and Walters to Allen, November 3, 1967, in Walters Papers, Presbyterian Church of America Historical Archives, St. Louis, Missouri.
3. James B. Allen, "The Significance of Joseph Smith's First Vision in Mormon Thought," *Dialogue: A Journal of Mormon Thought* 1 (Autumn 1966): 29–45.
4. James B. Allen and Leonard J. Arrington, "Mormon Origins in New York: An Introductory Analysis," *BYU Studies* 19, no. 3 (Spring 1969): 241–42. Truman G. Madsen to Dallin H. Oaks, January 25, 1968, and Madsen to Stanley B. Kimball, January 25, 1968; Truman G. Madsen to Frederick G. Williams, February 22, 1968, TGM Papers.
5. Truman G. Madsen to Daniel H. Ludlow, November 10, 1967, TGM Papers.
6. Bushman, "The First Vision Story Revived," 83. Truman G. Madsen to Ruth Shinsel, October 30, 1967; Truman G. Madsen to Robert B. Flanders, January 24, 1968, TGM Papers.
7. Truman G. Madsen to Ruth Shinsel, October 30, 1967. Truman G. Madsen to Nancy Richards, September 25, 1967, TGM Papers.
8. Truman G. Madsen to Ruth Shinsel, October 20, 1967, TGM Papers.

9. Truman G. Madsen to First Presidency, April 17, 1968; Truman G. Madsen to John Wilde, January 4, 1967, TGM Papers.

10. Truman G. Madsen to Craig A. Hanson, October 22, 1968, TGM Papers.

11. Truman G. Madsen to Richard L. Bushman, October 18, 1968; Truman G. Madsen to Ruth Shinsel, November 25, 1968, TGM Papers.

12. Truman G. Madsen, "Guest Editor's Prologue," *BYU Studies* 9, no. 3 (Spring 1969): 235–40. Truman G. Madsen to Craig A. Hanson, October 22, 1968, and Madsen to Eugene England, October 16, 1968, TGM Papers.

13. James B. Allen and Leonard J. Arrington, "Mormon Origins in New York: An Introductory Analysis," *BYU Studies* 9, no. 3 (Spring 1969): 241–74, mentions Walters on pp. 271–72.

14. Truman G. Madsen to Dean Jesse[e], March 4, 1968, TGM Papers.

15. Wesley P. Walters, "New Light on Mormon Origins from the Palmyra Revival," *Dialogue: A Journal of Mormon Thought* 4 (Spring 1969): 61.

16. Milton V. Backman Jr., "Awakenings in the Burned-over District: New Light on the Historical Setting of the First Vision," *BYU Studies* 9, no. 3 (Spring 1969): 301–20; Richard L. Anderson, "Circumstantial Confirmation of the First Vision through Reminiscences," *BYU Studies* 9, no. 3 (Spring 1969): 373–404. Quote is from p. 404.

17. Helen Walters, "Wesley Walters, Sleuth for the Truth," 1, unpublished manuscript in Presbyterian Church of America Historical Archives, St. Louis, Missouri.

18. Joe Jeppson of *Dialogue* sent Walters word in February 1969 that the journal planned to publish his essay in the next issue, followed by Bushman's reply (which Jeppson included), and invited Walters to reply to Bushman. He informed Walters, "Bushman is a Harvard PhD who taught at B.Y.U. until he won the 'Bancroft Prize' . . . & moved to a full professorship at Boston Univ. He's LDS & pretty orthodox." Joe Jeppson to Wesley Walters, February 17, 1969, Walters Papers, Presbyterian Church of America Historical Archives, St. Louis, Missouri.

19. Truman G. Madsen to Richard L. Bushman, October 18, 1968, and Madsen to Eugene England, October 16, 1968, TGM Papers.

20. Bushman, "First Vision Story Revived," 83.

21. Wesley P. Walters, "New Light on Mormon Origins from Palmyra (N.Y.) Revival," *Bulletin of the Evangelical Theological Society* 10, no. 4 (Fall 1967): 238.

22. Bushman, "First Vision Story Revived," 85.

23. The quote is from David Middleton and Derek Edwards, *Collective Remembering* (London: Sage, 1990), 4. The idea owes much to David Lowenthal, *The Past Is a Foreign Country* (Cambridge, UK: Cambridge University Press, 1989).

24. The quote is from Middleton and Edwards, *Collective Remembering*, 4. The idea owes much to David Lowenthal, *The Past is a Foreign Country* (1989).

25. See Richard L. Bushman, "On the Uses of Psychology: Conflict and Conciliation in Benjamin Franklin," *History and Theory* 5 (Fall 1966): 225–40 and "The Inner Joseph Smith," *Journal of Mormon History* 32, no. 1 (Spring 2006): 65–81.

26. Bushman, "First Vision Story Revived," 83–85.

27. Walters, "Wesley Walters, Sleuth for the Truth," 6.

28. David O. McKay, "Present Responsibility of the Church in Missionary Work," *Conference Report*, April (1954): 22–26.
29. James B. Allen, "Eight Contemporary Accounts of Joseph Smith's First Vision-What Do We Learn From Them?" *Improvement Era* 73, no. 4 (April 1970): 4–13.
30. Milton V. Backman Jr. *Joseph Smith's First Vision: The First Vision in Its Historical Context* (Salt Lake City: Bookcraft, 1971).
31. Chris Crowe, "Chris Crowe," unpublished manuscript, used by permission.
32. Chris Crowe, "Chris Crowe," unpublished manuscript, used by permission.
33. Chris Crowe, "Chris Crowe," unpublished manuscript, used by permission.
34. Walters, "New Light on Mormon Origins from Palmyra (N.Y.) Revival," 241.

26

Our Whole Strength

Our whole strength rests on the validity of that vision. It either occurred or it did not occur. If it did not, then this work is a fraud. If it did, then it is the most important and wonderful work under the heavens.

—Gordon B. Hinckley, 2002[1]

Early on a midsummer morning in 1975, an anxious boy in his midteens walked into a grove in western New York, planning to kneel as if to pray.[2] Unlike Joseph Smith, he was not alone. Movie producer and director David Jacobs was there with his crew of filmmakers, capturing the shots they needed for a short film sponsored by the church.

Jacobs wanted the film to be historically accurate and to convey spiritual power. He worried about how to represent Smith's canonized description of feeling oppressed by an evil, unseen power just before the vision. On the plane to New York Jacobs read Dean Jessee's edition of Smith's 1835 journal entry, noting the passage, "I heard a noise behind me like some one walking toward me. I strove again to pray, but could not; the noise of walking seemed to draw nearer. I sprang upon my feet and looked around but saw no person or thing." Jacobs knew he could capture that on film. "This was how I wanted to get into the darkness scene," he said. "It was dramatic. It was true."[3]

Meanwhile, more and more scholars were seeking truth about Joseph Smith. Their object was truth but not drama. They sought neither to defend nor to defame the church, but to understand its past. They were eager to capture Smith's complexity. Their writings generated a "New Mormon History," as it was dubbed in 1969.[4] James Allen's essay, "The Significance of Joseph Smith's 'First Vision' in Mormon Thought," was this movement's benchmark for first vision studies.[5]

In 1974, Jan Shipps, a Methodist scholar of American religion, contributed the lead essay in the inaugural issue of the *Journal of Mormon History*, "The Prophet Puzzle: Suggestions Leading toward a More Comprehensive

Interpretation of Joseph Smith."[6] She began by noting how Wesley Walters had opened a floodgate, leading to "a steady stream of articles, essays, and books on the early period in Mormon history."[7] Much of it was old, polemical history, Shipps noted. And though much of it was significant and novel, she argued, Joseph Smith remained a puzzle. Shipps selected from and related the evidence and arguments of Joseph Smith, Fawn Brodie, Dale Morgan, the Tanners, Wesley Walters, and James Allen—resulting in an interpretation of Smith she called "a larger than life *whole* man."[8]

"Around 1820 he probably did have a vision," Shipps concluded, interpreting the event in naturalistic terms. But she also conceded, in a nod to Morgan and Walters, that revivalism may have led him to "doubt his earlier conclusion about the Protestant churches, leading him to inquire about the matter a second time, thereby stimulating a second vision around 1824."[9] Her thesis accounted for complexity. Earlier writers had generally rejected the records of Joseph Smith and others that explained his revelations in supernatural terms. Shipps took the historical record seriously without accepting it at face value.

The immensely important new historiography—with its critical and contextual interpretations of Joseph Smith's first vision, and of his complexity generally—made almost no difference in the short term. For the few saints in the know, it offered solutions to the problems the prophet posed. For most, however, there were no historical problems, no prophet puzzles at all. But the truth in David Jacobs's film and the truth in the new historiography were on a collision course as Smith's first vision entered an era of internet, digital media, and social media—an era characterized by accessibility, where almost anyone could become a selector and relater.

■ ■ ■

On the evening of September 2, 1976, Spencer W. Kimball, then the church president, together with dozens of other general authorities, their families, and other invited guests, took their seats in the Promised Valley Playhouse in downtown Salt Lake City.[10] David Jacobs stood and welcomed them to the premier of *The First Vision*. The film was made, he said, "to particularly strengthen the testimonies of the young people throughout the Church."

The script derived mainly from the canonized account. The vision scenes were shot on site in the grove. Every member of the cast and crew shared the goal of being true to the event. They had done their homework, Jacobs said, "then fervently prayed for the inspiration of heaven to enlarge our understandings and to bless our efforts."[11] He hoped the miracle of film could add some "new insight, a new breath of life, a better understanding or even a confirming feeling to the reality of the vision." Then he showed the film.[12]

It opened with Stewart Peterson as Joseph Smith running through a vibrant green meadow with the grove in the background as a narrator announced that God had always called prophets, and "after centuries of darkness and apostasy from Christ's teachings, God once again chose to reveal himself to mankind." As Joseph arrived at a home bustling with family, the narrator added, "The revelation came in answer to a humble prayer by the fourteen year-old-boy, Joseph Smith, in the year 1820 near Palmyra, New York. This is the story of the visitation of God the Father and his son Jesus Christ to the boy prophet Joseph as told in his own words."

The next scene shifted to a younger narrator of Smith's canonized account in first person as Peterson acted it out and occasionally delivered a line himself. Even those who disbelieve Smith's telling can find it a captivating story. Jacobs depicted it well. The musical score matched the message. The handsome Peterson played his part convincingly. In the end the old narrator assured viewers that the vision led to restoration of the gospel and church of Jesus Christ.[13]

The film was well received. Church employees in charge of curriculum were enthusiastic about it.[14] Apostles praised it as "beautifully done." One said, "The darkness scene was just great" and "I hope this will be shown in seminaries." Another said, "It's going to be powerful in the missionary use."[15] Anecdotal evidence began to accumulate, justifying their optimism. Ann Crowell wrote from Nova Scotia to the editor of the *New Era*. "I saw the film *The First Vision* shortly before I was baptized, during the time I was trying to get permission for baptism. It helped to strengthen my testimony." Shanna Moss wrote from Colorado, "My seminary class and I viewed that film this last week, and it is very spiritual and very moving. It is a great missionary tool and a wonderful testimony builder."[16]

Jeane Woolfenden, an editor of *New Era*, wrote to Jacobs saying that she and her colleagues all loved it. "Even the most dyed-in-the-wool critics of almost anything good," she said, "even people I've heard criticize the architecture of the temple were praising the film." A friend wrote to Jacobs that he had been teaching one of the men who acted in the film and his wife the restored gospel, and they had converted as a result of learning Smith's vision story. "I first read to him from Joseph's account of the 1ˢᵗ vision. As I read aloud that narrative the Spirit came in rich abundance and we were seemingly transferred through time and place into the Sacred Grove experiencing the revelation with Joseph."[17]

Some students at Brigham Young University were shown the film and surveyed about it. Their response was overwhelmingly positive. "Very uplifting," one wrote. "I felt as if I had really just watched the First Vision." Dozens of students noted their spiritual or emotional responses. They were moved, uplifted, and inspired, and felt the Holy Spirit warm their hearts. Some even wept. "It has a very moving emotional impact," one wrote, and another noted, "It affected me mostly through feelings, emotions."[18]

The film was a highly effective memory modulator because it got viewers' attention, linked it with powerful emotions, and associated those emotions neurologically with the specific story of Smith's vision.[19] "It really made me feel very spiritual," one said. "I became very involved during the portrayal of the vision and was very impressed by the photography," a typical student wrote. "I loved it. I loved it."[20] "It reminded me of a visit I made to Palmyra and the feeling I had then," one reported. Subsequent thoughts of the vision for these viewers would tend to work the same way by evoking the positive feelings the film produced in them.[21] It is hard to overstate how powerfully the film solidified and strengthened the saints' memory—and contributed to that memory's vulnerability.

Viewers left the film assured that it "was an excellent portrayal," but these viewers were generally ignorant of what the historical record said about Smith and his vision. One viewer noted, "I've never seen a film more outright of Joseph Smith."[22] Another thought "it portrayed well the setting and circumstances that led to the restoration of the Church." They had seen a film that depicted elements described in his 1835 and 1838/39 vision accounts, yet few if any knew there was more than one account or which elements each included. Few if any were conscious of the questions Morgan, Brodie, and Walters had raised, or of Allen's discovery that early saints were largely unaware of the vision. Few of the film's viewers knew anything of the complicated past, new findings, or recent arguments. Yet they felt sure they knew—knew in the depths of their souls—that the vision happened as the film depicted it.

The saints' collective memory, shaped and solidified by Jacobs's 1976 film, experienced little change for a generation. But with the birth of the internet and other media, including commercial feature films by and about Latter-day Saints, things were changing. The shift is evidenced in a landmark October 2002 sermon, where then-prophet Gordon B. Hinckley declared

> without equivocation that God the Father and His Son, the Lord Jesus Christ, appeared in person to the boy Joseph Smith. . . . Our whole strength rests on the validity of that vision. It either occurred or it did not occur. If it did not, then this work is a fraud. If it did, then it is the most important and wonderful work under the heavens.[23]

In 2000, Richard Dutcher wrote, directed, and acted in *God's Army*,[24] which tells the story of missionaries in Los Angeles. Mature Elder Dalton (Dutcher) mentors Elder Allen, who struggles to find meaning in, and stay on, his mission. Meanwhile Elder Kinegar, one of their roommates, grows increasingly skeptical as he reads "anti-Mormon literature."

Over a light-hearted lunch at a restaurant, Kinegar, who has been glancing at a book, changes the mood when he says, "Hey, did you guys know that Joseph Smith gave four different accounts of the first vision?" The missionaries look down. "Did you?" Kinegar presses.

"Why don't you put that stuff away man?" his companion replies. "That's really starting to get on my nerves."

"I just thought you might want to learn about your own religion," Kinegar responds.

Dalton, who has been observing the exchange, deliberately says, "He gave different accounts because he was talking to different audiences in different circumstances." Dalton's reconciliation of varying accounts had been selected, related, and repeated enough to become part of a collective memory for saints who knew of the various accounts.

Kinegar counters, "That must be why the First Presidency never even mentioned that God and Jesus Christ appeared until after the 1900s."

"It's not true," Dalton replies.

"It says it right here," Kinegar offers.

Dalton leans in and says, "Look it's not true. Orson Pratt and John Taylor both taught it repeatedly." Allen and the other missionary watch the high-stakes debate as Dalton demands, "Why don't you look it up in our books for a change. How many lies do you have to find in there before you're going to get it?"

Kinegar tries to de-escalate the tension. "Just forget it okay."

"No I'm not going to forget it," Dalton responds. "Look at this stuff," he says, grabbing the book. "Who are these people? Don't they have anything better to do with their time? I mean we've got drugs, disease, people living out on the street and these people spend their time trying to tear down other people's faith." He tosses the book in Kinegar's lap and says, "Doesn't that give you a clue?"

Kinegar smiles and calmly asks, "Why are you getting so upset Elder?"

"I'm getting upset because you're wasting your time with that garbage instead of doing your work," Dalton answers.[25]

The scene ends in unresolved tension, highlighting increasingly complicated memories of Smith's first vision at the beginning of the twenty-first century. With more information available to select and relate, and with mass media and the internet giving voice to new, unofficial but powerful selectors and relaters, the laity was beginning to learn that there were multiple accounts that varied from each other. Those facts were freighted with implications.

Not long after the lunch debate in the movie *God's Army*, Elder Dalton has a seizure and Kinegar abstains from giving him a healing priesthood blessing, indicating that he has lost his faith. Later, Allen and Kinegar have a late-night discussion. Kinegar is convinced by now that "not just Mormonism, but Christianity, the whole thing," is all a big lie. "Damn them if it's not true," he says of the prophets. "Damn them to hell."

In a later scene, Kinegar leaves the apartment in the middle of the night, having left his antagonistic books for Allen. When Dalton confronts Kinegar at the bus station, they have a physical fight. Dalton pins Kinegar against the wall and tells him he's read it all, "every stupid accusation." Before boarding the bus Kinegar appeals to Allen to join him. The young missionary refuses, but in the next scene he questions Dalton. "He is wrong, isn't he?"

Dalton appeals to Allen to seek and receive his own inner conviction. Allen subsequently receives a testimony from the Holy Spirit as he sincerely prays and asks God for it.

Smith's first vision plays an even more pivotal role in resolving the plot of the 2003 movie *The Best Two Years*. Two pairs of American missionaries share an apartment in Amsterdam. Elder Rogers is the most seasoned among them but has turned skeptical because his parents have divorced and his girlfriend has married his former fellow missionary. The transformation comes when Rogers and new, naïve Elder Calhoun teach Smith's first vision to an American student. As Rogers repeats the words of Smith's canonized account, words he has said before but never with such effect, he feels their power and knows the story is true and that his mission is meaningful.[26] In *God's Army* and *The Best Two Years*, Smith's first vision was at the crux of testimony, missionary work, and conversion.

That narrative was challenged, however, in Grant Palmer's 2002 book *An Insider's View of Mormon Origins*. "For thirty-four years I was primarily an Institute director for the Church Educational System (CES) of the Church of Jesus Christ of Latter-day Saints," Palmer wrote, inviting the laity to trust him. Then he set forth the problem his book aimed to solve: "We like to hear confirmation that everything is as we assumed," but church curriculum didn't touch the complex past. Palmer promised readers he would "introduce church members who have not followed the developments in church history during the last thirty years to issues that are central to the topic of Mormon origins."[27]

The book's timing and tone were well suited to disrupt the saints' memory. As a selector and relater of elements newly available for making memory, *An Insider's View* worked like Fawn Brodie's *No Man Knows My History*. They are both poor examples of the historical method, but some readers gained from them an identity-stabilizing relationship to the past. Jan Shipps described this phenomenon: "In some (perhaps many) instances," she wrote,

> study of the community's history appears to be a surrogate for lost faith. In other instances, however, it becomes an effort to find hard evidence that can serve as justification for abandoning the community's creedal base. If it is the latter and if the interest in history becomes a preoccupation that leads to writing about the community, very often the outcome is history that is tendentious in the extreme—history the community dismisses as "apostate."[28]

In *An Insider's View*, Palmer reassured readers that he had no agenda but truth. With disarming potency, he cast considerable doubt on the saints' simple, shared memory. He didn't just question Smith's vision. Palmer confessed that his own heartfelt youthful feelings of the Holy Spirit had been a delusion, or at least a misguided way to discern truth.[29]

Around the same time, Hinckley delivered his 2002 sermon on the all-or-nothing historicity of Smith's first vision. He called out "a so-called intellectual who said the Church was trapped by its history." Palmer—the type of person Hinckley had in mind—advocated that the church should follow the example of the Independence, Missouri-based Community of Christ, the second-largest church under the restoration umbrella, which was distancing itself from Joseph Smith's first vision in contrast to Hinckley's stand.[30]

* * *

Critiques like Palmer's multiplied online, where more and more saints encountered claims that disrupted their shared memory. Why are there no accounts of the vision at the time it occurred? Why does the 1832 account only mention the Lord? Why are there so many accounts, and why do they make conflicting claims about Smith's age, what he was worried and praying about, and what he learned from God?

Of the saints who learned of the newly selected and related knowledge, many dismissed or disregarded it. But many experienced dissonance that led to deeper investigation. Some successfully incorporated new knowledge and consolidated a more complex but still orthodox memory. For others, however, a high degree of unresolved dissonance eroded their faith. They could no longer believe that Joseph Smith experienced a vision, but because it had become the seminal event underpinning their faith, they could agree with Gordon B. Hinckley: "It either occurred or it did not occur. If it did not, then this work is a fraud."[31]

Notes

1. Gordon B. Hinckley, "The Marvelous Foundations of Our Faith," October 2002, accessed August 25, 2018, https://www.lds.org/general-conference/2002/10/the-marvelous-foundation-of-our-faith?lang=eng.
2. The actor portraying Joseph Smith was Stewart Peterson. His memory, including feelings of anxiousness, is in Elise Petersen, interview of Stewart Petersen, November 25, 2013, in the author's possession. For other details of the filming see Production Schedule, July 28, 1975, David Kent Jacobs Collection on Mormon Films, UA 5625, L. Tom Perry Special Collections, Harold B. Lee Library, Brigham Young University, Provo, Utah (hereafter LTPSC, BYU).

3. Jeane Woolfenden, "Lovely Was the Morning," draft article sent to David Jacobs for corrections, in carton 60, folder 2, David Kent Jacobs Collection on Mormon Films, UA 5625, LTPSC, BYU.

4. This emerging historiography was dubbed "New Mormon History" by Moses Rischin in "The New Mormon History," *American West* 6 (March 1969): 49. Also see Gregory A. Prince, *Leonard Arrington and the Writing of Mormon History* (Salt Lake City: University of Utah Press, 2016).

5. James B. Allen, "The Significance of Joseph Smith's 'First Vision' in Mormon Thought," *Dialogue* 1 (Autumn 1966): 29–45.

6. Jan Shipps, "The Prophet Puzzle: Suggestions Leading toward a More Comprehensive Interpretation of Joseph Smith," *Journal of Mormon History* 1 (1974): 3–20.

7. Shipps, "The Prophet Puzzle," 4.

8. Shipps, "The Prophet Puzzle," 20.

9. Shipps, "The Prophet Puzzle," 11.

10. "A Sacred Morning," September 11, 1976, newspaper clipping from unknown paper, in David Kent Jacobs Collection on Mormon Films, UA 5625, LTPSC, BYU.

11. Jacobs's files include copies of the latest scholarship, as well as a report of a May 1, 1975, production meeting in which crew members emphasized the need to be not only professional but also spiritually sensitive. "Our homework is to repent of our own sins," Sterling Van Wagenen said, "so that we, ourselves, have an eye single to the Lord's work." Karl Wesson "suggested that we read several sources of the same material to get more of a feel of what we're doing." Production meeting #231 The First Vision, May 1, 1975, David K. Jacobs, notes for the premier of "The First Vision," in David Kent Jacobs Collection on Mormon Films, UA 5625, LTPSC, BYU.

12. David K. Jacobs, notes for the premier of "The First Vision," in David Kent Jacobs Collection on Mormon Films, UA 5625, LTPSC, BYU.

13. "The First Vision (1976)," published on October 9, 2015, by Hard-to-Find Mormon Videos, accessed October 25, 2018, https://www.youtube.com/watch?v=nqq9lDUpduU.

14. David K. Jacobs to Stewart Peterson, May 10, 1976, in David Kent Jacobs Collection on Mormon Films, UA 5625, LTPSC, BYU.

15. Comments from second showing to Advisors to the Correlation Committee, May 14, 1976, in David Kent Jacobs Collection on Mormon Films, UA 5625, LTPSC, BYU.

16. "Dear Editor," *New Era* 7, no. 10 (October 1977): 3.

17. Jeane Woolfenden to David Jacobs, September 24, 1976; Peter Johnson to David Jacobs, July 28, 1875, in David Kent Jacobs Collection on Mormon Films, UA 5625, LTPSC, BYU.

18. "Film Evaluation Summary," in David Kent Jacobs Collection on Mormon Films, UA 5625, LTPSC, BYU.

19. Besides cognitive attention, "emotion modulates the selection and relation of specific memory items, and subsequent activation of those memory items arouses emotion." Thomas J. Anastasio, Kristen Ann Ehrenberger, Patrick Watson, and Wenyi Zhang, *Individual and Collective Memory Consolidation: Analogous Processes on Different Levels* (Cambridge, MA, and London: MIT Press, 2012), 107.

20. "Film Evaluation Summary," in David Kent Jacobs Collection on Mormon Films, UA 5625, LTPSC, BYU.

21. Anastasio et al., *Individual and Collective Memory Consolidation*, 107.

22. "Film Evaluation Summary," in David Kent Jacobs Collection on Mormon Films, UA 5625, LTPSC, BYU.

23. Gordon B. Hinckley, "The Marvelous Foundations of Our Faith," October 2002, accessed August 25, 2018, https://www.lds.org/general-conference/2002/10/the-marvelous-foundation-of-our-faith?lang=eng.

24. "Richard Dutcher: *film auteur,*" last modified October 22, 2004, accessed May 25, 2018, http://www.ldsfilm.com/directors/Dutcher.html.

25. *God's Army*, directed by Richard Dutcher (Ventura Distribution, 2000), DVD.

26. *The Best Two Years*, directed by Scott S. Anderson (HaleStorm Entertainment, 2000), DVD.

27. Grant H. Palmer, *An Insider's View of Mormon Origins* (Salt Lake City: Signature, 2002), vii–x.

28. Jan Shipps, *Sojourner in the Promised Land: Forty Years among the Mormons* (Urbana and Chicago: University of Illinois Press, 2000), 179–80.

29. Palmer, *An Insider's View of Mormon Origins*, 131–32, 235–54.

30. Palmer, *An Insider's View of Mormon Origins*, 263. On the Reorganized Church of Jesus Christ of Latter-day Saints/Community of Christ historical shift, compare Joseph Smith III and Heman C. Smith, *History of the Church of Jesus Christ of Latter Day Saints* (Lamoni, IA: Reorganized Church of Jesus Christ of Latter Day Saints, 1908), 1:6–12, with Mark A. Scherer, *The Journey of a People: The Era of Restoration, 1820–1844* (Independence, MO: Community of Christ Seminary Press, 2013), 51–67.

31. Gordon B. Hinckley, "The Marvelous Foundation of Our Faith," October 2002, https://www.lds.org/general-conference/2002/10/the-marvelous-foundation-of-our-faith?lang=eng.

27

I Did Not Know

I did not know there are multiple first vision accounts. I did not know
of their contradictions or that the Church members did not know
about a first vision until 12-22 years after it supposedly happened.
                                                    —Jeremy Runnells, 2013[1]

Jeremy Runnells was a lifelong Latter-day Saint and "fully believing" former
missionary in early 2012 when he read an online article reporting that
saints were "leaving in droves" over historical problems.[2] Shocked, Runnells
began what he described as "a year of intense research and an absolute rabid
obsession with Joseph Smith."[3] The result was an extended April 2013 letter
to a director in the LDS Church Educational System (CES), an associate of
Runnells's grandfather, who they both hoped could answer his questions.

Runnells described a dozen major concerns including the first vision. He
listed facts and issues raised by Morgan, Walters, Jessee, Allen, and others,
none of which were new, but all of which were new to him. He wrote,

> I did not know there are multiple first vision accounts. I did not know of
> their contradictions or that the Church members did not know about a
> first vision until 12-22 years after it supposedly happened. I was unaware
> of these omissions in the mission field, as I was never taught or trained in
> the Missionary Training Center to teach investigators these facts.[4]

Before sending his manuscript to the CES director, Runnells shared it
online, where it began to circulate widely.[5] By then the collective memory
buffer had enlarged exponentially in two ways. Historical research had multiplied many times over the known information about Smith's first vision.
Then the internet made it available to millions of saints for the first time
and everyone became a selector and relater. Runnells was one of many.

Apologetic sites selected new items and related them in support of the
shared memory, adding complexity and resolving dissonance with little
disruption. Critical sites selected and related information in ways that

undermined the shared memory. Bloggers and vloggers and tweeters and trolls weighed in, some posing as objective analysts, others blatantly partisan.

An anonymous saint said, "I was very distraught when I started learning these things. I felt as if my entire world had collapsed." This person began studying for a few hours a day, trying to figure out whom he or she could trust to tell the truth. Deciding that "both sides are guilty of making errors and misrepresenting facts," the anonymous saint started mormonthink.com as a place to post pro and con arguments along with their point of view.[6] In this environment the LDS Church could no longer quarantine information about the vision if it wanted to. It was no longer the sole selector and re-later with a vested interest in shaping and transmitting a version of Joseph Smith's first vision.

At the turn of the twenty-first century church leaders and educators took for granted that Latter-day Saints shared the memory of Smith's vision as their origin story and that it would be automatically transmitted to the next generation. Church curriculum hardly touched it. It was taught in Sunday school only once every four years—probably less regularly to children and teens. High school students who chose to attend seminary would hear it once in four years. College-aged students at the church's universities or Institutes of Religion, though required to take sixteen credits of religion, commonly did so without covering Smith's first vision.

The manual published in 1989 for Religion 341, the elective early church history course, selected some new elements and related them to the can-onized account. It included Anderson's picture of the grove captioned, "the exact location where Joseph Smith experienced his first vision is unknown. The grove across the street from the family home is assumed to be the most likely spot."[7]

The chapter silently incorporated elements from all four primary ac-counts of Smith's vision. However, nothing but the endnotes told students there was more than one account. The manual said nothing about when the accounts were written, why, or how they compared. The manual didacti-cally emphasized that the vision really occurred, God and Christ were sep-arate, Satan opposed Joseph Smith, sectarians persecuted him, and saints could trust that "all else of which he spoke is true."[8]

It was more catechism than history. There was no description of sources, nor of historical problems or even complexity. The chapter claimed that "eventually he [Smith] confided his theophany to other family members" and wrongly implied that his brother William was referring to hearing Joseph relate his vision when he said, "Father and Mother believed him, why should not the children."[9]

The manual for instructors suggested approaches to the lesson. First on the list was to use the 1976 film. Another was to use quotes from recent prophets. The last one on the list cautioned teachers to "be prepared to *briefly* answer questions that may come up about the historicity of the first vision" and summarized orthodox arguments by Backman, Allen, and others. It was hoped and expected that students would be ignorant of the issues, and if they wanted to become educated about them that teachers would discuss them quickly and emphasize more important points, including prophetic witnesses of the historicity of the vision.[10]

Compared to some of the material published on the ever-changing and accessible internet, the manual was a poor memory modulator. It had little power to fuse knowledge and emotion in ways that would consolidate memory. Jeremy Runnells could have taken the class and dutifully done his reading and still concluded, "I did not know there are multiple first vision accounts."[11]

Another selector and relater, John Dehlin, graduated from BYU in 1993. "I didn't learn until well after I graduated from college that there was anything other than one version of the Joseph Smith story," he remembered in a conversation with Richard Bushman.[12] At the time, Dehlin was in the middle of a journey from volunteer seminary teacher to skeptic to critic to advocate for disenchanted saints. He and Runnells and others felt a bitter sense of betrayal when they learned truths about the vision from outsiders and realized that the insiders they trusted to teach them truth had concealed significant facts from them.[13]

These issues were not addressed in the LDS Church's 2008 movie *The Restoration*. It integrated all of Smith's accounts and was viewed widely, but it concealed rather than revealed the findings of the historiography. It worked like the 1976 film as a memory modulator, though probably not as powerfully. Viewers did not learn there were multiple vision accounts, not to mention what each one said or when or why it was composed. Viewers did not learn that early saints generally did not discuss the vision—that it only became a common memory around 1880, and that it had been seriously challenged in recent decades.[14]

■ ■ ■

The Joseph Smith Papers raised the bar of the new historiography. Building on Dean Jessee's pioneering work, by 2005 the project had institutional support from The Church of Jesus Christ of Latter-day Saints and generous funding from Larry H. and Gail Miller. The resulting volumes have been critically acclaimed for meeting the highest standards of documentary editing. What they lacked, however, was accessibility. The books were large and expensive. Some volumes sold extremely well but were not generally or widely digested.

Then in October 2013 all of the first vision accounts in the known historical record were published together in a new open-access website, josephsmithpapers.org. These documents were already online and in volumes of *The Joseph Smith Papers*, but pulling them together made them easier to access and signaled to Latter-day Saints and others that the church was forthcoming. Relatively few saints or anyone else knew of the documents, however, or paid any attention to efforts to publicize them.

Then, without fanfare, on November 20, 2013, the LDS Church published "First Vision Accounts" at lds.org. It was an unattributed essay including candid statements of all the issues raised over the years, counterarguments to Brodie and Walters, links to images of all the known accounts, and the epistemology the feature films displayed and Grant Palmer disputed:

> Neither the truth of the First Vision nor the arguments against it can be proven by historical research alone. Knowing the truth of Joseph Smith's testimony requires each earnest seeker of truth to study the record and then exercise sufficient faith in Christ to ask God in sincere, humble prayer whether the record is true. If the seeker asks with the real intent to act upon the answer revealed by the Holy Ghost, the truthfulness of Joseph Smith's vision will be manifest.[15]

The essay had been in the works for a few years, though its timing made it seem like a direct response to Runnells. His letter was being downloaded thousands of times every day. Many saints were experiencing increasing doubt that the vision happened as Smith described, along with distrust that the church was a reliable source of truth on the matter.

The quiet publication of "First Vision Accounts" indicated some ambivalence about how best to respond to the issues raised by the new historiography and now selected and related in myriad ways online. Blogger David T. argued with the essay premise by premise.[16] Never neutral, mormonthink.com tried to undermine confidence in the essay and to cast doubt on Joseph Smith's memory.[17]

The Church of Jesus Christ of Latter-day Saints did not exert all its potential power as a selector and relater of the first vision story. Perhaps there was not a consensus among decision makers about whether to focus attention on facts that would disrupt the shared memory, which most Latter-day Saints had not questioned nor doubted.

The option existed to return to methods like James Allen's 1970 *Improvement Era* article, which featured all the evidence in accessible prose and an accompanying chart that compared all the accounts.[18] "First Vision Accounts" was a variation on that. It selected all the accounts and related them as a shared memory that was resilient to critics but still orthodox. Still, the way it was presented and the lack of attention drawn and paid to it meant that, like the 1970 article, too few saints read it, or remembered it if they did, to make any massive change.

The status quo was another option: tell the standard story rarely and generally so tepidly and didactically that it wouldn't modulate memory well. But sometimes tell it powerfully via the best available media, taking for granted that such methods would ensure its persistence and transmission. That would perpetuate a shared memory that was widely shared but now so easily disrupted that it would lead, for many, to doubt and distrust.

The church could maintain its line in the sand. Or it could adopt the "evolutionary development" interpretation of Mark A. Scherer, the Community of Christ world church historian, who argued in 2013 that spiritual truths, not historicity, are the more important product of Smith's vision accounts.[19]

In the end, The Church of Jesus Christ of Latter-day Saints chose not to try the 1970 approach again, or to tell the old story in new ways, or to maintain unequivocally that Joseph Smith saw God and Christ in the woods in 1820, or to emphasize the spiritual message in the historical record. It chose, instead, to do all these and more.

Notes

1. Jeremy Runnells, "Letter to a CES Director: Why I Lost My Testimony," April 2013, accessed June 1, 2018, https://cesletter.org.
2. Peter Henderson and Kristina Cooke, "Special Report: Mormonism Besieged by the Modern Age," *Reuters*, January 31, 2012, accessed June 1, 2018,

https://www.reuters.com/article/us-mormonchurch/special-report-mormonism-besieged-by-the-modern-age-idUSTRE80T1CM20120131; Jeremy Runnells, "Letter to a CES Director: Why I Lost My Testimony," April 2013, accessed June 1, 2018, https://cesletter.org.

3. Jeremy Runnells, "Letter to a CES Director: Why I Lost My Testimony," April 2013, accessed June 1, 2018, https://cesletter.org.

4. Jeremy Runnells, "Letter to a CES Director: Why I Lost My Testimony," April 2013, accessed June 1, 2018, https://cesletter.org.

5. Jeremy Runnells, "Letter to a CES Director: Why I Lost My Testimony," April 2013, accessed June 1, 2018, https://cesletter.org.

6. D. Jeff Burton, "Anonymous Confessions of an LDS Webmaster," *Sunstone* no. 150 (July 2008): 67–69.

7. *Church History in the Fulness of Times* (Salt Lake City: The Church of Jesus Christ of Latter-day Saints, 1989), 33.

8. *Church History in the Fulness of Times*, 2nd ed. (Salt Lake City: The Church of Jesus Christ of Latter-day Saints, 1993), 28–36. Quote is on p. 29 and is mirrored by the chapter-closing quote of Joseph F. Smith: "Having accepted this truth, I find it easy to accept of every other truth that he enunciated and declared." The only difference in "Chapter Three: The First Vision" between the original and the second edition is that the first opens with a quote from Spencer W. Kimball: "That a new day dawned when another soul with passionate yearning prayed for divine guidance. A spot of hidden solitude was found, knees were bent, a heart was humbled, pleadings were voiced, and a light brighter than noonday sun illuminated the world—the curtain never to be closed again." The second edition replaced that with this Gordon B. Hinckley quote: "This glorious first vision . . . was the parting of the curtain to open this, the dispensation of the fulness of times. Nothing on which we base our doctrine, nothing we teach, nothing we live by is of greater importance than this initial declaration. I submit that if Joseph Smith talked with God the Father and His Beloved Son, then all else of which he spoke is true. This is the hinge on which turns the gate that leads to the path of salvation and eternal life."

9. *Church History in the Fulness of Times*, 2nd ed., 34.

10. *Church History in the Fulness of Times Instructor's Guide* (Salt Lake City: The Church of Jesus Christ of Latter-day Saints, 1991), 4–5. Emphasis in original.

11. Jeremy Runnells, "Letter to a CES Director: Why I Lost My Testimony," April 2013, accessed June 1, 2018, https://cesletter.org.

12. A transcript of the Dehlin and Bushman interview is at "Multiple First Vision Accounts," *Mormon Heretic*, posted June 10, 2012, accessed June 15, 2018, https://mormonheretic.org/2012/06/10/bushman-on-the-multiple-first-vision-accounts/.

13. See Dehlin's talk at "Featured Speaker: John Dehlin, Ph.D. – 'How Mormonism Led Me out of Mormonism,'" published on January 29, 2016, by Kansas City Oasis, accessed June 15, 2018, https://www.youtube.com/watch?v=-ov-1hyodY8. Also see Dehlin's three-part interview of Jeremy Runnells: John Dehlin, "480-482: Jeremy Runnells and His Letter to a CES Director," posted June 18, 2014, accessed June 15,

2018, https://www.mormonstories.org/podcast/jeremy-runnells-and-his-letter-to-a-ces-director/.

14. "The Restoration," *LDS Media Library*, accessed October 26, 2018, https://www.lds.org/media-library/video/2008-06-01-the-restoration?category=feature-films&&lang=eng#d.

15. "First Vision Accounts," part of *Gospel Topics Essays* series, originally published November 2013, accessed June 15, 2018, https://www.lds.org/topics/first-vision-accounts?lang=eng.

16. David T., "The First Re-Vision of Joseph Smith," *Mormon Disclosures*, posted December 3, 2013, accessed October 26, 2018, http://mormondisclosures.blogspot.com/2013/12/the-first-re-vision-of-joseph-smith.html.

17. "The First Vision," MormonThink, accessed June 15, 2018, http://www.mormonthink.com/firstvisionweb.htm; "The First Vision – Response to LDS.org," MormonThink, accessed June 15, 2018, http://www.mormonthink.com/essays-first-vision.htm.

18. James B. Allen, "Eight Contemporary Accounts of the First Vision—What Do We Learn from Them?," *Improvement Era* 73 (1970): 4–13.

19. Mark A. Scherer, *The Journey of a People: The Era of Restoration, 1820–1844* (Independence, MO: Community of Christ Seminary Press, 2013), 65–67.

28

Gone Are the Days

I am not worried that the Prophet Joseph Smith gave a number of versions of the First Vision.

—Gordon B. Hinckley, 1983[1]

In his 2005 biography of Joseph Smith, Richard Bushman incorporated the findings of the new Mormon history. He saw change over time in Smith's vision accounts and granted the critics that point, just not their interpretation that it meant Smith did not experience what he claimed. Bushman had been active for half a century in the contest over Smith's first vision. He argued graciously and with confidence. He was patient, not polemical, and he knew Smith's life and times better than anyone else.

Bushman did not question whether Smith told the truth about his vision, only what truth he told each time he recorded it. Bushman's Joseph Smith is therefore not the deceived or deceiving one of Fawn Brodie or Wesley Walters or contemporary biographer Dan Vogel. But neither is Bushman's Joseph Smith the simplified teenage prophet of the movies and manuals.

Bushman's Joseph Smith struggled to choose between his parents' opposing views, experimented with deism, and wrestled with two versions of the same question: "which church was right, and how to be saved."[2] Bushman's Joseph Smith prayed in the woods, "probably in early 1820," and in his earliest recorded account of what happened as a result of that prayer, Smith "explained the vision as he must have first understood it, as a personal conversion."[3]

In later, more confident accounts, Smith shared more, including details of a dark power. He also shifted the emphasis to apostasy of the existing churches at the expense of earlier emphasis on personal redemption. Bushman's Joseph, in other words, is consistent with the historical record. Bushman's presentation of Smith, moreover, was neither didactic nor polemical, just historical.[4]

Bushman's Joseph was not warmly welcomed into church curriculum.[5] Bushman's colleagues chose him to defend Smith's first vision in the 1960s because he was a well-informed believer but not dogmatic or defensive.[6] Those same attributes made his biography generally unattractive to the Church Educational System, whose personnel were advised not to teach it.

In February 2016, a decade after the publication of Bushman's biography, Elder M. Russell Ballard, of the Quorum of Twelve Apostles, announced a sea change. Giving the annual address by a senior church leader to church educators, he said:

> As Church education moves forward in the 21st century, each of you needs to consider any changes you should make in the way you prepare to teach, how you teach, and what you teach if you are to build unwavering faith in the lives of our precious youth. Gone are the days when a student asked an honest question and a teacher responded, "Don't worry about it!" Gone are the days when a student raised a sincere concern and a teacher bore his or her testimony as a response intended to avoid the issue. Gone are the days when students were protected from people who attacked the Church. . . . It was only a generation ago that our young people's access to information about our history, doctrine, and practices was basically limited to materials printed by the Church. Few students came in contact with alternative interpretations. Mostly our young people lived a sheltered life. Our curriculum at that time, though well-meaning, did not prepare students for today—a day when students have instant access to virtually everything about the Church from every possible point of view.[7]

Ballard explicitly directed the educators to seek, and help their students seek, accurate history from experts, and acknowledged that he did so. He compared this to inoculating missionaries before sending them abroad "so they will be protected against diseases that can harm or even kill them. In a similar fashion, please, before you send them into the world, inoculate your students by providing faithful, thoughtful, and accurate interpretation of gospel doctrine, the scriptures, our history, and those topics that are sometimes misunderstood," including "different accounts of the First Vision."

Elder Ballard said that the church had made "extraordinary efforts to provide accurate context and understanding" and pointed to the gospel topics essays as "a prime example of this effort." Then he told the teachers, "It is important that you know the content of these essays like you know the back of your hand."[8]

Ballard had indicated a deliberate shift in the way the first vision was taught to the youth of the church. Soon after, in a worldwide broadcast to young adults, Nancy and Richard Maynes modeled the new approach. In May 2016, Nancy Maynes spoke from the packed tabernacle on Temple Square in Salt Lake City, telling about her young adult search for purpose and direction. She was a believer in Jesus Christ. She attended different churches "hoping to find some answers," and finally knelt at her bedside and asked God for help. Then she met Richard Maynes, who introduced her to the restored gospel.

"The First Vision was an important part of my conversion," she said. "I felt a connection with Joseph Smith because he had the same question that I had: Where do I find the truth? Heavenly Father answered his sincere prayer, and He answered my prayer."[9] Maynes's autobiographical testimony showed how Smith's first vision both catalyzed conversion and modeled Mormon epistemology.

Her husband, Elder Richard J. Maynes, a general authority, then spoke, selecting and relating as Orson Pratt had done repeatedly in that same space. Maynes situated Smith's vision relative to Old Testament prophecies and a providential reading of American history, leading to the restoration of God's truth. But then he did something no general authority had ever done before in that space or anywhere else: he cited and quoted extensively from "First Vision Accounts," reviewing the four primary accounts in detail, selecting and relating, noting variation and differences, but emphasizing their "consistent, harmonious story."[10]

Maynes ended his address by testifying of Smith's first vision and inviting audience members to share their thoughts and feelings about it on social media, noting that missionaries all around the world were sharing the same "sacred information" that converted Nancy years earlier. This message helped shape a resilient, shared memory among the audience. Elder Maynes showed that an updated understanding of the first vision based on the historical record did not negate the role the event could play in personal conversions.

In fact, spiritual experiences like Nancy Maynes's were not only important for personal conversion but also rewarding. In November 2016, a group of scholars published findings they hoped would contribute to "a neuroscience of religious and spiritual experience." They had scanned the brains of nineteen devout former missionaries in their mid- to late twenties. The study aimed to identify neurological elements of a typical saint's spiritual experience. It showed "that religious experience, identified as 'feeling the Spirit,' was associated with consistent brain activation across individuals." The test subjects' spiritual experiences lit up brain regions linked to reward.[11] The experiment, in other words, proved that spiritual experience, neurologically speaking, feels good. When Latter-day Saints feel the Spirit associated with Smith's first vision, as Nancy Maynes did, they typically cherish that association and remember it often.

■ ■ ■

Richard Bushman spoke to students at BYU–Hawaii in November 2016. He chose as a topic, "What can we learn from the First Vision." He began by guiding the students on a virtual tour of a brand-new exhibit at the Church History Museum in Salt Lake City. It tells the story of the restoration, he said, a story of people who yearned for direction from heaven and could not find it.

> Then the exhibition displays a picture of Joseph Smith searching the scripture and invites you into a theater where the First Vision is reenacted in film. The film is projected in a round room to show a wooded grove surrounding you about 270 degrees. A tall young man walks into this grove, prays, and the light appears. The revelation that was looked for by so many seekers has at last come.[12]

Bushman described other exciting new aspects of the old story. "As the film begins, words appear on the screen explaining that there are nine versions of the First Vision and this presentation draws on all of them." That represented a major departure from earlier films, which drew on multiple accounts without revealing the fact to viewers. Moreover, as Bushman described to the students,

> as you exit the theater is a notebook containing all of these accounts in full, with the parts that are incorporated into the film script printed in bold. That is a new addition to the story—nine accounts of the First Vision when previously we had known only one, the one that appears in Pearl of Great Price.[13]

Bushman then told a detective story. "I thought you might be interested in hearing how it came about that we have these other accounts when for so long there was just one. Even more important, how does this new knowledge affect our understanding of Joseph Smith and the Gospel." This was Richard Bushman at his best as selector and relater of "new knowledge."[14]

The problem, Bushman said, was Fawn Brodie's thesis that Smith made the vision story up late. "Church historians of course could not leave that challenge unanswered. They thought Brodie made a weak argument but without evidence of an earlier account, her conjecture might persuade some. And so the hunt was on."

In Bushman's telling, newly discovered accounts solved the problem. The 1832 and 1835 accounts "effectively dispelled" Brodie's argument, he said, "but the acquisition of other records of the First Vision had an added value." In Bushman's telling, differences in the accounts were interesting, expected, and revealing. He noted that the 1832 account was incomplete but he liked it for what it had, not what it lacked. It had forgiveness. "The first thing the Savior did was forgive Joseph and urge him to repent," Bushman noted. "The first act of the restoration was to put the soul of the Lord's prophet in order. After granting forgiveness, Christ went on to remind Joseph of the atonement."[15]

"This account throws new light on the Restoration," Bushman declared. "The 1838 account, the traditional one emphasized the problem of churches: which church is true? The 1832 story bring redemption to the fore—forgiveness and atonement. Even the prophet of the Lord stands before God in need of forgiveness." Bushman was offering a new memory of the seminal story. In the twenty-first century, it could be less about feeling embattled and persecuted and the one true church. Attention could shift instead to the universal message of redemption through Christ. Bushman emphasized the second point very much. "Likely no more than a handful of Latter-day Saints had even heard of the First Vision before 1839," he said. The message of the restored gospel, Bushman declared, was Christ, as the Book of Mormon proclaimed on its title page. "That is what Joseph would want to come out of his work: for us to believe in Christ."[16]

The problem, Bushman noted, is that

some people's faith is based more on Joseph Smith than on Jesus Christ. When they begin to question the Prophet, they lose faith in the Savior. We all know of Latter-day Saints whose faith is shaken by new facts, such as the existence of the alternate accounts of the First Vision which I have talked about today. When this new information builds up, they grow concerned. Could it all be wrong? Their consternation goes so far that they consider leaving the church, painful as that would be.[17]

He said he had tried for a long time to answer the specific questions of those who worried about having different accounts of Smith's vision, but he had changed his approach. "I have taken to asking the doubters a question. How do you feel about Jesus Christ?" He told the students:

> Those who lose faith in Christ because they have lost faith in Joseph Smith have things backward. Joseph's mission was to increase faith in Christ, not in himself. He thought of himself as one of the weak things of the world who came forth that faith might increase in the earth and that Christ's everlasting covenant might be established. He would want us to develop faith in his teachings, in Christ and the atonement, in prayer and adhesion to high moral standards, not in him as a man. He would want us to believe in the principles independent of the man, as the Saints in the first decade did. We honor him as a prophet, to be sure, but as one who testified of the Savior. His revelations pointed beyond himself to Christ and the Father. I believe in Joseph Smith as a prophet of God, and most of you here today do too. But we must place our faith first in Christ, and believe in him apart from our faith in his messenger. Christ should be the anchor when we struggle and question. We now benefit from having not just one but many accounts of the First Vision, each one offering a different perspective. The Vision is a powerful source of faith. It helps my faith to know that someone in our own era saw God. But we should keep in mind the Vision's purpose: it was to testify of the Lord. That Christ will come first in our faith, that he will be the foundation, that we will enjoy forgiveness and renewal through His atonement.[18]

■ ■ ■

On May 31, 2018, the LDS-owned *Deseret News* published "Defending the Faith: The Supposed Scandal of Multiple First Vision Accounts," an essay by well-known apologist Daniel Peterson. He dismissed the widespread criticisms that the multiple accounts show that Joseph Smith "simply couldn't get his story straight" and that "the LDS Church has sought to hide these differing accounts."

He said two accounts were published in Smith's lifetime, and "two other accounts, recorded in Joseph's earliest autobiography as well as in a later journal, were essentially lost and forgotten until the 1960s, when historians working for the LDS Church rediscovered them and very quickly published them." The article linked to "First Vision Accounts" at lds.org and quoted from it at length, emphasizing its point that "the various accounts of the First Vision tell a consistent story."[19]

Comments on the article began to accumulate. Most attacked Peterson's premises. One found Joseph Smith's accounts "very inconsistent." Some said Peterson should have faulted Joseph Fielding Smith for suppressing evidence and credited Jerald and Sandra Tanner with finding it. Soon the commenters were waging a war of words about Joseph Smith's memory and about whether Joseph Fielding Smith really suppressed evidence and about whether God has a body and whether anyone had ever seen God.

Then apm22 from Sparks, Nevada, interrupted to post a lament and to ask a question. "I was never aware of differing 1st vision accounts," though he had been a missionary and later served in bishopric and had read all seven volumes of *History of the Church*. Peterson's article emphasized how early and often the accounts had been published and publicized by the church, yet this mainstream member repeated, "I never knew about the differing accounts." He expressed sadness and wondered, "Why don't the leaders write articles in the *Ensign* or speak about the details of these things in General Conference?"[20]

In response to Peterson's article, on June 5, 2018, John Dehlin assembled what he called "a really brilliant panel" for a Mormon Stories podcast and Facebook Live, to be aired June 18. Panelists objected to Peterson's statement that there was "no suppression." One panel member, Sandra Tanner, challenged Peterson's version of how "historians working for the LDS Church rediscovered" first vision accounts in the 1960s "and very quickly published them," telling how her appeals to see Smith's earliest vision account had been refused.[21]

The panelists objected to "First Vision Accounts" as well.[22] They argued that Smith's story was inconsistent and discordant. "It wasn't just one story like the church wants to make it seem," Tanner said. "It was an evolving story—evolved as to who was there, what was said, what year it happened, why he went to pray, what he concluded from the vision. It all changed through the years."[23]

Dehlin declared it "deceitful" of the LDS Church to present the 1832 and 1838 accounts as complementary, the way Bushman had selected and related them in his biography of Joseph Smith and for the student body at BYU–Hawaii. Dehlin's panel of selectors and relaters offered a tendentious alternative memory, one his followers would likely share but mainstream saints would identify as apostate.[24]

Dehlin wasn't the only one who charged deceit in the church's handling of the vision accounts. IronChild9 from Boise, Idaho, had responded to Daniel Peterson's *Deseret News* article, saying that by emphasizing how scholars had known of the vision accounts for half a century, he had obscured the fact that the laity did not know.

> When was the last time this was discussed from the pulpit, Sunday school lesson, or visiting teaching visit? Why is it only mentioned in an essay that is essentially buried deep on the church website? Sure, this info can be found by those that go looking, but why should they have to go looking? Why isn't this part of the standard narrative that is taught?[25]

In a devotional address days later, apostle Quentin L. Cook announced a new standard narrative. In his June 12, 2018, address to BYU–Idaho students, Cook declared, "For the first time in nearly a hundred years, a new multi-volume history of the Church is being issued under the direction of the First Presidency." Titled *Saints*, it had been in the works for a decade, he told them, and the first few chapters had already been serialized online and in the church's magazines. Cook described it as a narrative history—the true story of ordinary people who became saints. He said the first volume was being translated into fourteen languages for worldwide distribution beginning in September 2018.[26]

The new history would now begin with the spring 1815 cataclysmic eruption of Mount Tambora in Indonesia, signaling "to God's children everywhere" by its opening scene and worldwide distribution "that it is the story of their covenant with God, who knows their hardships," and who would, despite cataclysmic or private tragedies, "endow our lives with transcendent meaning, promise healing through the Savior's Atonement, and assure us that relationships we cherish here on earth can endure in eternity, coupled with eternal glory."[27]

Cook aimed to persuade the students that *Saints* was not old-fashioned, but a story for them and about them, one that located them relative to the epic story of God renewing his covenant to redeem mankind because of love. "As you read you will discover new insight and meaning even in stories you have heard before"; he then illustrated by selecting and relating Joseph Smith's first vision in a new way, drawing on the way Bushman related the 1832 and 1838 accounts and adding an interpretation that resolved the problem B. H. Roberts handled—before the world could access high-resolution images of all the accounts with a search engine and a few mouse clicks—by deleting a troublesome line.[28] Cook explained:

> No scene in Church history is better known than Joseph Smith's First Vision, but *Saints* helps us better understand how Joseph struggled to reconcile what he felt in his heart with what he thought in his mind. Joseph's heartfelt desire to feel the Savior's forgiveness had gone unfulfilled because he observed that none of the existing churches taught "the gospel of Jesus Christ as recorded in the New Testament."[29] In his mind Joseph pondered which church was right, or if they were all wrong. In his heart he desperately hoped that one of them was right so he could find the peace he sought. With his head and his heart at odds, Joseph discovered that he could ask of God. He went to the woods to pray. There he saw the Father and the Son, who forgave him and resolved his dilemma in a way he had never imagined.[30]

Indeed, as Cook had indicated, Joseph Smith's first vision is the inciting incident in this new narrative. The first chapter sets it up. Smith is an appealing protagonist. Like many others in his world, he is afflicted by disease and disruption. Like many others, he wonders if his sins have displeased God, and he seeks to be reconciled to God lest he be damned at death. He is frustrated until he discovers a new way to read an old verse. Chapter 2 shows the young hero going to the woods to pray for wisdom. He is opposed by an unseen power but prevails at the last moment, when "a pillar of light appeared over his head" and descends, "filling him with peace and joy unspeakable."

Smith sees God in the light, who calls him by name and introduces his Beloved Son, who says, "Joseph, thy sins are forgiven thee." Smith asks, "What church shall I join?" Christ answers, "Join none of them. They teach for doctrines the commandments of men, having a form of godliness, but they deny the power thereof." They converse further, Smith sees a host of angels, and he is finally left looking into heaven. The narrative is captivating and blends the accounts harmoniously, drawing on the most descriptive and dramatic elements of each. The next passage tells how Smith's story was rejected by the minister.

Then comes some exposition, explaining that Smith kept the vision to himself after being rejected, and later tried to record it. "He wrote the words out himself, in halting language, trying earnestly to capture the majesty of the moment." He recorded it again later, with help from scribes, saying "less about his own search for forgiveness and more about the Savior's universal message of truth and the need for a restoration of the gospel. With each effort to record his experience, Joseph testified that the Lord had heard and answered his prayer."[31]

In the new narrative, the answer to Smith's prayer launches a quest that transforms him from an obscure boy into a prophet with power from God to seal relationships so that they transcend even death.

Notes

1. Gordon B. Hinckley, "God Hath Not Given Us the Spirit of Fear," November 1983 address to students at Salt Lake Institute of Religion, *Ensign,* October 1984), also at https://www.lds.org/ensign/1984/10/god-hath-not-given-us-the-spirit-of-fear?lang =eng&para=p50#p50.
2. Richard Lyman Bushman, *Joseph Smith: Rough Stone Rolling* (New York: Knopf, 2005), 38.
3. Bushman, *Joseph Smith,* 38–41.
4. Bushman, *Joseph Smith,* 38–41. Bushman had arrived at this general interpretation of Smith's first vision by the time he published *Joseph Smith and the Beginnings of Mormonism* (Urbana: University of Illinois Press, 1984).
5. Bushman, *Joseph Smith,* 38–41.
6. Truman G. Madsen to Richard L. Bushman, October 18, 1968, Truman G. Madsen Papers, Wheatley Institution, Brigham Young University, Provo, UT; TGM to Eugene England, October 16, 1968, TGM Papers.
7. M. Russell Ballard, "The Opportunities and Responsibilities of CES Teachers in the 21st Century," address to CES Religious Educators, February 26, 2016, Salt Lake Tabernacle, accessed August 25, 2018, https://www.lds.org/broadcasts/article/ evening-with-a-general-authority/2016/02/the-opportunities-and-responsibilities- of-ces-teachers-in-the-21st-century?lang=eng.
8. Ballard, "The Opportunities and Responsibilities of CES Teachers in the 21st Century," address to CES Religious Educators, February 26, 2016, Salt Lake Tabernacle, accessed August 25, 2018, https://www.lds.org/broadcasts/article/

evening-with-a-general-authority/2016/02/the-opportunities-and-responsibilities-of-ces-teachers-in-the-21st-century?lang=eng.

9. Nancy J. Maynes, "Finding My Purpose," Worldwide Devotional for Young Adults, May 1, 2016, https://www.lds.org/broadcasts/article/worldwide-devotionals/2016/01/finding-my-purpose?lang=eng.

10. Richard J. Maynes, "The Truth Restored," Worldwide Devotional for Young Adults, May 1, 2016, https://www.lds.org/broadcasts/article/worldwide-devotionals/2016/01/the-truth-restored?lang=eng.

11. Michael A. Ferguson, Jared A. Nielsen, Jace B. King, Li Dai, Danielle M. Giangrasso, Rachel Holman, Julie R. Korenberg, and Jeffrey S. Anderson, "Reward, Salience, and Attentional Networks Are Activated by Religious Experience in Devout Mormons," *Social Neuroscience* 13, no. 1 (November 2016): 104–16, DOI: 10.1080/17470919.2016.1257437.

12. Richard L. Bushman, "What Can We Learn from the First Vision," Devotional given at Brigham Young University–Hawaii, November 15, 2016, accessed August 25, 2018, https://devotional.byuh.edu/media161115.

13. Richard L. Bushman, "What Can We Learn from the First Vision," Devotional given at Brigham Young University–Hawaii, November 15, 2016, accessed August 25, 2018, https://devotional.byuh.edu/media161115.

14. Richard L. Bushman, "What Can We Learn from the First Vision," Devotional given at Brigham Young University–Hawaii, November 15, 2016, accessed August 25, 2018, https://devotional.byuh.edu/media161115.

15. Richard L. Bushman, "What Can We Learn from the First Vision," Devotional given at Brigham Young University–Hawaii, November 15, 2016, accessed August 25, 2018, https://devotional.byuh.edu/media161115.

16. Richard L. Bushman, "What Can We Learn from the First Vision," Devotional given at Brigham Young University–Hawaii, November 15, 2016, accessed August 25, 2018, https://devotional.byuh.edu/media161115.

17. Richard L. Bushman, "What Can We Learn from the First Vision," Devotional given at Brigham Young University–Hawaii, November 15, 2016, accessed August 25, 2018, https://devotional.byuh.edu/media161115.

18. Richard L. Bushman, "What Can We Learn from the First Vision," Devotional given at Brigham Young University–Hawaii, November 15, 2016, accessed August 25, 2018, https://devotional.byuh.edu/media161115.

19. Daniel Peterson, "Defending the Faith: The Supposed Scandal of Multiple First Vision Accounts," *Deseret News*, May 31, 2018, https://www.deseretnews.com/article/900020151/the-supposed-scandal-of-multiple-first-vision-accounts.html

20. Peterson, "Defending the Faith," see comments at https://www.deseretnews.com/user/comments/900020151/the-supposed-scandal-of-multiple-first-vision-accounts.html.

21. Peterson, "Defending the Faith."

22. Mormon Stories #944: "Smith's First Vision, and How the Church and Apologists Mislead, Part 1," published by Mormonstories on June 18, 2018, accessed October 26, 2018, https://www.youtube.com/watch?v=3LQY5EytqLg.

23. Mormon Stories #945: "Smith's First Vision, and How the Church and Apologists Mislead, Part 2," published by Mormonstories on June 18, 2018, accessed October 26, 2018, https://www.youtube.com/watch?v=UOVPoPSbLF4. Tanner's quote is around the 50-minute mark.

24. Mormon Stories #944 (https://www.youtube.com/watch?v=3LQY5EytqLg), 945 (https://www.youtube.com/watch?v=UOVPoPSbLF4), 946 (https://www.youtube.com/watch?v=3ZutK-mPY-U): "Smith's First Vision, and How the Church and Apologists Mislead, Parts 1, 2, and 3," published by Mormonstories on June 18, 218, accessed October 26, 2018. Jan Shipps described the kind of history done by the panel in *Sojourner in the Promised Land: Forty Years Among the Mormons* (Urbana and Chicago: University of Illinois Press, 2000), 179–80.

25. Peterson, "Defending the Faith"; see the June 1, 2018, comment at https://www.deseretnews.com/user/comments/900020151/the-supposed-scandal-of-multiple-first-vision-accounts.html.

26. Quentin L. Cook, "Out of Obscurity: How Merciful the Lord Has Been," BYU–Idaho devotional address, delivered June 12, 2018, Rexburg, Idaho, https://video.byui.edu/media/%E2%80%9COut+of+ObscurityA+How+Merciful+the+Lord+Has+Been%E2%80%9D+Elder+Quentin+L.+Cook/0_7zbuqubv.

27. Quentin L. Cook, "Out of Obscurity: How Merciful the Lord Has Been," BYU–Idaho devotional address, delivered June 12, 2018, Rexburg, Idaho, https://video.byui.edu/media/%E2%80%9COut+of+ObscurityA+How+Merciful+the+Lord+Has+Been%E2%80%9D+Elder+Quentin+L.+Cook/0_7zbuqubv.

28. Joseph Smith, History, circa June 1839–41, handwriting of James Mulholland and Robert B. Thompson, in Joseph Smith, History, 1838–56, vol. A–1, Church History Library, Salt Lake City. Compare to "History of Joseph Smith," *Times and Seasons* 3, no. 11 (April 1, 1842): 748; Joseph Smith, "Church History," *Times and Seasons* 3, no. 9 (March 1, 1842): 706. On p. 3 of his "History of Joseph Smith from the Millennial Star," Roberts wrote the following in pencil: "contradiction with statement in ~~Wentworth letter [one illegible word] see~~ preceding." *History of Joseph Smith*, 3 vols., in B. H. Roberts collection, MS 1278, Church History Library, Salt Lake City.

29. "History, circa Summer 1832," 2, *The Joseph Smith Papers*, accessed February 16, 2018, http://www.josephsmithpapers.org/paper-summary/history-circa-summer-1832/2.

30. Quentin L. Cook, "Out of Obscurity: How Merciful the Lord Has Been," BYU–Idaho devotional address, delivered June 12, 2018, Rexburg, Idaho, https://video.byui.edu/media/%E2%80%9COut+of+ObscurityA+How+Merciful+the+Lord+Has+Been%E2%80%9D+Elder+Quentin+L.+Cook/0_7zbuqubv.

31. *Saints: The Story of the Church of Jesus Christ in the Latter Days*, vol. 1, *1815–1846* (Salt Lake City: The Church of Jesus Christ of Latter-day Saints, 2018), 18–19. Also available at https://www.lds.org/languages/eng/content/history/saints-v1/02-hear-him.

Afterword

Deep Learning

In September 2018, sixteen-year-old Anna Godfrey sat in her seminary class in Farmington, Utah. As the school year began she listened to the excited teacher talk about Joseph Smith's first vision. She had been questioning for some time whether to believe all she had been taught. At times, the vision story seemed so far from her reality that she doubted it.

Her teacher said this year would be different from previous ones. This year Anna and her classmates would experience deep learning. Curious, she paid attention as the teacher explained that students could passively come to class, or they could choose to engage a variety of resources. He showed them a website on which the words "what can I learn from Joseph's First Vision?" overlaid a painting of Smith keeling in the grove and looking into a pillar of light. A header asked, "Got questions?"

Below the painting, a photo of diverse, happy, attractive teens appeared next to the words:

Have you ever told your best friend about an exciting experience you had? What if you were to tell your grandparents about that experience? Would you emphasize different parts of the story to them? What about when you record it in your journal? . . . Do you think that perhaps after years of experience and learning you might choose to emphasize different parts of your original experience as you retell it later on in your life?

That led to this:

After Joseph Smith saw and spoke with God in what we now call the Sacred Grove, he related the experience various times over the next 25 years. We currently have 4 of Joseph's recorded accounts of his experience in the Grove. Each one emphasizes different details as Joseph's own experience and circumstances changed over the years. For example, the first account (recorded in 1832), written by Joseph in an autobiography, highlights Joseph's desire to be forgiven of his sins and the redemption brought through Jesus Christ's atoning sacrifice.

This, Anna realized, was a new approach. Her teacher showed the class how to link to the accounts of Smith's vision from the site and encouraged them to do so, as well as to Bushman's BYU–Hawaii devotional. "You guys should definitely be reading *Saints*," the teacher encouraged. Expecting boredom, Anna found *Saints* delightfully readable and Joseph Smith surprisingly relatable. The combined effects of these resources and teachings on Anna were an increased sense of belonging to the group and increased confidence in Smith's story.[1]

■ ■ ■

Three years earlier in 2015, *The Joseph Smith Papers* published translations of the first vision accounts in nine languages.[2] At about the same time, the church issued new curriculum for college-age students, including the required course "Foundations of the Restoration." The first objective, the new instructors' manual said, is to help students rely on the atonement of Jesus Christ.[3] The first lesson set up the second, which is devoted to Smith's first vision. Instructors were directed to candidly discuss the multiple, differing accounts.

The example of differences in the accounts is a line from "First Vision Accounts" derived from Bushman's 2005 biography: "You might tell students that 'whereas the 1832 account emphasizes the more personal story of Joseph Smith as a young man seeking forgiveness, the 1838 account focuses on the vision as the beginning of the 'rise and progress of the Church.'" The assigned student reading is "First Vision Accounts." Instructors are to remind students of this reading and help them understand "that the multiple accounts of Joseph Smith's First Vision enable us to learn more about this sacred experience than we could if it were less well documented."

Curriculum a generation earlier had avoided any potential first vision controversies. Bushman had been banned from the classroom. Now Bushman's interpretation of Smith's accounts was the curriculum. It had been officially selected, related, and repeated in powerful ways via media that was much more likely than a lecture or a textbook to modulate memory in students like Anna, who has an autobiographical memory of learning it in seminary.

Neurologically speaking, memory of an event like Anna's seminary class recruits areas of the brain above and beyond those required for her to remember some of the facts she learned that day.[4] It is possible, even likely, that she will always associate the lesson and the vision because she judged the experience unusually engaging and emotionally evocative and because she subsequently shared it.[5]

As with Anna individually, a more resilient cultural memory is consolidating among Latter-day Saints generally based on the new, unabashed selection, relation, and repetition of Smith's accounts in church curriculum. Consolidation of collective memory takes time. The recursion process by which elements are added or subtracted and new memories form requires powerful forces to select, relate, and repeat information in ways that make it sink deep into individuals like Anna who belong to the group.

At the 1920 centennial of Smith's vision, students including Mildred Boyer at Brigham Young University internalized the story and made it their own.[6] As the 2020 bicentennial of Joseph Smith's first vision approached, Anna typifies another generation of saints poised to repeat the process because of the selection, relation, and repetition of new and old items woven seamlessly into a new narrative. Elements in the buffer are being integrated into their individual memories and increasingly into the cultural memory. Often this occurs in ways saints associate with spiritual experience, which, neurologically speaking, feels good. Those who experience that association typically cherish Smith's vision and remember it robustly.[7]

Such memory is remarkably stable and always changing. It is both resilient and vulnerable to disruption. It is impossible to predict when something as seemingly inconsequential as a teenager's crisis of faith, as dramatic as a newly discovered document, or as transforming as an information age will reshape what gets remembered.

Maybe the most surprising lesson of this history is not how Latter-day Saints and others have remembered Joseph Smith's first vision, but how quickly a group can forget. Because of the powerful and pervasive selection, relation, and repetition of Joseph Smith's first vision as told in the saints' new narrative, before long most of them may not remember a time when it was not common knowledge. If so, perhaps this book will preserve old memories and show how those that have come and gone came to be.

Notes

1. Accessed November 21, 2018, https://www.ldsscripturepower.org/learningactivities/dc/jsh/.

2. "First Vision Accounts Translated," *The Joseph Smith Papers,* accessed October 26, 2018, http://www.josephsmithpapers.org/site/first-vision-accounts-translated?p=1&highlight=first%20vision%20accounts.

3. "Introduction to the Foundations of the Restoration Teacher Manual (Religion 225)," 2015, accessed October 26, 2018, https://www.lds.org/manual/foundations-of-the-restoration-teacher-manual/introduction-to-the-foundations-of-the-restoration-teacher-manual-religion-225?lang=eng.

4. See George D. Pyper, *Stories of Latter-day Saint Hymns: Their Authors and Composers* (Salt Lake City: Deseret News Press, 1939), 33–38.

5. Steven Harper interview of Anna Godfrey, November 10, 2018, recording in author's possession. Anna's memory may fade based on the fact that "autobiographical memory for the time and place when a particular event occurred is easily disconnected from the factual knowledge acquired during the event." Larry R. Squire, "Biological Foundations of Accuracy and Inaccuracy in Memory," in *Memory Distortion: How Minds, Brains, and Societies Reconstruct the Past,* ed. Daniel L. Schacter (Cambridge, MA: Harvard University Press, 1995), 217–19. For an example of a reinforced autobiographical memory of learning about Smith's first vision, see Micah Trentman, "Knowing God: The First Vision," April 21, 2018, posted April 21, 2018, accessed November 21, 2018, https://commondaisy.com.

6. "The Return of Truth Triumphant," in Sketches Commemorating the Centenary of the Prophet Joseph Smith's First Vision, *Brigham Young University Quarterly* 14, no. 4 (May 1, 1920).

7. Michael A. Ferguson, Jared A. Nielsen, Jace B. King, Li Dai, Danielle M. Giangrasso, Rachel Holman, Julie R. Korenberg, and Jeffrey S. Anderson, "Reward, Salience, and Attentional Networks Are Activated by Religious Experience in Devout Mormons," *Social Neuroscience* 13, no. 1 (November 2016): 104–16, DOI: 10.1080/17470919.2016.1257437.

Index

Note: Tables, figures, and boxes are indicated by an italic *t, f,* and *b* following page number

9 780199 329472